COSTUMING COSPLAY

DRESS, BODY, CULTURE

Books in this provocative series seek to articulate the connections between culture and dress which is defined here in its broadest possible sense as any modification or supplement to the body. Interdisciplinary in approach, the series highlights the dialogue between identity and dress, cosmetics, coiffure, and body alternations as manifested in practices as varied as plastic surgery, tattooing, and ritual scarification. The series aims, in particular, to analyze the meaning of dress in relation to popular culture and gender issues and will include works grounded in anthropology, sociology, history, art history, literature, and folklore.

ISSN: 1360-466X

PREVIOUSLY PUBLISHED IN THE SERIES

Helen Bradley Foster, *"New Raiments of Self": African American Clothing in the Antebellum South*
Claudine Griggs, *S/he: Changing Sex and Changing Clothes*
Michaele Thurgood Haynes, *Dressing Up Debutantes: Pageantry and Glitz in Texas*
Anne Brydon and Sandra Niessen, *Consuming Fashion: Adorning the Transnational Body*
Dani Cavallaro and Alexandra Warwick, *Fashioning the Frame: Boundaries, Dress and the Body*
Judith Perani and Norma H. Wolff, *Cloth, Dress and Art Patronage in Africa*
Linda B. Arthur, *Religion, Dress and the Body*
Paul Jobling, *Fashion Spreads: Word and Image in Fashion Photography*
Fadwa El Guindi, *Veil: Modesty, Privacy and Resistance*
Thomas S. Abler, *Hinterland Warriors and Military Dress: European Empires and Exotic Uniforms*
Linda Welters, *Folk Dress in Europe and Anatolia: Beliefs about Protection and Fertility*

Kim K.P. Johnson and Sharron J. Lennon, *Appearance and Power*

Barbara Burman, *The Culture of Sewing: Gender, Consumption and Home Dressmaking*

Annette Lynch, *Dress, Gender and Cultural Change: Asian American and African American Rites of Passage*

Antonia Young, *Women Who Become Men: Albanian Sworn Virgins*

David Muggleton, *Inside Subculture: The Postmodern Meaning of Style*

Nicola White, *Reconstructing Italian Fashion: America and the Development of the Italian Fashion Industry*

Brian J. McVeigh, *Wearing Ideology: The Uniformity of Self-Presentation in Japan*

Shaun Cole, *Don We Now Our Gay Apparel: Gay Men's Dress in the Twentieth Century*

Kate Ince, *Orlan: Millennial Female*

Ali Guy, Eileen Green and Maura Banim, *Through the Wardrobe: Women's Relationships with their Clothes*

Linda B. Arthur, *Undressing Religion: Commitment and Conversion from a Cross-Cultural Perspective*

William J. F. Keenan, *Dressed to Impress: Looking the Part*

Joanne Entwistle and Elizabeth Wilson, *Body Dressing*

Leigh Summers, *Bound to Please: A History of the Victorian Corset*

Paul Hodkinson, *Goth: Identity, Style and Subculture*

Leslie W. Rabine, *The Global Circulation of African Fashion*

Michael Carter, *Fashion Classics from Carlyle to Barthes*

Sandra Niessen, Ann Marie Leshkowich, and Carla Jones, *Re-Orienting Fashion: The Globalization of Asian Dress*

Kim K. P. Johnson, Susan J. Torntore, and Joanne B. Eicher, *Fashion Foundations: Early Writings on Fashion and Dress*

Helen Bradley Foster and Donald Clay Johnson, *Wedding Dress Across Cultures*

Eugenia Paulicelli, *Fashion under Fascism: Beyond the Black Shirt*

Charlotte Suthrell, *Unzipping Gender: Sex, Cross-Dressing and Culture*

Irene Guenther, *Nazi Chic? Fashioning Women in the Third Reich*

Yuniya Kawamura, *The Japanese Revolution in Paris Fashion*

Patricia Calefato, *The Clothed Body*

Ruth Barcan, *Nudity: A Cultural Anatomy*

Samantha Holland, *Alternative Femininities: Body, Age and Identity*

Alexandra Palmer and Hazel Clark, *Old Clothes, New Looks: Second Hand Fashion*

Yuniya Kawamura, *Fashion-ology: An Introduction to Fashion Studies*

Regina A. Root, *The Latin American Fashion Reader*

Linda Welters and Patricia A. Cunningham, *Twentieth-Century American Fashion*

Jennifer Craik, *Uniforms Exposed: From Conformity to Transgression*

Alison L. Goodrum, *The National Fabric: Fashion, Britishness, Globalization*

Annette Lynch and Mitchell D. Strauss, *Changing Fashion: A Critical Introduction to Trend Analysis and Meaning*

Catherine M. Roach, *Stripping, Sex and Popular Culture*

Marybeth C. Stalp, *Quilting: The Fabric of Everyday Life*

Jonathan S. Marion, *Ballroom: Culture and Costume in Competitive Dance*

Dunja Brill, *Goth Culture: Gender, Sexuality and Style*

Joanne Entwistle, *The Aesthetic Economy of Fashion: Markets and Value in Clothing and Modelling*

Juanjuan Wu, *Chinese Fashion: From Mao to Now*

Annette Lynch, *Porn Chic: Exploring the Contours of Raunch Eroticism*

Brent Luvaas, *DIY Style: Fashion, Music and Global Cultures*

Jianhua Zhao, *The Chinese Fashion Industry: An Ethnographic Approach*

Eric Silverman, *A Cultural History of Jewish Dress*

Karen Hansen and D. Soyini Madison, *African Dress: Fashion, Agency, Performance*

Maria Mellins, *Vampire Culture*

Lynne Hume, *The Religious Life of Dress*

Marie Riegels Melchior and Birgitta Svensson, *Fashion and Museums: Theory and Practice*

Masafumi Monden, *Japanese Fashion Cultures: Dress and Gender in Contemporary Japan*

Alfonso McClendon, *Fashion and Jazz: Dress, Identity and Subcultural Improvisation*

Phyllis G. Tortora, *Dress, Fashion and Technology: From Prehistory to the Present*

Barbara Brownie and Danny Graydon, *The Superhero Costume: Identity and Disguise in Fact and Fiction*

Adam Geczy and Vicki Karaminas, *Fashion's Double: Representations of Fashion in Painting, Photography and Film*

Yuniya Kawamura, *Sneakers: Fashion, Gender, and Subculture*

Heike Jenss, *Fashion Studies: Research Methods, Sites and Practices*

Brent Luvaas, *Street Style: An Ethnography of Fashion Blogging*

Jenny Lantz, *The Trendmakers: Behind the Scenes of the Global Fashion Industry*

Barbara Brownie, *Acts of Undressing: Politics, Eroticism, and Discarded Clothing*

Louise Crewe, *The Geographies of Fashion: Consumption, Space, and Value*

Sheila Cliffe, *The Social Life of Kimono: Japanese Fashion Past and Present*

Linda Welters and Abby Lillethun, *Fashion History: A Global View*

DRESS, BODY, CULTURE: CRITICAL SOURCEBOOKS

Rebecca Mitchell, *Fashioning the Victorians: A Critical Sourcebook*

COSTUMING
COSPLAY

Dressing the Imagination

THERÈSA M. WINGE

BLOOMSBURY VISUAL ARTS
LONDON • NEW YORK • OXFORD • NEW DELHI • SYDNEY

BLOOMSBURY VISUAL ARTS
Bloomsbury Publishing Plc
50 Bedford Square, London, WC1B 3DP, UK
1385 Broadway, New York, NY 10018, USA

BLOOMSBURY, BLOOMSBURY VISUAL ARTS and the Diana logo are trademarks
of Bloomsbury Publishing Plc

First published in Great Britain 2019

Cover design: Adriana Brioso
Cover image: Fans dress up in costume during the London Film and
Comic Con day 2 at Olympia London on July 29, 2017 in London, England.
(© Danny E. Martindale/Getty Images)

A catalogue record for this book is available from the British Library.

A catalog record for this book is available from the Library of Congress.

ISBN: HB: 978-1-3500-3590-4
PB: 978-1-3500-3591-1
ePDF: 978-1-3500-3592-8
ePub: 978-1-3500-3589-8

Series: Dress, Body, Culture, 1360-466X

Typeset by Deanta Global Publishing Services, Chennai, India
Printed and bound in India

To find out more about our authors and books visit www.bloomsbury.com
and sign up for our newsletters.

CONTENTS

LIST OF ILLUSTRATIONS

Figures

Plates

ACKNOWLEDGMENTS

I would like to express my deepest appreciation to all of the amazing Cosplayers I have met over the years, but especially want to thank those who participated in this study. A special thanks to Cosplayers Jodie Gustafson, Phoenix Kincaid, and the Deep Dive team and photographer Eron Rauch, who were invaluable in their in-depth and diverse insights into the Cosplay fandom.

I am grateful to everyone at Bloomsbury Publishing, in particular Frances Arnold and Joanne B. Eicher, as well as the reviewers, for all of their assistance and expert guidance. Some of the images in this book were possible because of the support from the Michigan State University, College of Arts and Letters' Humanities Arts and Research Program Production grant.

I owe a special debt of gratitude to Dr. Marybeth C. Stalp, who was so supportive during the early years of this research study and who never let me slack off on my research goals. I also am grateful to Rebecca E. Schuiling for tolerating my sardonic humor and continuously interrupting me throughout the writing of this book, despite her not reading a single draft of this book. I would also like to acknowledge Angie, Para, and Rachel for being amazing research assistants, who followed up on my strange requests without the smallest complaint.

I am immensely thankful to my devoted husband and our kitties, who were wonderful and annoying with their distractions and peculiar encouragement. Fergus and Bill, I am exceptionally grateful for your edits, suggestions, and snuggles. And, Heather, there are not words to express how much I appreciate you for being the dearest friend who came when I needed you.

DISCLAIMER

All the images of fan costumes used in this academic research were reproduced with the permission of the creators, photographers, and/or Cosplayers. In cases where images of fan costumes or text references include details of characters, logos, objects, and/or symbols from popular media, where a third party holds the copyright and/or trademark of such materials, this representation and use: (a) is regarded by the author and publishers as fair dealing and/or fair for the purposes of criticism and review only; and (b) does not imply any form of approval, endorsement, and/or sponsorship on the part of third-party copyright and/or trademark holders.

1
LET'S COSPLAY!

Sitting in a humid, poorly ventilated hotel ballroom in Bloomington, Minnesota, in 2000, I waited for something called "the masquerade." My good friends at the annual gaming convention called CONvergence had encouraged me to attend the masquerade costume competition, assuring me that I would enjoy the spectacle of Cosplayers' costumes because of my interest in fashion and dress. I, however, was not convinced because their descriptions of Cosplay sounded silly and childish, but I was seated there just the same. My expectations were low, but I hoped the Cosplayers would provide at least as much entertainment value as those I had seen in the hallways of the hotel that hosted CONvergence. While I had previously met several individual costumed Cosplayers in the early 1990s, this was my first official organized Cosplay event.

Unsure about what to expect, the masquerade was already forty minutes late in starting, and my seat was becoming increasingly uncomfortable, but at least my friends and I were not on the folding chairs haphazardly placed in the back corners of the expansive ballroom because more people were attending than anticipated. Finally, the lights dimmed. An awkward emcee welcomed everyone to CONvergence's masquerade. The presentation that followed was nearly two hours of Cosplay action—costumed performers portraying beloved characters from *The Wizard of Oz* to *Star Wars*, from *Final Fantasy* to *Pokemon*. The performances were mostly straightforward and predictable; performers wore handmade costumes depicting key characteristics in order to establish well-known fantasy characters. Taking signature poses and delivering shaky but well-known dialogue and catchphrases, these amateur performances were punctuated with numerous humorous and self-deprecating skits, which the Cosplayers' roleplay drew on the audience's understanding of the characters. The audience frequently interacted with the performers by shouting in a call-and-response manner, and this exchange further increased the enjoyable ruckus (and tongue-in-cheek satire). Having been warmly received by the audience, the masquerade concluded with the presentation of awards recognizing the judges' selections for originality, costumes, and performances.

When the house lights came back up again, I listened as the audience around me immediately began to debate who should have won which award, many disagreeing with the judges' selections usually based on esoteric fan information about storylines or character details. Many Cosplayers had fans and friends in the audience and the politics of the event were being revealed in their discussions, but this debate quickly dissolved into character and costume discussions. Everyone became interested in knowing how the more intricate or the largest costumes were constructed, and how did the winning group create such a humorous skit and engaging costumes. As the Cosplayers emerged from backstage, convention attendees quickly surrounded them for pictures, autographs, and praise, despite no one in the competition being a Cosplay celebrity.

While this masquerade was my first encounter with a Cosplay event, it remains the most memorable. I was impressed with their discernible efforts for the multiple dimensions of their craft, as well as the Cosplayers' obvious love for character and story. For the first time, I felt like I understood multiple aspects of Cosplay and how Cosplay enhanced fan experiences at a fan convention. Cosplay encompasses a person's fantasies, costumes, socializing, competitions, and, of course, play. Cosplayers select and research fictional characters to portray to friends and in competitions with authenticity, humor, and passion, as well exhibiting traits of being resourceful, creative, and inventive. Cosplay is an expensive and time-consuming activity; however, Cosplayers are devout to the re-creation and depiction of their selected characters and the performance art of Cosplay. Cosplay extends beyond the assumptions about fandoms to performance art that embraces various forms of media from popular culture.

Origins of Cosplay

When I first saw Cosplayers at conventions and eventually began judging competitions, I assumed Cosplay began in Japan (similar to many other fans). After speaking with several scholars of Japanese popular culture, and numerous Cosplayers, I was convinced that its origins were in Japan. I occasionally met Cosplayers, however, who insisted Cosplay began not in Japan but instead it originated in North America, specifically the United States. Subsequently, I set out to research the origins of Cosplay, and in 2006, I wrote an article—"Costuming the Imagination: Origins of Anime and Manga Cosplay"—with my findings.

The exact origins of Cosplay are highly debated among Cosplayers and their fans, as well as among some scholars. The origin story, however, is far more mundane than most of the outlandish speculations I heard over many years. The earliest evidence of Cosplay may be in 1877, when Jules Verne hosted a "masked ball" where guests were dressed as characters from Verne's novels (Unwin 2005: 223). Then, in the early 1900s, there are at least two documented examples in Cincinnati, Ohio, and Monroe, Washington, where fans created costumes of Mr. Skygack for masquerade balls (Miller 2013; Ashcroft and Plunkett 2014). Costumed fans dressed as Mr. Skygack, a Martian from the first science-fiction comic strip *Mr. Skygack, from Mars* (1907–12) by cartoonist A. D. Condo (Miller 2013; Veach 2010). The latter example was documented with a photograph and short newspaper article from the *Tacoma Times* (Washington, United States) noting that the Mr. Skygack costume won first prize (Miller 2013). Accordingly, Cosplay originated in the United States and is more than 100 years old.

Forrest J. Ackerman is credited with being the first fan to dress in a "furturisticostume" similar to the costumes worn in the film *Things to Come* (1936) for a science-fiction fan convention in 1939 (O'Brien 2012: 24). Quickly after his appearance, fans dressing in costume had more formalized activities within fandom conventions. In 1940, Worldcon (a science-fiction convention) held the first masquerade ball, where attendees who wore costumes were awarded prizes for the best costumes (Resnick 2009: 106–10).

Cosplay was practiced in the United States before it had an official name. In 1984, Nobuyuki Takahashi was a guest at Worldcon in Los Angeles, California. He was impressed with the sci-fi and fantasy characters roleplaying and especially the performances at the masquerade (i.e., costumed competition) and parades (a.k.a. fashion show; see Lamerichs 2011: 2.3).[1] Takahashi wrote about his experiences when he returned to Japan, but found it necessary to create the general term understandable in Japanese culture (Bruno 2002, 2002a). Subsequently, Takahashi created the term "kosupure," or Cosplay, to describe the costume masquerade and competition; "Cosplay" is a term created from combining "costume" and "play" (roleplaying) (Winge 2006: 66). The term aptly describes the most basic components of Cosplay: dressing in costume and roleplaying a fantastic character. Cosplay, however, represents far more complexities and layers than its name implies.

History of Cosplay

Once introduced to Japan in the mid-1980s, Cosplay gained recognition as a subcultural phenomenon that quickly grew in popularity among the youth and adults. Generations of Japanese embrace Cosplay with great enthusiasm that they continually infuse back into the subculture. The most important contribution to Cosplay is Japanese anime (animation) and manga (comics), where artists create fantastically gorgeous characters, exotic and seductive environments, and innovative storylines.

Cosplay continued to evolve from its early beginnings where Cosplayers created their own costumes reflecting the careful character research. Today, Cosplayers are drawn to characters from more sources than ever before,

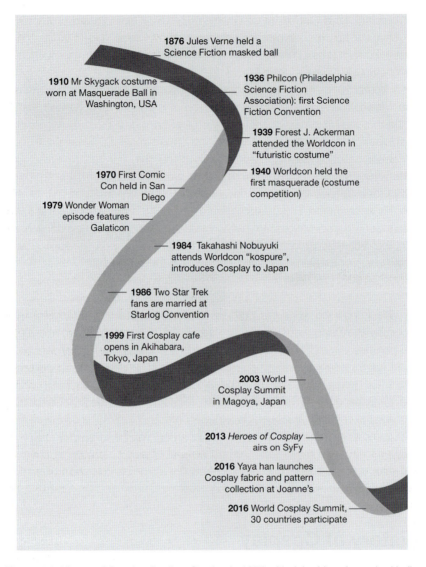

1876 Jules Verne held a
Science Fiction masked ball

1910 Mr Skygack costume
worn at Masquerade Ball in
Washington, USA

1936 Philcon (Philadelphia
Science Fiction
Association): first Science
Fiction Convention

1939 Forest J. Ackerman
attended the Worldcon in
"futuristic costume"

1970 First Comic
Con held in San
Diego

1940 Worldcon held the
first masquerade (costume
competition)

1979 Wonder Woman
episode features
Galaticon

1984 Takahashi Nobuyuki
attends Worldcon "kospure",
introduces Cosplay to Japan

1986 Two Star Trek
fans are married at
Starlog Convention

1999 First Cosplay cafe
opens in Akihabara,
Tokyo, Japan

2003 World
Cosplay Summit
in Magoya, Japan

2013 *Heroes of Cosplay*
airs on SyFy

2016 Yaya han launches
Cosplay fabric and pattern
collection at Joanne's

2016 World Cosplay Summit,
30 countries participate

Figure 1.1 History of Cosplay timeline. Starting in 1876 with Jules Verne's masked ball where he asked guests to dress as science-fiction characters, Cosplay has a rich global history with a promising future. Graphic: Therèsa M. Winge and Rachel Brunhild.

and their options for creation of character costumes seem nearly infinite. The increasing expenses associated with costume materials, props, and weapons reflect the popularity of Cosplay. In addition to the initial financial cost, Cosplayers also dedicate endless hours in character research, performance practice, and costume construction. Moreover, Cosplayers invest copious money to travel to and attend conventions and participate in Cosplay events.

In the "Spaced Out" episode (January 26, 1979) from the television series the *New Adventures of Wonder Woman*, the plot involves a science-fiction convention with fans dressed as favorite characters. The "Spaced Out" episode uses actual convention footage from the 1978 GalatiCON held in Los Angeles, California. In this episode, the sci-fi movie *Logan's Run* is referenced, and Robby Robot from *Lost in Space* hosts the masquerade. Many homemade costumes for characters also appear; some are similar to Jawas from *Star Wars* and Sardor from *Wonder Woman*'s "Mind Stealers from Outer Space" TV episode (1977). In the "Spaced Out" episode, the character Diana Prince and others who are clearly not identified as fans engage with the convention attendees as novelties, and critique convention-goers dressed in character costumes with eye rolls, smirks, and giggles. This 1979 episode is one of the first times a large and diverse television audience is shown a science-fiction convention (see Figure 1.1).

Global Cosplay

Cosplay is now a phenomenon spanning the globe, where Cosplayers from all parts of the world travel, compete, and socialize with other Cosplayers. Cosplay benefits from the cross-pollination of participants from various cultures drawing on numerous forms of media. Cosplay activities and events happen in person at conventions and parties primarily and online. Most significantly impacting Cosplay is the reach of the media, Internet, and Japanese popular culture, both to the benefit (and detriment) of the fandom.

In the few decades, Cosplay is so popular that print magazines, such as *CosMo* (Costume Model), *Cosmode* (Costume Mode), and *Anime Costumer*, are entirely dedicated to this phenomenon. These magazines include detailed descriptions and instructions, ranging from makeup and hair tips to color photographs of the finished character, for creating almost any anime, manga, and/or video game character. Some magazines even include patterns and instructions for sewing/constructing the actual costume for the character. In addition, many of the anime and manga magazines, such as *NewType* and *Animerica*, have sections dedicated exclusively to Cosplay, including candid reports about Cosplayers and their activities at conventions and always includes color photographs of individuals dressed as their favorite characters. Furthermore, unrelated magazines, such as *Lee's Toy Review*, which specializes in collectible toys, issued a request for readers to send in Cosplay-related photographs and stories for publication (November 2004).

While the connections between the media and Cosplay fan community seem symbiotic and mutually beneficial, their relationship actually exists more parasitic. At a superficial level, the relationship reads as the media securing images of Cosplayers for sales and ratings, and in turn the Cosplay subculture gains more recognition and popularity. The benefits granted the fandom, however, come with negative impacts for Cosplayers and the same cannot be said for the media. In fact, the media gains benefits from Cosplayers being harassed and from internal conflicts because these negative aspects provide fodder for sensational articles.

Cosplay's popularity is evident in the Syfy channel's *Heroes of Cosplay*, which chronicles selected Cosplayers at various conventions and their successes and failures in Cosplay competitions. This documentary series follows Cosplay celebrities, such as Yaya Han. Each weekly episode features different Cosplayers, who develop characters complete with detailed costumes, makeup, props, and poses.

In addition, the Internet contributes to the popularity of Cosplay by not only allowing Cosplayers to share love of a particular character with images of costumed portrayals, but also allowing fans to interact with Cosplayers and communicate with anyone interested in Cosplay. Subsequently, anyone with Internet access has the ability to learn more about Cosplay and Cosplayers; perhaps more importantly, the Cosplayers readily use the Internet to connect with other Cosplayers (and resources).

Online Cosplayers exchange images of themselves dressed as specific characters, share information about Cosplay events and activities, and seek suggestions from the fan community for character and costume choices, as well as offer how-to advice about costume construction or weapon design. Some popular Cosplay websites supporting the fandom are CosplayLab.com, Cosplay.com, and Fanpop.com/Clubs/Cosplay. Other websites that support the costuming's technical detailing (i.e., wigs, cosmetics, costumes, accessories, etc.) of Cosplayers are CosplayFU.com, EZCosplay.com, HelloCosplay.com, and CosplayHouse.com.

Cosplay retail venues around the world specialize in constructing, tailoring, or selling costumes, props, prosthetics, and supplies. In Japan, Cosplay is a subcultural activity practiced by teenagers and young adults; however, the promise of financial profits encouraged commercial retail ventures. In recent years, some celebrity Cosplayers released Cosplay fabrics and patterns in the United States. Michael Bruno draws an apt comparison between Japanese and American Cosplay retailers:

Japan has . . . seen the rise of Cosplay specific stores known as Cospa. These stores cater to cosplayers carrying character specific costumes and accessories. Many Cospa also carry fabric and other supplies for making your own costumes and often have a professional in-house who will do custom costume work. While American cosplayers do not have access to these officially licensed cosplay products they do have easier and greater access to wider variety of costume making supplies. (2002a)

Although now somewhat outdated, Bruno's comparison highlights the differences in the ways Cosplay resources differ between countries and cultures. Despite the significant positions of the United States and Japan in the Cosplay fandom, the major Cosplay retailers are from China (CRI 2014).

In 2009, the International Cosplay Day was established as an annual event, occurring on the last Saturday of August. The organizers utilize Facebook and other social media to share the event, where they encourage Cosplayers around the world to dress as their favorite character and live their everyday routine while dressed as Cosplayers. Through this group's Facebook page, Cosplayers are also encouraged to create Cosplay events in their region and invite other members of related fan communities to participate.

The global appeal of Cosplay is further evident worldwide in its events, conventions, and media coverage, as well as in its prominence on social media. Cosplay exists as a transcultural (Ortiz 1947) and transnationalism phenomenon, where it creates spaces for interconnections and intersections of social, (sub) cultural, political, and economic values and impacts to converge without concern for or awareness of national or geographic borders. Cosplayers benefit from the resources and diversity available because of globalization.

Japan and Cosplay

During the late twentieth century, anime (animation/cartoons) and manga (comics/graphic novels) gained immense popularity (McCarthy 1993; Napier 2000; Poitras 2001). This is evident in the growing consumption of anime movies, such as *Vampire Hunter D* (1985), *Akira* (1988), and *Spirited Away* (2001); anime television serials, such as *Speed Racer* (1967) and *Dragon Ball Z* (1984–95); and manga (that eventually became anime) such as *Nausicaa of the Valley of the Wind* (1982–94) and *Sailor Moon* (1992–97) (Drazen 2002; Napier 2000). As a result, there is an alternative and popular market for a vast range of anime and manga merchandise, including plush toys, action figures, fashion, art, and costumes.

Japan's relationship with Cosplay is complicated and frequently convoluted even within the fan community; there are common misconceptions and assumptions about the associations between Japan and Cosplay. While Japan makes two significant contributions to Cosplay, it is not intrinsically tied to the fandom, and Cosplay takes even less common forms within Japanese culture. From Japan, Cosplay gets its name, and many Cosplayers are devoted to anime and manga characters and genres generated from Japanese popular culture. These fantasy characters are packaged with dynamic appearances and captivating storylines, which are quite seductive to many Cosplayers. Fans' dedication and allegiance to anime touches on obsession, with adherence to every detail and nuance regarding costumes, gestures, and storylines.

In addition, Japan wrestles with the limited position of Cosplay within popular culture, as well as with its fundamental practice in the rest of the world. Over the years, the novelty of Cosplay became a subcultural activity, as less of the dominant Japanese culture participated in it. For years, Cosplayers were rejected by the parent culture because they dressed and behaved in ways that did not conform to mainstream expectations. Additionally, Japanese conventions contend with the ways Cosplay is practiced in the rest of the world. While the world's largest fan convention—Comiket (Comic Market) with an attendance of 590,000 in 2015—is held twice a year in Japan, Cosplay here is distinctively different than it is in other parts of the world. At this convention, Cosplayers are limited to a designated area called Cosplay Square, but the Cosplayers are not as enthusiastic about posing for photographers as they are in the United States. Similarly, 2016 AnimeJapan boasts itself as the world's largest anime convention, which is held in Tokyo, Japan, with 135,323 attendees (Otakumode. com 2016). The convention features Cosplayers' World, a designated area (indoor and outdoor) for Cosplayers to pose for photographs. These examples are in stark contrast to similarly themed fan conventions held elsewhere around the world, where Cosplayers are able to move throughout the convention freely, but the landscape of Cosplay at conventions is changing.

Capitalizing on the connections between anime/manga and the Cosplay fandom, as well as with Cosplay's transnational appeal, Japan organized the World Cosplay Summit (WCS) to garner international friendship in 2003 (WSC 2016). Each country is allowed two Cosplayers to compete in the WCS. Since 2003, each year more countries are competing. In 2016, thirty countries and regions submitted Cosplayers for competition (WCS 2016). The WCS features numerous Cosplay events including a parade of Cosplayers in Osu, Nagoya, Japan, a well-known shopping district friendly to anime/manga and Cosplay subcultures. Non-Japanese summit attendees assume that because Osu is a Cosplay-friendly environment during the WCS that all of Japan is the same (see Figure 1.2).

In addition, the media is eager to manipulate the conspicuous connections between Japan and Cosplay, which leads to the continued exoticism of Japan and related exploitation of the Cosplay fandom. The exoticism of Japanese youth's Cosplay dress provides the media fuel for sensational images, which is compounded by the eagerness of the Cosplayers to pose for such photographs. Furthermore, Cosplayers draw on these linkages made by the media to create further spheres of influence. It is a cycle that Cosplayers feed and seem unaware of the negative consequences.

By establishing Japan as something to be consumed, the media has done the country and its connections to Cosplay a disservice. In 2001, for example,

Figure 1.2 WCS Cosplayer contestants pose at a parade for the World Cosplay Summit in Nagoya, Japan, 2009. Photo: AFP PHOTO/Frank Zeller/Getty Images.

numerous fans of Japanese popular culture adopted identifiers such as "weebs" and "otaku."[2] Cosplayers who are fans of anime/manga also use these designations. Unfortunately, both of these terms have origins as derogatory insults that non-Japanese do not completely understand or acknowledge. Many fans argue that "weeaboo" (and its shortened form weeb) is a term used in Nicholas Gurewitch's newspaper and web comic *Perry Bible Fellowship*. Weebs, however, is openly acknowledged as a derivation of "wapanese" (or "wannabe Japanese"), which is considered a derogatory term. In fact, filters on some Internet sites change "wapanese" to "weeaboo" to minimize negative feedback. In Japan, "otaku" is also recognized as a slur, meaning someone who places obsessions with fantasy-related media and products before family and community.[3] Some Cosplayers, however, use these terms both proudly to identify their obsession with all things Japanese and as teases to themselves and peers for the same fanaticism.

The exoticization of Japanese popular culture and its connections to Cosplay (and Western culture) lead to further eroticization and exploitation of both. Scholars casually but inaccurately credit Cosplay as originating or being sustained as a Japanese popular culture (see Cherry 2016: 36; Lamerichs 2011: 2.1). A superficial read of Cosplay suggests deep connections to Japan; however, a closer examination reveals that Japan is one of many countries in the world participating in the Cosplay fandom and anime is but one of many genres that inspire Cosplayers.

Fan conventions

The fandom convention, or "con" for short, is a temporary and ephemeral fan space created within a physical venue (hotel, arena, or convention center) to facilitate the gathering of fans around a specific theme, activity, and/or genre. These conventions are held around the world, typically once a year, and have attendance ranging in numbers from a few hundreds to more than half a million. Conventions are commonly fan organized and managed to include panels with featured guests and fan experts within the programs. In recent years, however, the profit-making potential has changed some formats. Some conventions award prestigious honors, such as Worldcon, which presents the Hugo Awards (Coppa 2006). Conventions also offer merchandise for sale, such as original artwork located in the artists' alley and costume merchandise from vendors'/dealers' room or expo floor.

The earliest documented fan conventions were science-fiction conventions: 1936 Philcon (Philadelphia Science Fiction Conference), 1937 Leeds Science Fiction League (eventually becoming British Science Fiction Association), and 1939 Worldcon (World Science Fiction Convention) (Willis 1952). There are fan conventions held around the world at all times of the year. Examples of such conventions are Lucca Comics and Games Convention in Tuscany, Italy; Games Con in Cologne, Germany; Japan Expo held in Paris, France; and Wizard World in the United States. Still, online databases for fandom conventions report that the United States hosts more conventions that encourage or promote Cosplay fandom events than any other country.

Fan conventions benefit from the popularity of Cosplay and the Cosplayers' desire to perform. Every year, conventions feature Cosplay masquerades (competitions) for the entertainment of convention attendees. Conventions provide Cosplayers with a venue to gather, socialize, and share their most recent Cosplay character(s). While some conventions focus on Cosplay, many others circulate around all things related to gaming, science fiction, and comic books, such as Comic-Con and Worldcon. The conventions that include many fandoms also typically include Cosplay events or at least a parade of costumed attendees.

A Cosplay masquerade may be as simple as a parade of Cosplayers walking along a designated route through the convention space for viewers, or, as more commonly seen at modern fan conventions, the masquerade may be elaborate competitive exhibitions, replete with judging panels and awards. Cosplay masquerades are one of the most widely attended events at the fan convention. An individual Cosplayer or team will display the fictional character costumes with poses, performances (often humorous), and stunts. The masquerade judges are usually famous or well known within the fan community, ranging from Cosplay celebrities to comic book writers to costume designers for science-fiction television series.

Due to the lack of fan conventions focused solely on Cosplay, Cosplayers attend other fandom's conventions. With the growing numbers of Cosplayers, however, it is not surprising to find fandom conventions devoted entirely to Cosplay or feature it prominently. The Cosplay Mania convention held in Mandaluyong City, Philippines, in 2008, may be the first Cosplay fan convention (Bakamann 2010). Additional Cosplay conventions are being created monthly to meet the growing demands of the fandom.

Within the convention, the Cosplayers function as carnivalesque attractions, promotions for characters and related media, and celebrities. Accordingly, Cosplay activities, such as competitions and masquerades, were added to most fan conventions' itineraries and draw as large crowds similar in numbers to those who attend featured celebrities' presentations. Cosplay is practiced around the globe, and the cross-pollination from various forms of media and cultures benefit the fan community who enjoy Cosplay.

Why Cosplay?

The reasons for cosplaying characters are as varied as the people who participate; still, there are common nuclei composing the Cosplay experience. Cosplayers create individual and shared environments and communities both online and in person. Through the use of elaborate costumes and detailed characters, Cosplayers negotiate fictional identities out of place and time (primarily at fan conventions).

The social structures created by Cosplayers and their fans are not unique to this subculture; however, there are distinctions that facilitate Cosplayers in creating their individual and shared environments. Cosplayers build social systems supportive of friendships and Cosplay competitions at the same time. Socializing provides Cosplayers with ways to share their inspirations and encouragement, while challenging each other to choose more complicated characters or tackle more technical props.

In addition, Cosplayers enjoy the benefits of the escapism provided within the costumes and activities of the chosen characters. Adopting the dress of a character, for example, provides a "disguise" from which the Cosplayer may be more adventurous or simply act bolder than without the costume. Cosplayers find power and agency residing within their chosen characters. This text will continually return to Cosplay dress and appearance for the ways it contributes to Cosplay experiences.

Conventions offer a conduit for fans to create escapism bubbles outside of the reality of space and time. Cosplayers assist in creating these socially and culturally structured zones with their portrayals of fantastic characters and social interactions with fans from other fandoms. A fantastic reality is created where the Cosplayer assumes the character's identity: she or he is not acting but manifesting a character. These moments are occasionally captured in videos and photographs of a child interacting with a superhero Cosplayer. For the child fan, Spiderman is as real as her mother or father, and this reality extends to and engulfs the Cosplayer beneath the red Lycra bodysuit.

The social rituals associated with Cosplay are numerous, providing Cosplayers with expected experiences before, during, and after Cosplay-related activities. Rituals associated with Cosplay often begin with selecting the character; dressing in the costume; practicing poses in the mirror; posing for pictures; and performing in front of an audience for a Cosplay competition. These Cosplay rituals are discussed in detail in the latter half of the book.

Cosplayers are highly motivated by their love for their chosen characters, as well as the characters' associated storylines and genres. Cosplayers share online how they watch episodes featuring their characters repeatedly in order to practice and perfect their speech, poses, and performances before cosplaying (Winge 2006a). They also review original media and fan art to design the costume and overall character appearance. Consequently, external stimulus propels the fandom forward.

Fantastic characters

Character selection is an important part of the Cosplay experience. There are no ethnic, racial, spiritual, or geographic limitations or expectations when choosing a character to Cosplay. Gender is also of little consideration when choosing a character. In the Cosplay fandom, "crossplay" refers to cosplaying a character of gender differing from which the Cosplayer identifies. There are, of course, negative critiques from some peer Cosplayers when ethnic, gender, racial, and size lines are crossed or challenged.

The selection of Cosplay characters comes from animation, books, comic books, graphic novels, movies, podcasts (see Plate 1.3), and videogames. Original characters are drawn from a variety of sources, and Cosplayers are afforded liberties in their portrayal. Characters from literature (who have not been extensively portrayed or merchandised like Harry Potter), for example, pose unique challenges because readers interpret the exact details of the costume in differing ways. Choosing a literary character is a laborious challenge, where a Cosplayer has more latitude to create a truly unique interpretation. While at conventions, I have seen many interpretations of Alice from *Alice's Adventures in Wonderland* (Carroll 1865). She commonly has long blonde hair wearing an iconic blue dress with white apron, but stylistic differences range from a demure depiction of a teen Victorian girl with a stuffed white rabbit under her arm to a punky portrayal of a Mohawk hairstyle, tattered clothing, and combat boots, to a humorous representation of Alice crossplayed by a large man whose body hair could not be contained in the tightfitting Lycra dress.

In recent years, Cosplayers create their own characters drawn from a variety of sources, which furthers the agency acquired through Cosplay activities. Sometimes they are the amalgamation of two or three established characters and are called a "mash-up" character. These unique characters also originate from fan fic(tion), evolving out of a well-known storyline or plot instead of their original creator's intentions. Additionally, in 1999, at an anime convention, a portly bearded male was photographed wearing a yellow wig and blue and white dress, humorously portraying the beloved female character Sailor Moon (WikiMoon 2014; Tomberry 2014). The sensation around this parody created a new character of Sailor Bubba, who is now commonly cosplayed by various individuals at fan conventions.

Character costumes

The role of the Cosplay costume, including clothing, makeup, wig or hairstyle, prosthetics, and accessories and props, is paramount in successfully portraying a given character. The costume is all encompassing of the Cosplayer's physical body and identity. While some Cosplayers even lose or gain weight and muscle mass to more accurately portray a character, most Cosplayers embrace their physical appearance and work with it for a given character. Cosplayers take advantage of their physical traits, which contribute to portraying a specific character, such as a very tall person playing Groot (from *Guardians of the Galaxy*) or Rubeus Hagrid (from *Harry Potter*).

Cosplayers also use costumes to establish the tone of a character (despite the actual character's persona), whether the Cosplayer is attempting to nonverbally communicate humor or satire or drama. The character Freddy Krueger from *A Nightmare on Elm Street* films, for example, could be portrayed as a sexy character wearing a distressed green and red-striped sweater dress on a female Cosplayer or a humorous mash-up Santa Freddy character, who is wearing a Santa costume that was red and green striped with Freddy Krueger's burned face prosthetic and razor finger glove.

Cosplayers spare no expense or effort in creating costumes that accurately reflect chosen characters with precision. Originally, Cosplayers were forced to create their own costumes because there were no retailers/merchandisers who sold costumes beyond those used for Halloween or themed parties. In recent years, Cosplayers have numerous resources online and in brick-and-mortar stores that cater solely to Cosplayers. Still, many Cosplayers create most portions of their costumes in order to maintain control over the final details and overall composition, while enjoying the creative process. Furthermore, fans who own a "costume [from a movie or TV series] is distinct from cosplay" (Brownie and Graydon 2016: 114). These types of costumes are often far too valuable or fragile to wear or use for prolonged periods around conventions but some may be suitable for photographs or competition(s). In addition, most Cosplayers could not financially afford nor have access to authentic television or film costumes.

Roleplay

In addition to the visual appearance of the character, Cosplayers learn signature poses and catchphrases. Some Cosplayers even develop skits for competition and social interactions. In order to convincingly roleplay, Cosplayers spend endless hours analyzing physical traits, gestures, and movements within the context of a character's milieu persona, as well as costumes and props.

Cosplayers commonly "stay in character" when roleplaying their characters even within the chaos of conventions; the exception is when famous Cosplayers pose with their fans for photographs and autographs. Once in the "real world," Cosplayers in costume may choose to maintain their character depending on the situation. Cosplaying outside of designated events or activities can cause issues, as is the case with any subculture member who displays their subcultural affiliation without the protection of the group or their (geographic) domain.

Humor is a common part of roleplaying characters, and Cosplayers must strike a balance between interactive humor with the audience and the actual dialogue of a character who may have grave and humorless traits. Cosplayers use calculated demonstrations of self-effacing humor to acknowledge the fan's understanding of the foibles of the character or tropes of the given medium. Humor, based on the Cosplayer's perception of the character in a social situation, also allows audience members to be active participants with the performance.

Cosplay subculture

The Cosplay fandom subculture is comprised primarily of Cosplayers and their fans (who may also participate in Cosplay activities), but spectators, judges, critics, and even harassers have the ability to influence the internal structure of the nebulous group. The duality of the Cosplayers' identities and symbiotic relationships among them are distinct characteristics to this subculture. The fluidity of the Cosplayer allows her or him to be either participant or fan, and sometimes both at the same time where the Cosplayer in costume interacts with a Cosplayer she or he admires and/or emulates.

Cosplay is a sizable encompassing subculture; within it there are subset groups reflecting specific areas of interest and genres, such as anime and science-fiction movies, or television series (e.g., *Firefly*) or video games (e.g., *World of Warcraft*). Cosplayers easily cross the fluid boundaries between the subsets and genres within the subculture (and into other fandoms as well). For example, during a three-day fan convention, an individual Cosplayer may dress and participate in activities as Princess Leia from *Star Wars* on day one while enjoying science-fiction activities with friends; on day two, the Cosplayer performs Bellatrix Lestrange from *Harry Potter* in a Cosplay competition; and for the last day, she is Tinkerbell from *Peter Pan* convincing attendees to clap loudly if they really believe she will fly around the convention area (Winge 2006a). Over the span of a long weekend, this Cosplayer intersected with multiple fan communities while cosplaying characters from three distinct genres.

The Cosplay fandom is a meritocracy, where members establish their position within the group grounded on demonstrated skills and talents valued for Cosplaying activities (costumes, performances, recognitions, creativity). In this way, the meritocracy allows for social mobility within the Cosplay fandom. Cosplayers are awarded for meritorious costumes and performances, as well as acknowledged for skills mastered to create the characters' costumes.

Critics and judges further shape the Cosplay subculture. While judges' official reviews and acknowledgments of Cosplayers' costumes and performances have the power to create Cosplay celebrities, critics' more informal evaluations stir Cosplayers and fans to action and reaction. Harassers also impact the Cosplay communities and the conventions where Cosplayers frequently congregate and socialize.

The Cosplay fan subculture demonstrates resiliency when faced with most recent challenges (e.g., harassment and sexual assault) and stimuli (e.g., social media and news reports) by adapting and adjusting. Furthermore, Cosplayers embrace diversity, novelty, and exposure, which serve the fandom as strengths regardless of accompanying issues. The inventive ways the fan subculture responds to both members and outsiders suggest it is a highly dynamic and vibrant system, which indicates Cosplay's potential for growth and longevity.

Cosplay and popular culture

Cosplay's impact on popular culture has a wide-ranging effect ranging from museum exhibitions to fashion designs to television series to movies. In most of the world, Cosplay is still a subcultural activity; in spite of this, Cosplay has a growing presence in popular culture and the media: most notably, the growing presence of superheroes and villains. In 2008, for example, the Metropolitan Museum of Art (MET) in New York City featured the *Superheroes: Fashion and Fantasy* exhibition featuring superhero and villain fashions. The MET presented the superhero costumes as the ultimate representation of fashion, empowering the wearer with superpowers. In the same year, the MET gala's theme was "Superheroes: Fashion and Fantasy," which encouraged guests to dress as their favorite superhero or create a new or a mash-up superhero costume for the event (Wilson 2008). Essentially, guests were asked to attend a very expensive Cosplay event. In addition, *Vogue* magazine featured comic book characters re-envisioned by fashion designers as avant-garde versions of Cosplayers (Vogue 2008).

In addition, Cosplay is finding its way into television series and is regularly referenced and displayed by the characters on the comedy television series *Big Bang Theory* (2007 to present). In "The Middle Earth Paradigm" episode (2007), Sheldon references a "costume parade" and costume evaluations; and in "The Bakersfield Expedition" episode (2013), Sheldon, Leonard, Raj, and Howard are stranded in the desert, on their way to a fan convention, while dressed in *Star Trek* costumes. Furries (i.e., anthropomorphized fantasy animals), for example, are depicted on the television drama *CSI: Crime Scene Investigation* (2003) and Moby's music video "Beautiful" (2005). Movies such as *Galaxy Quest* (1999) and *Ted 2* (2015) include Cosplayers as part of the plot. And, of course, there are documentaries and documentary-style films about Cosplay, including *Cosplayers: The Movie* (2009), *Cosplayers UK: The Movie* (2011), and *My Other Me: A Film about Cosplayers* (2013). In America, the Public Broadcast Service aired a documentary titled *Cosplay! Crafting a Secret Identity* (2013) focusing primarily on Cosplayers, costumers, and prop makers in Atlanta, Georgia. The Syfy network featured two television series devoted entirely to Cosplay, titled *Heroes of Cosplay* (2013–14) and *Cosplay Melee* (2016). On the Game Show Network *Steampunk'd* (2015) aired, with the theme of Steampunk for costumes and other decorations. Other reality series feature Cosplay events within the greater scheme of the show: *King of the Nerds* (TBS) featured a Cosplay competition as two of its challenges in individual seasons with Yaya Han as the judge (2013; 2015). Also, a Honda Civic commercial (2016) featured Cosplayers driving to a convention with all of their gear in the roomy trunk; the full version of the advertisement has Cosplayer Laura Cee explaining what a "Cosplayer" is.

The allure of comic books and graphic novels comes from their dynamic graphics, high-concept plots, and compelling characters. Still, comic books simultaneously occupy a place in popular and low culture. Furthering its mass appeal are the storylines, which often parallel real life to reach and resonate with diverse audiences. In recent years, some comic book/graphic novel writers challenge stereotypes often associated with these types of media (and their mainstream cultures) and included diverse characters and storylines that reflect the sociopolitical complications of global society. Another example of comic book and the graphic novel's mass appeal is their ability to inspire the creation of live-action movies. *Kick-Ass* (2010) is a movie about everyday people who donned superhero-style costumes and assumed superhero or heroine personas to defeat the bad guys terrorizing their city. Since most characters in animation, comic books, graphic novels, movies, and videogames are firmly positioned as an archetype, the everyday comic book heroes or heroines both defy and fulfill the Jungian archetypes (1972; 1977), such as the Maiden (Snow White), Trickster (Joker), Villain (Cruella de Vil), Hero (Superman), and Anti-hero (Batman) (see Plate 1.4).

The media has a highly contentious, complex, and self-serving relationship with the Cosplay fan community. Cosplayers are enticed and seduced to pose for photographs and interact with media for the fleeting moments of assumed (and realized) fame. And, the media is eager to exploit Cosplayers for exoticism in their body-contouring and revealing colorful costumes, which often are spectacularly portraying fantasy characters not commonly seen in everyday life.

Cosplay celebrities

"Cosfamous" is a term that refers to Cosplayers who gain notoriety or fame for their costumes and/or performances, and if they become famous enough to become Cosplay celebrities known beyond the subculture. Some of the most popular Cosplayers around the world are Alodia Gosiengfiao, Yaya Han, Jan Illenberger, Jenni Källberg, Linda Le, Kaname, Jessica Nigri, Iiniku Uushijima, and Spiral Cats (a Cosplay team). Cosplay professionals (i.e., celebrities, models, spokespersons, and experts) are commonly asked to serve as emcees and judges for Cosplay competitions. Additionally, Cosplay professionals may also host other Cosplay-related events as emcees and spokespersons. At times, they are paid for their time and expertise, but more often these professionals accept these positions in exchange for free airtime and recognition of them dressed as their characters. On the other hand, some Cosplay celebrities become Cosplay models and spokespersons, where there are under signed contracts to be paid for advertisements and promotional activities.

Introductions to the Cosplay fan subculture

I was introduced to Cosplay in the early 1990s at Gen Con in Milwaukee, Wisconsin.[4] While there was not a formal Cosplay masquerade or competition at the time, numerous attendees were dressed in costumes of their favorite characters from cartoons, television series, video games, and movies. In 2000, I attended my first Cosplay masquerade and competition at CONvergence. In 2003, I judged with Marc Hairston[5] my first Cosplay competition at the Schoolgirls and

Mobilesuits: Culture and Creation in Manga and Anime academic conference at the Minneapolis College of Art and Design in Minneapolis, Minnesota.[6] In 2005, I was invited to and joined the Anime Detour convention's Cosplay panel. In 2009, I attended an academic conference in Hong Kong, where I met with Cosplayers from around the world.

In 2004, I began an ethnographic study of Cosplay dress/costumes, documenting Cosplayers at fan conventions with photographs, interviews, and observational field notes. I launched a second study in 2015, in which I collected the same types of data and noted new information about the Cosplay fandom and Cosplayers. As part of these studies, I attend fan conventions (e.g., Anime Detour, Anime Expo, Comic-Con, CONvergence, Fan Expo, Gen Con, Shuto Con, etc.) to meet and speak with Cosplayers, as well as academic conferences (e.g., Schoolgirls and Mobilesuits and Extraordinary Dress Codes) that attracted/ included Cosplayers.

Prior to this research, I realized that fans and participants, or people capitalizing on the costumed body's inherent exotic nature, produced most of the information about Cosplay. While fans and participants offer the most accurate information, they focus tightly on areas of Cosplay that specifically interest them and ignore or subtly suggest anything not within their sphere of interest and influence. Also, fans and participants are so familiar with the craft and practice of Cosplay that they frequently offer vague information in blog articles/posts or interviews, where outsiders need deep details to fully understand the information presented. Even Cosplayers who offer insights, in an attempt to enlighten the general public, acknowledge the unique and sometimes indecipherable existence of the group. Then there are those individuals, usually those from outside the Cosplay fandom, who exploit Cosplayers with exotic and "glamorous" photographs for websites, magazines, and even books. There is, of course, photographic documentation of most subcultures in this manner. This is most evident in the work of Eron Rauch, whose photographs capture raw and gripping moments of a Cosplayer's life at fan conventions.

Cosplay research

"Fanthropology" is the study of fandoms, fans, and related experiences and material culture(s), which is practiced by professional researchers and journalists interested in fan studies (including fans themselves). Fan studies span all activities and media that attract fans, such as sports, films, music, and dolls. Fans (without formal research training) who study members of fan communities also produce fanthropology data, which reflects their internal positions. Fans have intimate access to their fandoms and the Internet is fertile ground for sharing "research" findings, but some fan studies lack academic rigor and produce only anecdotal information. Frequently, fan-produced "research" amounts to photographs or videos including commentary but without specific purpose or analysis.

I position myself as an academic fan, or "aca-fan," whose research contributes to fanthropology about Cosplayers. I began as a fan of science fiction and fantasy literature, graphic novels, and films, with which I eventually found my way to researching fan subcultures. As with all of my research about subcultures and related dress, I seek to learn and share insights into subcultural dress within the context of the voices in and around the subculture.

While research on fandoms is increasing, there is still limited Cosplay-focused research beyond the sharing of photographs of Cosplayers. In recent years, scholars began disseminating research on Cosplay from around the world, such as Cosplay from Australia (Bainbridge and Norris 2013), China (Xiaomi 2006), Hong Kong (Rahman, Wing-sun, and Cheung 2012), Indonesia (Rastati 2017), the Netherlands (Lamerichs 2011), and Taiwan (Chen 2007). Research about North American Cosplay (Duchesne 2005; Anderson 2014; Thomas 2014) is also limited. Although these studies offer valuable information about Cosplayers and the Cosplay fandom, they do not offer comprehensive descriptions of the fandom and lack discussions about the roles of costumes for Cosplayers' experiences.

My research offers a framework for understanding Cosplayers' experiences with costumes and characters in social situations and competitions at fan conventions. The significance of this study is its inclusion of information that provides a broader context of Cosplay, including Cosplayers' narratives and observations at fan conventions in order to present a comprehensive understanding of the Cosplayers' experiences and the significance of their dress (i.e., costumes, props, makeup).

Fandom ethnography

I gathered ethnographic research about the Cosplay fan subculture for more than a decade. Ethnography allows for utmost unobstructed access to the Cosplay fandom and promises the best potential for securing visual and material culture, as well as representing Cosplayers accurately with interview narratives. I secured Cosplayers for interviews and photographs in two ways. First, I posted advertisements requesting Cosplayers for a research study with my contact information and, if posted online, I also included information about which upcoming convention I was attending. Given that conventions range in duration from one day to a week and may span several locations in proximity, the advertisements alerted Cosplayers that I was at a given convention on a specific day and provided a way to contact me if they missed me at the convention. Once at a convention, I found that when a Cosplayer completed an interview and photo session with me, there was another waiting. Since fan conventions are popular places for media and, more recently, researchers, once I started photographing and interviewing Cosplayers, a line of Cosplayers usually formed. Since I collected 98 Cosplayer interviews with 400+ photographs, it was necessary to collate corresponding images with interview narratives and surveys, and label each set with alphanumeric codes for analysis. I was unable to completely protect participants' identities in this study because some costumes/characters reveal the Cosplayer's face or some other identifying trait. Participants were aware of this factor before participating in the study.

As with all research, assumptions and limitations frequently dictate the direction of research more than the researcher's initial plans. In this research, the assumptions include my bias as a researcher; my personal connections to Cosplayers; and my status as a fan of the greater fandom communities including anime/manga, fantasy, science fiction, and Cosplay. Recognizing my bias about the Cosplay fandom, I am a fan of Cosplay who interacts personally with friends who are Cosplayers. Yet, since I am not a Cosplayer, I entered this research with a narrow understanding of the intimate Cosplayer experiences not limited to performance and entertainment for fan audiences.

According to Eventbrite 2015 Fan Survey (2,600 respondents), 60 percent of Cosplayers are between twenty-three and thirty-nine years of age, and 65 percent identified as female (Eventbrite 2015a). It is not uncommon to meet Cosplayers in their fifties and sixties at conventions, and even older, such as the 103-year-old Wonder Woman.[7] My research data was similar to these survey results; however, my participant ages ranged from eighteen to fifty-six years, and seventy-four participants identified as female Cosplayers (of those who identified with a gender).[8]

Researcher bias

While I am not a Cosplayer, I have, at times, been part of fan communities who attend the same conventions as Cosplayers. Furthermore, once introduced to the Cosplay fandom, I attend Cosplay events and support Cosplayers with costume consultations. In professional capacities, I serve as a Cosplay judge and sit on fan panel discussions. Accordingly, I have friends and acquaintances who are Cosplayers, as well as friends who organize, promote, and volunteer for fan conventions.

I also contended with limitations regarding this research including restricted financial resources, Cosplayers' expectations, and the confines/regulations of fan conventions. The lack of financial resources limited how many conventions I attended and how many Cosplayers I interviewed. Cosplayers were occasionally confused about my research despite detailed release forms and careful explanation of the details, because they anticipated research interviews to be carried out similarly to media coverage or media interviews. Access to fan conventions and human subjects' permissions limited most of my research to the United States, with additional observational data from Hong Kong and Japan. I did, however, interview Cosplayers from Australia, Brazil, Canada, China, Germany, Japan, South Korea, Puerto Rico, and the United Kingdom, who were in the United States attending fan conventions. They shared anecdotal stories about Cosplay practices in other parts of the world. While it is impossible to obtain a specific or official count of Cosplayers, the popularity of Cosplay assures thousands and thousands of Cosplayers around the world. In this study, I interviewed only a small number of Cosplayers compared to the greater members of the fandom worldwide.

Methodology

My Cosplay research study was guided by three overarching questions:

- What are the Cosplay(er) experiences?
- What are the roles of dress/costume within the Cosplay subculture?
- What are the positions of the Cosplay subculture within the greater fandom communities/subcultures?

In order to address these questions, I employ empirical qualitative research methods including observations, surveys, interview narratives, and photography and visual analysis. Observations were collected into field notes (analog and digital) during or directly after Cosplay events, typically at fan conventions. Surveys and interview narratives were given to Cosplayers at fan conventions in the United States. I collected photographs in connection with surveys and interviews for documentation of costumes and later analysis. The data from these methods assist in constructing a comprehensive examination of the Cosplayer's worlds and experiences.

My observations of Cosplayers and Cosplay activities were primarily gathered at fandom conventions and surrounding areas during these conventions. Due to limited time availability during conventions, I also interacted with Cosplayers at other locations for some of the interviews and photographs collected in this study. I documented these observations with notes both in print and digital journals, which support interview narratives and photographic evidence. The field notes include convention details and dates; notes about Cosplay events; descriptions of Cosplayers' costumes/appearances and performances; and information about Cosplay-related rules, signage, and organizations.

I collected Cosplayer narratives by interviewing individual Cosplayers. When Cosplayers were part of a team, I documented the team members in photographs and made notations on individual interview scripts. The interviews focused around my guiding research questions, but the actual query process was organic in nature, which allowed for follow-up questions that probed deeper into the Cosplayers' answers and resulted deeper reflections in their responses. Most Cosplayers were enthusiastic to be interviewed and photographed, giving lengthy and highly informative answers/responses.

Photographs of Cosplayers were significant to my research because these images provided visual documentation of their dress, more specifically, how the costumes were worn, styled, posed, and performed. These photographs offer information beyond simply analyzing their costumes as artifacts; they launch discussions about construction, technologies, and rituals. I had difficultly documenting Cosplayer costumes because the Cosplayers were accustomed to posing dramatically for media publicity photos and constantly trying to meet the continuous demands of fans when at conventions. After attending a few fan conventions where I met several Cosplayers, I learned to communicate specifics about the type of documentation that I needed for my research; I also discovered that the Cosplayers responded better to the request for "boring" documentation photographs after showing me their signature poses or in-action movements.

While this study focuses primarily on Cosplay in North America, it would be remiss not to discuss its presence elsewhere because Cosplay is a global phenomenon. In addition to this formal Cosplay research, I had exceptional opportunities to meet and interact with Cosplayers around the globe. In 2009, I met Cosplayers from China, England, Germany, Japan, South Korea, and Australia at the Dress Codes academic conference at the University of Hong Kong in Hong Kong, China. And, at the annual Schoolgirls and Mobilesuits academic conference at the Minneapolis College of Art and Design from 2003 to 2006, I judged Cosplay competitions and met Cosplayers from Brazil, Canada, Japan, and the United States. Interactions with these varied Cosplayers impressed upon me the global appeal of Cosplay, as well as demonstrating the potential for Cosplay to galvanize Cosplayers and fans into a global subculture.

Cosplay themes

After reviewing the interview narratives, field notes, and photographs, I utilized thematic analysis to complicate and reduce (Siedel and Kelle 1995: 30) the data in order to reveal ten themes (or patterns found across the collected data) about the Cosplay fandom subculture. Using data-driven thematic coding, themes emerged from the collected data by examining the parts to the whole and back again. Theme and subtheme names reflect common concepts from the Cosplay fan subculture.

These themes were reviewed for accuracy in revealing the complexities and patterns evident within the Cosplay subculture and their experiences. Subsequently, the themes were further discussed and explored utilizing quotations from Cosplayers' interviews and observations as supporting data. The result is a "thick description" (Geertz 1973: 3–30) for each theme and subtheme that is incorporated into a report describing and elucidating the Cosplayer's experiences.

Book overview

In Chapter 2, I introduce components of Cosplay contributing to the construction of the subculture and its growing popularity. I establish the significance of fan conventions and fandoms to the longevity and reputation of Cosplay fan subculture. In addition, I explore the ways the subculture is mediated and exploited through professional and amateur photographs and videos that are often disseminated on the Internet without compensation or consideration for the Cosplayer(s). For the average Cosplayer, the attention from fans and media is initially flattering, but eventually presents complications, and female Cosplayers contend with particular difficulties not as prevalent in other fandoms. Cosplay celebrities and professionals, however, rely on the media exposure in order to gain, continue, and expand their popularity among fans.

I discuss the fantasy genres of characters commonly portrayed by Cosplayers, including the controversial Furry and the popular Steampunk genres. Cosplay characters are inspired from animation, comic books, movies, books, or even videogames. In Cosplay fan community, no single person has exclusive ownership portrayal over a specific character, nor is a Cosplayer regulated by the fandom to portray any single (or multiple) character(s) from a specific genre. Establishing the character genres provides the reader with a deeper understanding for the Cosplay subculture and how the characters contribute to the diversity of the subculture while also reflecting common popular culture themes.

In Chapter 3, I focus on the thematic analysis of ten themes and subthemes emerging from my Cosplay subculture dress research. The themes are Costume Makes the Superhero (Cosplay Costume), Mirror, Mirror on the Wall (Constructed Representations), A Picture Is Worth 140 Characters (Photographs and Videos), You Gotta Have Friends (Social Networks and Communities), I Am Just Roleplaying My Character (Performativity and Roleplaying), Cosplay Is the Mother of Invention (Creativity), With Great Powers Come Great Powers (Empowerment and Self-Determination), Toto, We're Not in the Convention Anymore (Escapism),

It's Not Just a Costume: Cosplay Is a Way of Life (Devotion and Obsession), and Have Fun! (Fun and Play).

Each theme is individually analyzed and discussed for complexities and patterns in order to provide a more accurate representation and a deeper understanding of Cosplay. For example, the theme Mirror, Mirror on the Wall (Constructed Representations) revealed information about character selection, transnational identity or identities, and visual representations, as well as issues such as racism, sexism, sizism, and crossplay (i.e., donning a character with a different gender other than which the Cosplayer identifies). The theme and resulting analysis are supported with specific examples and narratives from interviews and collected data. By exploring the themes revealed within Cosplay experiences, it is possible to understand how Cosplay is multidimensional and layered than simply just comic book nerds dressing in Halloween-style costumes.

In Chapter 4, I explore Cosplay dress including all aspects of the Cosplayer's appearance when dressed as a chosen character. I begin by discussing the importance of the Cosplay character and the process a Cosplayer commonly uses to select an individual character or create an original character. I further discuss how roleplaying, signature poses, and dialogue contribute to the portrayal of the character for accuracy, humor, fun, and/or competitions.

A majority of this chapter focuses on the Cosplay costumes (dress/appearances). I discuss all of the aspects of the costume, from makeup to clothing to prosthetics to weapons. I draw on specific examples from my research to explore Cosplay costumes in depth. I examine the highly controversial practice of purchasing all or most of a character's overall costume, in contrast to the do-it-yourself construction of most aspects of the costume by the Cosplayer. Purchased or constructed, the Cosplayer's costume is a significant expense of time and money.

Furthermore, I address the ways the Cosplayer's body plays an integral role in achieving an accurate character portrayal, at the same time having the potential to be an area of contention and conflict. Cosplayers, for example, who are not the same height, weight, race, species, and/or gender as their selected character may go to extreme lengths to achieve accuracy in portrayal. These discrepancies between reality and fantasy have led to face-to-face and online debates usually focused on three primary issues: weight, race, and gender.

In Chapter 5, I focus on the powerful and controversial positions of specific groups and individuals within the Cosplay fan subculture, firmly situated within the larger fandoms, such as comic book fans, anime and manga fans, roleplayers, and reenactors. In this chapter, I provide statistics and data establishing how males were the primary attendees to fan conventions and members of related subcultures until the last fifteen years when the number of women began to grow to nearly equal proportions. This shift in demographics should create a power shift, but that has not happen yet.

Gender constructs and the corporeal body are complicated, sexualized, and often ritualized within the Cosplay fandom subculture. Female-representing Cosplayers and characters further struggle with internal and external conflicts regarding the body and identity. In addition, Cosplayers struggle with size, race, and ethnicity limitations in the array of contemporary fantasy characters from which to select and reflect fandom's diversity. Cosplayers also face challenges and criticisms regarding representations of size, race, and ethnicity within costumes and performances.

These challenges and criticisms come from outsiders, convention attendees, and spectators who harass female and female-representing Cosplayers in costume. Since crossplay characters are further eroticized as the exotic Other by outsiders, this judgment presents additional situations of vulnerability for female Cosplayers. Some Cosplayers speculate that the harassment toward female Cosplayers happens because those outside the Cosplay subculture interpret costumes as implied consent. Subsequently, spectators and non-Cosplayers touch and grope costumed female Cosplayers with inappropriate and sometimes illegal behaviors. Most Cosplay groups and conventions have now instituted strict rules about interactions with Cosplayers, which has been familiarized to "Cosplay is NOT Consent." I conclude Chapter 5 with a discussion about the ways Cosplay offers unconventional gender, sexuality, and identity constructs within the tropes of fantastic characters, creating ritualized transformational spaces ripe with potential for conflict and agency.

In Chapter 6, I concentrate on the contextualizing Cosplay beyond the subculture. I position the Cosplay subculture within the larger fandom communities/subcultures, as well as ascertain its place within popular, Internet, and global cultures. In addition, I discuss the opportunities and challenges that arise from Cosplay's continued recursion or rebounding associated with Japan.

Cosplay is growing in popularity, both inside and outside the subculture. This popularity is directly traced to social media and continued external media coverage, increasing membership and outsiders' interest in the fandom. Unfortunately, there are also negative consequences for the fandom, where outsiders exploit Cosplayers without permissions, compensation, or consideration.

I also outline the impacts Cosplay's popularity has on economies, popular culture, and fan subcultures. Accordingly, I address the economic predictions directly connected to Cosplayers and the fandom. I explore related continuing debates in regard to the popularity, consumption, and economic expectations related to Cosplay.

The future of Cosplay has exciting possibilities if the subculture is able to address disconcerting issues concerning its female members and acknowledge itself as a global phenom (instead of being tied to an individual country or genre). Cosplayers' enthusiasm crosses language, geographical, and cultural boundaries and Cosplay continues to effect and influence popular culture.

2
COSPLAY FANDOM SUBCULTURE

When I began researching the Cosplay subculture for my article "Costuming the Imagination: Origins of Manga and Anime Cosplay" (2006), I discovered that Cosplay was first practiced in the United States at fan conventions and eventually transculturally was exported to Japan. For years, Cosplayers only dressed in their character costumes during one night of the convention in order to participate in a costume contest, masquerade, or parade. By the late 1990s, however, fan conventions around the world welcomed costumed fans and Cosplayers throughout the convention. By the 2000s, Cosplay grew in popularity, and Cosplayers and the related activities continue to be major attractions at fan conventions.

My research also revealed that most literature about Cosplay lack in-depth research with information and insights about the subculture, their costumes, experiences, and lifestyles. Instead, these books primarily include photographs of Cosplayers or how-to guides for costume construction. Frequently, these texts also focus on Japanese-centric Cosplay experiences, leading to sweeping generalizations and misunderstandings regarding the global phenomenon that are Cosplay fan experiences. That is not to suggest these sources are without merit in documenting the seductive and captivating visual qualities of the Cosplay subculture. More authentic to experiences of Cosplayers than most text, however, are the Internet sites for Cosplayers composed by Cosplayers or fans. Unfortunately, these websites frequently lack objectivity.

Cosplay celebrities, models, photographers, fans, and other Cosplayers shape the Cosplayers' experiences within the subculture and greater fandoms at conventions. Cosplay celebrities and models also have Internet sites allowing them to connect with their fans as well as serve as areas of promotion. The Cosplayers' spheres are additionally affected by outside influencers, such as members from other fandoms, the media, researchers, harassers, and exploiters. Further adding to the complexities of the subculture is the Cosplayers' and fans' use of social media and online forums. Subsequently, the Cosplay subculture is a dynamic, organic fandom system continuously impacted by internal and external forces, making it challenging to represent Cosplayers with any accuracy in a fixed, static form (i.e., the representations in this book).

Cosplay fandom subculture

Subcultures are distinct from mainstream society and identifiable by the members' loosely collective style and dress (Hebdige 1979). Mike Brake argues subcultures are distinguishable by their argot (language), demeanor (behaviors), and image (styles and appearances) (1985: 11–18). J. Patrick Williams suggests understanding subcultures moves beyond Hebdige and Brake by thinking about subcultural "style" as "cultural practices and cultural objects" (2011: 67–9). At a fundamental level, a subculture is a group whose individual (formal or informal) members distinguish themselves from the mainstream culture/society with dress, politics, music, language, technology, geography, and activities (Winge 2012: 5).[1]

Daisuke Okabe states the Cosplay fandom subculture is "a distinct community with shared values and boundaries" (2012: 227). Individuals are drawn to the Cosplay subculture because the Cosplay fandom offers social and cultural spaces to explore and express the love of characters and genres through creative expressions in costume and performances. Within this subcultural arena, Cosplayers have numerous opportunities for belonging, acceptance, and appreciation for their Cosplay identities and activities, which may be misunderstood or rejected in other areas of their "real" lives by non-Cosplayers. Cosplayers define the parameters of their fandom with their use of social networks, activities, and even physical spaces (e.g., fan conventions and cafés). These recognized spaces also encourage active participation in the fan community even when critiques of Cosplayers are harsh and discouraging.

Most contemporary fandoms informally expect active participation on the part of the fan (see Brownie and Graydon 2016; Cherry 2016; Cubbinson 2012; Jenkins 2006; Lamerichs 2011), instead of being passive observers within the system. Moreover, this participation is ritualized in its actions and outcomes, whether in the rules of tabletop or online gaming or tropes of Cosplaying a character in the public spaces of a convention. Fans also socialize newcomers with humor and support until they are guided to the proper station and behave within the broad sphere the specific fandom occupies. Fans reward their peers who understand the rituals and unwritten rules with camaraderie, support, and even awards and sanction those fans who disregard the guidelines and respect demanded by Cosplayers. Even nonconformers are rarely excluded from Cosplay activities; instead, these outliers are encouraged through affable peer pressure to modify their behaviors to align with the fandom's expectations.

Frequently, Cosplayers extend beyond their understood ritualized participation to more specific expectations of themselves and one another. This is most evident in Cosplay teams, where the group expects individual Cosplayer contributions to lead to the overall performance of the team. If one Cosplayer performing a character improvises or steals the audience's attention outside of the agreed-upon skit, the team members may socially admonish the violating Cosplayer or compete against each other trying to regain the audience members' attention for the entire team or moving the attention to a different individual. And the obverse is observed when a Cosplayer interacts with another Cosplayer to enhance her performance or better visually communicates a relationship between two characters where the Cosplayers had no previous introduction. For example, consider a *Star War*'s Luke Skywalker's chance meeting with a Darth Vader outside an artist gallery at a convention. Their improvisational interactions about Luke's "healthy handshake" and Father's Day jokes lead to humorous banter and storyline ripe for any nearby *Star Wars* fan to enjoy.

Cosplayers identify as "fans" of specific genres and characters, as well as members of the Cosplay fandom. The term "fandom" is used to describe all things and activities associated with the subcultures of fans, and functions as an extension of the fan (Jenkins 1992: 192). Fandoms spawn from an area of common interest or activity that attracts people's fascination and is generally associated with a devotion to an obsession or interest. The activities and outcomes from the fandom also support individual fans within social groups, in which the individual may attend and/or participate. Fans may also choose to pursue their shared interest alone and only be associated to the corresponding fandom in the most informal sense. A fandom is a subcultural group where individuals (fans) join together or intersect into subsets, which are categorized by genres (i.e., science fiction, anime/manga, or horror) commonly found at conventions.

Fandoms are constructed around people who have similar interests. While the term "fan" is short for "fanatic," today's fantasy and science fiction fans are typically stereotyped by the media as sweet and endearing, but socially awkward nerds (e.g., *The Big Bang Theory* 2007–present and *Fanboys* 2009); there are examples of the fan as a dangerous, disturbed stalker (e.g., *Swimfan* 2002 and *Misery* 1990). Typically, Cosplayers are not considered to be this menacing type of fan, but it may be due to the cute, nonthreatening factor provided by the costumes and animated performances. Cosplayers participate in select social group settings (such as anime conventions), with costumed appearances portraying idealized bodies, donning dynamic, and flattering clothing with perfectly coifed hairstyles and immaculate makeup for consumption by a like-minded audience.

A "superfan" is a person who is deeply dedicated (possibly even obsessed) with a specific fandom. These superfans are the first in line for their fandom events, preorder merchandise, and religiously attend fandom conventions. They also contribute significantly to their preferred fan community(ies) by setting high standards for devotion and fervor. Superfans can also devalue their fan community by exhibiting behaviors that promote extreme behaviors that are then associated with the fandom, which may appear aggressive, childish, or obsessive. Overall, superfans *live* for their love of the fandom and, in exchange, they nourish the fandom with enthusiasm, exuberant performances, and revenue but at a repercussive social cost to the individual and fandom.

According to the 2015 Eventbrite Fan Survey (annual survey), 50 percent of Cosplayers who participated in the online survey identify as superfans (Eventbrite 2015a). Cosplay superfans exhibit intense devotion and passion for the fandom with their extensive knowledge of specific genres, characters and storyline, and Cosplay professionals, as well as construction skills or makeup techniques. Superfans often have significant online presences where they proselytize the virtues of Cosplay, as well as displaying their enthusiasm, commitment, and fanaticism for their favorite genres and characters, or criticizing flaws with specific story arcs or inconsistencies between different generations or incarnations of a series or franchise.

The Cosplay subculture is a fandom overlapping and existing in concert with other fan communities, especially in the context of the convention. Unlike members of many fandoms, such as Beatlemaniacs (fans of the Beatles), Sherlockians (fans of Sherlock Holmes), and Sneakerheads (fans of athletic shoes), Cosplayers are highly visible, perform in public settings, and even seek out media attention. Even fandoms with recent media visibility and rich storylines from which to draw characters, such as Bronies (fans of *My Little Pony: Friendship Is Magic*), are not necessarily dressing in costumes and participating in Cosplay activities. This is not to suggest that each fandom is so distinct that there are buffers between each or they resist overlapping. Consider, for instance, a Potterhead (fan of *Harry Potter*) who cosplays Snape, a Whoovian (fan of *Doctor Who*), who cosplays the fourth Doctor, or a Trekkie (fan of *Star Trek*), who cosplays Mr. Spock. In this way, Cosplay creates a space for interactions and overlappings with other fandoms represented with specific character portrayals.

Costume or Cosplay?

Is everyone who wears a costume a Cosplayer? Some scholars, such as Brownie and Graydon (2016), Cherry (2016), and Lamerichs (2011), group all costumed performances together (i.e., historic reenactment, theatre, LARPing, and Renaissance Faires). Pravina Shukla states, "Costume—like dress—is the clothing of who we are but signals a different self" (2015: 3). Nicolle Lamerichs further proposes that Cosplay is a combination of sci-fi fandom and Renaissance faire and/or historical reenactment practices in the roleplay (2011: 2). Brownie and Graydon add to Lamerichs's argument by suggesting that in addition to drawing on these costumed events/activities, Cosplay is an extension of childhood, stating, "These [Cosplay activities] are all practices that extend childhood play into adulthood" (2016: 110). Gunnels also examines Cosplayers' motivations, where she continually returns to childhood motivations (2009: 1.2, 4.11–12, 5.2). I argue that while there may be superficial similarities, Cosplayers' intentions, expectations, and outcomes are distinct from historic reenactments and theatric performances. My research suggests that these latter arguments are most plausible considering the origins of even the term "Cosplay" (i.e., costume + play). Furthermore, Cosplayers express that their experiences are greatly enhanced by participating in "play" and "humor."

The assumption that all costumed events/activities are similar leads to other fan communities commonly misidentified as Cosplayers and vice versa, as well as misunderstandings. While members of the Society for Creative Anachronism (SCA) and Live Action Roleplayers (LARPers) may appear similar to Cosplayers by dressing in costumes to perform characters, they actually differ greatly from members of the Cosplay fandom. The SCA is an international organization dedicated to researching and reenacting pre-seventeenth-century European history; its 30,000 members primarily dress as historical fictitious characters from the Dark Ages and Medieval Europeans (SCA.org). LARPers create fantasy personas or characters with fictitious backstories for the purposes of roleplaying within a live action game (i.e., system; roleplaying games [RPGs]), and may also interact in-character social purposes "out of game." Typically, the LARP and RPG personas are not exact representations of characters from existing literature, films, or video games; instead, these characters have context within the roleplaying game.

In *Cosplay Girls: Japan's Live Animation Heroines* (2003), there is a brief discussion about Cosplayers being interested in RPGs as other sources for additional characters for them to portray when they Cosplay (Aoyama and Cahill 2003: 85–91). It should be noted that a SCA member, Renaissance actor or actress, or LARPer may also be a Cosplayer, but as a Cosplayer she or he would most likely portray a different type of character, one drawn from a source media (usually science fiction or fantasy). The rare exceptions are original characters (OCs) who would satisfy the requirements for SCA or another group in addition to the Cosplay fandom. The latter has the most lenient requirements for character representations, which has encouraged Cosplayers to perform their characters in a variety of settings beyond the fan convention.

Is anyone who roleplays in costume automatically a Cosplayer? When Cosplayers extend the existences of their fantasy characters beyond the physical spaces of conventions and private gatherings, they may transition their characters into participation in well-known tabletop RPGs, such as

Call of Cthulhu, *Dungeons & Dragons*, *Pathfinder*, and *World of Darkness*, with all types of roleplayers beyond Cosplay. They also play online games (i.e., ORPG [online roleplaying game] and MMORPG [massively multiplayer online roleplaying game]), such as *Echo of Souls*, *Final Fantasy*, and *World of Warcraft*. Furries, for example, play *Bunnies and Burrows* (a tabletop RPG based on the novel *Watership Down* [1972]) and *Ironclaw* (tabletop RPG and online game).

The Cosplayer conducts extensive research for her selected character, noting even the minutest details. The Cosplayer's meticulous approach to consuming the character and associated storylines provides an intricate yet formidable foundation from which Cosplay may flourish and take shape in costumed performances. The ability to transition the character (and the self) from the source media into a physical reality for Cosplay purposes and then (if they desire) into a fantasy character suitable for game formats (and back again when needed) suggests that the Cosplayer has malleable and fluid identities despite the bedrock identity of the chosen character.

The genre of source media that fans read, watch, and engage with in any way is frequently regarded as "text" (Jenkins 1992; Hills 2014; Cherry 2016). In fact, several scholars suggest that fans engage with the source media as "text" (similar to reading and writing fanfic)[2] even if the media is visual, which extends to Cosplayers when portraying characters (Cherry 2016; McCudden 2011; Turk 2011). According to Rauch and Bolton, Cosplay is a feedback loop where the Cosplayer actively engages with the text (2010: 177). Brownie and Graydon argue that Cosplayers "interact with [source] text intradiegetically and extradiegetically," where Cosplayers are audience members who also become authors of their own characters and performances (2016: 111). Still, some scholars acknowledge Cosplayers diverge from text (Parrish 2007: 32) and even extend source text in creative ways (Cubbinson 2012: 144).

The ways the audience members interact and participate with Cosplayers reflect Jenkins's term "interactive audience" (2006: 234–37). Audience members play crucial roles in the Cosplay performance. At times, the audience's interactions with the Cosplayer while roleplaying are similar to "call and response," where the dialogue is so well known by the Cosplayer and audience that they become part of the performance. Audience members also participate in other ways, such as shouting humorous interactions and offering pertinent topics for improvisational dialogue.

Examining fandom from the assumption that all source media and resulting portrayals of characters can be understood as "text" is a Western approach, but overlooks and denies the ways Cosplayers experience a storyline where they draw significantly on its seductive visuals and imaginary fantastic qualities. The roles of visual culture are paramount to Cosplay fandom. From the costume to the photographs, Cosplayers engage in visual semiotics and communication more than most subcultures. Furthermore, this argument neglects to acknowledge the material artifacts primarily produced within the fandom, which is significant for the Cosplay fan subculture. The Cosplay fandom's material culture primarily focuses on the costume and accessories, which is understood as nonverbal or visual communication. For these reasons, a textual-only read of the Cosplay fandom disregards the essence of the subculture.

While Cosplayers are audience members who become authors, they also become actors engaged in telling a story. A contemporary version of a storyteller, the Cosplayer sculpts and embodies the 3D character (from 2D imagery), moving through physical space and speaking in audible tones to bring the fantastic character and story to life. In this way, Cosplayers are enacting their own live version of fan fiction that departs from the source media. Furthermore, they are extending the suspension of disbelief for their audience (and themselves) by bringing characters to life with creative interpretations and portrayals.

Cosplayers

In recent years, Cosplay appears to have gained nearly universal appeal, and its fans are from all types of social and economic strata and perspectives. The individuals who are drawn to Cosplay defy fitting into tidy categories because they are diverse in ethnicity, race, age, and economic backgrounds. Fans of Cosplay are equally diverse. For this reason, Cosplay is a transcultural fandom with the potential for transnational social, cultural, and economic impacts to both the fan subculture and outsiders who interact with Cosplayers.

Where fan convention attendees were primarily males for decades, in recent years females had a stronger showing (Eventbrite 2015). This increased female attendance is in part due to the Cosplayer fandom, which is now attracting more females than males. This changing demographic complicates and benefits the fan convention spaces, activities, and fandoms. Convention organizers and promoters, as well as vendors, artists, and merchandisers, are capitalizing on the presence of women by marketing to female fans as well as male fans. The same people also have to create spaces safer for Cosplayers who are experiencing harassment and exploitation. Accordingly, fans outside the Cosplay fandom are negotiating the changing convention spaces and their interactions with Cosplayers.

While the Cosplay subculture is rich with diversity and inclusivity, it finds that fantasy and fiction source materials lack racially diverse characters. Moreover, characters with disabilities or limitations are even scarcer in fandom genres. These character limitations create demands and situations ripe for tensions internal and external to the Cosplay community. Most notably, Cosplayers may alter their natural skin pigment with makeup when roleplaying a character of a different race or skin color. When Cosplayers utilize makeup to darken skin visibility (not covered by costume) in order to roleplay characters of differing ethnicities, they risk criticism regarding their practice of "blackface" or "brownface." While skin lightening is more acceptable, it also meets with harsh critiques within subsets. The critiques stem from two basic perspectives. First, there are limited numbers of characters of color for Cosplayers. Second, blackface is marred with a history of being associated with racism and discrimination especially within the Western culture (Strausbaugh 2006). Consequently, use of blackface currently has a complicated position within the Cosplay fandom.

Throughout the history of the fandom, Cosplayers exist as the exotic Other within fandoms and the general public, which attracts the media celebrating and exploiting members of the fandom as entertainment or at least the lighter side of the news. This Othering happens both inside and outside the subculture, ranging from marginalization and ridicule to celebration and celebrity to harassment and exploitation. Cosplayers capitalize on their reputation as the Other, which facilitates their distinctiveness within the greater fandom culture. Subsequently, it is particularly difficult for Cosplayers to distinguish when Othering serves to advantage the fandom and when it serves as exploitation, at the same time.

Being a Cosplayer is a seductive activity because Cosplayers dress in fantastic costumes, attract fans, and seek photography and some even acquire fame and/or popularity beyond the Cosplay fan community. Still, Cosplay has the potential to be a double-edged sword. On the positive side is the capacity for Cosplayers to gain fans, roleplay for audiences, compete against/with other Cosplayers, and pose for photographers. The negative side is the increasing likelihood of being exploited for other's profit or being harassed. Furthermore, as the subculture is continuously exposed to the mainstream culture, Cosplayers are vulnerable and lack protection even within the convention environment where fans often assume there is safety for attendees.

Cosplayers create clever monikers (or aliases) for each of their Cosplay characters, which represent their interpretations of the characters. The moniker frequently suggests the Cosplayer's interest in a character or genre and reflects the Cosplayer's personality, as well as protects the real identity of the Cosplayer on convention badges. Many Cosplay professionals incorporate the term "Cosplay" into their moniker, such as Effy Cosplay (Alexandra) and Kamui Cosplay (Svetlana Quindt). Some Cosplayers have more than one moniker, which may reflect specific characters or the Cosplayer's role, such as Australian Cosplayer's name of Variable Cosplay, which is her fandom identity, but she is also known as "That Lola Bunny" because of her exceptional portrayal of Sakimi-Chan Lola Bunny from *Space Jam* (1996).

In addition to providing character information and establishing Cosplay identities, Cosplay monikers conceal individual identities external from the fandom and general public. Their monikers commonly evolve from nicknames or a combination of terms from the latest and/or favorite fan obsession. While most Cosplayers are self-named (and this moniker carries markers of self-identification), their peers can have input as some ask for advice online or in peer-group conversations. A Cosplayer may acquire several monikers during their time in the Cosplay fandom. These monikers or nicknames serve as disguises and identifications at the same time.

When the Cosplayer adopts a Cosplay moniker, the process suggests rebirth of the self, which is celebrated within the subculture that "christens" the Cosplayer with his, her, or their new identity and name. Moreover, projecting from this rebirth, the Cosplayer's and the related character's identities merge with the character dominating the negotiation of identity when in costume and performance spaces. In time, the Cosplayers will come to be known by his, her, or their moniker, which may be problematic when the Cosplayer does not want to be too closely associated with a single character.

Cosplayers do not have fixed identities; instead they have collections of identities (Lunning 2011). Not only within the design of characters' costumes but also from the interpretations of each performance, Cosplayers are producing and reproducing their identities. The fandom benefits from these multiple identities embodied in each Cosplayer because it maintains a heightened level of dynamics for the overall social system.

As previously mentioned, Cosplayers create a socially structured bubble in which to perform their characters. However, the real world is continuously impacting the escapist worlds of Cosplay (Anderson 2014: 10–15), which creates tension and issues for Cosplayers attempting to attain and maintain a fantasy character identity. There are momentary reminders of reality, such as intruding sounds from emergency vehicle sirens or a baby's cry that, for the audience, disrupts the illusion created by the Cosplayer's performance. But rarely do these unwanted external stimuli impact the Cosplayer's concentration. More experienced Cosplayers may even improvise and incorporate the distraction into their performance, mingling fantasy with reality.

In turn, the Cosplay bubble expands and impacts fans from other fandoms. Some members of other fandoms are drawn into the performances and interrupt the audience member's social environment, conversations, and behaviors. The Cosplay bubble also has the ability to disrupt other fandoms' spheres by distracting their members or physically displacing the assemblies for another fandom.

Cosplayers frequently take liberties with their characters' performances and/or appearances, which is named "transformative Cosplay" (Hale 2014: 19). While Cosplayers are allowed some latitude in how they portray and perform characters, Cosplay critics, fans, and other Cosplayers evaluate these presentations in both informal and formal ways. The critiques' focus on "screen accuracy" and "character accuracy" may reference costume, performance, and/or demeanor. Humorous representations are also acceptable portrayals but are usually parody or satire/irony. Cosplayers are most critical on other Cosplayers who portray characters as a hypersexualized being, or one that presents a character disrespectfully (without the merit of humor).

In *Subculture: The Meaning of Style* (1979), Dick Hebdige offers the concept of subcultural "noise" to explain not only subcultural music but also the metaphoric "noise" created from activities or dress that draws attention to the subculture's members (152). In fact, the feedback and critiques Cosplayers receive about their choice of character and costume is a type of "noise" that attracts attention (while also repelling outsiders). Cosplayers further produce subcultural "noise" with their costumes, performances, and especially with the chaos surrounding photographers attempting to capture unplanned images of posing Cosplayers.

Nonetheless, the more successful Cosplayers become associated with specific genres and characters. On Cosplay.com, for example, forum participants commonly include their preferred genres and favorite Cosplay characters listed after their messages as online signatures. Cosplay celebrity, models, and professionals are well known for specific characters (and character types) and genres. Traci Hines, for example, wears elaborate costumes for characters inspired by Disney animations, such as Tinker Bell from *Peter Pan* and Anna from *Frozen*, while Jessica Nigri commonly portrays video game characters such as Juliet Starling from *Lollipop Chainsaw* and a female version of Captain Edward Kenway from *Assassin's Creed*. While this recognition is desired and assists in establishing identity and reputation, Cosplayers are always challenging themselves to portray new characters and genres. Yaya Han's characters, for example, range from Chun-Li (*Street Fighter* video game) to Jessica Rabbit (*Who Framed Rodger Rabbit* film [1988]) to Shampoo (*Ranma ½* manga) to Powergirl (*DC Universe* comic line).

Representation of the character and presentation of self are entangled within the Cosplayer, where the character becomes the dominant identity within the fandom. Cosplay is a form of "self-expression," where "characters are used as signifiers of the fan's own identity" (Lamerichs 2011: 5.2). The struggle between the character and the self is ongoing when the Cosplayer and/or audience continuously reinterpret both aspects in any given moment. In this way, the self is symbolically, metaphorically, and ritualistically embedded in the performance of the character. Accordingly, Jen Gunnels recognizes Cosplay as "performed identity" allowing for "individual agency and social commentary" about the "social stresses" facing Cosplayers (2009: 1.3).

Brownie and Graydon further suggest that "Cosplay creates multiplicity" for the Cosplayer's identities (2016: 5). Identity is self-determined, and individuals may live/experience multiple identities/roles at the same time (Tajfel 1982), such as being a girlfriend, sister, and student. Individuals experience multiple identities with the use of a hierarchy (Goffman 1959), which is evident in the Cosplayers' fandom when interacting with close friends versus audience members.

Cosplayers embrace the duality of their existence when in costume and appropriate spaces without completely denying the self. The Cosplayer brings something of themselves to the character, which creates a unique representation of the character and by extension their own identity(ies). Subsequently, the Cosplayer's positions within the subculture are multifaceted; sometimes, she or he fulfills more than one role at the same time (e.g., as the costumed Cosplayer becomes a fan securing an autograph in the presence of a more popular Cosplayer and then returns to pose for pictures as their character).

Cosplayers hold all of their characters internally, only freeing one at a time when in the appropriate costume and setting, unless portraying a mash-up character that allows for a combination of more than one character. The internalizing of characters impacts and modifies the self with agency and deterministic behaviors, as well as influences future characters' portrayals, performances, and overall appearances. Accordingly, Cosplayers present fluid and, at times, conflicted identities that may extend beyond the act of Cosplaying.

The importance of authenticity to the Cosplay fan community is paramount within the subculture and must be taken seriously by other fandoms. Brownie and Graydon argue how the commitment to character assists the Cosplayer in establishing authenticity (2016: 113–15). Additionally, the Cosplayer's knowledge of the character and associated genre(s) is critical to verifying fan status. Cosplayers may be criticized for not being a true fan of a character because while dressing as a character seen in a movie adaptation it is not as the character (or storyline) as it existed in its original source media (i.e., graphic novel or comic book).

Variable Cosplay, a professional Cosplayer from Australian, is an advocate for "causeplay" or "costume for a cause" (Epoch Talent 2016). Variable Cosplay performs her Cosplay characters in fundraisers for charities and hospital visits. Many Cosplayers are altruistic with their Cosplay performances for charities and the fandom. Most fandoms and conventions donate monies or services to charities, many being nonprofit organizations. Fan conventions typically donate portions of the ticket sales and/or organize events to channel monies directly to charities. Dragon Con hosts an annual blood drive during the convention, and Howler Con (convention for *Teen Wolf* fans) holds an art auction with all proceeds going to the Cystic Fibrosis Foundation. Furthermore, some fandoms support charity efforts external to conventions, such as Furries' "furmeets" that garner support for animal rights and welfare. Some fandom organizations hold events both internal and external to conventions to support and nurture specific aspects of a given fandom with a larger community. GPS (Geek Partnership Society, formally MiSFiTS—Minnesota Society for Interest in Science Fiction and Fantasy) currently holds writing competitions and other community events to promote science-fiction and fantasy literacy while partnering with CONvergence, the Minnesota science-fiction and fantasy convention, for numerous activities.

Figure 2.1 The Barbarian is an original character, and the Cosplayer created the weapons from children's toys and used secondhand fur for the bracer. Photo: Therèsa M. Winge.

Cosplayers are somewhat restricted in character choice and performance/roleplaying by their corporeal body. Still, Cosplayers are inventive with strong problem-solving skills; they frequently collaborate with other Cosplayers to address issues, such as costume construction that resembles machinery, such as oversized mechs or robots, or portraying a character who is top heavy with large arm-like structures but with no lower body or legs or even lacks corporeal form, such as all of the versions of Zeromus, one of the final bosses from the *Final Fantasy IV* video game. Many Cosplayers learn a variety of crafts and skills in order to create their costumes with accuracy. For weaponry or complicated props requiring highly specialized skills and equipment, however, Cosplayers may hire someone to construct these items (see Figure 2.1).

Cosplayers perform alone and/or in teams, and some do both. Cosplaying in teams presents practical challenges, which explains its short-lived existence. These Cosplayers contend with issues similar to most team activities, such as agreeing to a unified vision, finding times for everyone to meet, and difficulties determining leadership. Cosplay teams, however, also need to consider, for example, character selections best suited to the team's composition, consistency, and appropriateness in fabrics and construction, and weapons and props.

Cosplay celebrities and professionals

Unlike most subcultures, Cosplay has a growing legion of celebrities and professionals from around the world who are considered by some Cosplayers to be the most popular and "cosfamous." Some of the most popular Cosplayers include Yaya Han (United States), Alodia Gosiengfiao (Philippines), Marie-Claude Bourbonnais (Canada), Maria Ramos (Mexico), Variable Cosplay (Australia), and Jessica Nigri (United States). Despite the most popular Cosplayers being female dominated, there are popular male Cosplayers as well, including Kid Remington (Canada), Elffi Cosplay (Finland), Captain Cosplay (United States), Leon Chiro Cosplay Art (Italy), Reika (Japan), and Justin Acharacter (Australia). And, there are Cosplay teams, such as Spiral Cats (South Korea), Cosis (South Korea), LT3 (United States), and Official XX Girls (United States). Individual members of Cosplay teams may Cosplay a character without their team, and Cosplayers may temporarily create a team to portray a character group; for example, in 2008 at the Anime Expo, Yaya Han joined with Hannah Lees, Steph, and Joie to create a Cosplay team to create the Eternal Sailor Scouts from the *Sailor Moon* franchise.

These popular Cosplayers also function in many respects as Cosplay royalty or luminaries. They frequently serve as judges for Cosplay competitions, give media interviews, and are featured as special guests at conventions, as well as gain celebrity status beyond those in Cosplay. Yaya Han, for example, is a Cosplay celebrity/model/spokesperson who is known for her elaborate anime costumed characters and frequently judges Cosplay competitions. She starred in *Heroes of Cosplay* (Syfy 2013–14) and served as a judge on two episodes of the TBS television series *King of the Nerds* (2013 and 2014) as well as winning awards from judging many other Cosplay competitions. Currently, she has a line of Cosplay costume fabrics, notions, and patterns for sale at Jo-Ann Craft and Fabric stores.

Cosplay professionals are frequently employed as "models," who serve many roles as spokespersons for marketing merchandise, emcees for Cosplay competitions and events, and speakers and guests at conventions' Cosplay panels. Cosplay professionals are highly regarded by most of their Cosplayer fans, whose status then comes with elevated expectations. Subsequently, they evoke harsh criticism from fans when they fail to meet or exceed those expectations (see Lamerichs 2011: 4.4, 4.5). Cosplayers lament (primarily online) that some Cosplay celebrities, models, and spokespersons hire people to maintain their websites or do not personally respond to comments and feedback, which is considered disrespectful by many fans. Interactions with fans are crucial to assure a continued following at fan conventions and online. Some Cosplay models and spokespersons are also criticized for not attending fan conventions or performing before assuming their celebrity status among and representing Cosplayers.

Cosplayers are not always pleased with the ways they are represented in the media: as exoticized and hypersexualized geeks and nerds.[3] Cosplay celebrities and professionals, nevertheless, rely on the media exposure in order to gain, continue, and expand their popularity among other Cosplayers and fans. They also utilize social media to connect with all kinds of audiences, promote their chosen Cosplay characters, and encourage fans to join them at upcoming events and conventions.

Still, Cosplayers admire (and possibly covet) the positions of Cosplay professionals, models, and celebrities and strive to attain their own celebrity status. Obviously, the renown, attention, and fame, frequently inherent with these positions, are desirable. Also, they have an opportunity to financially profit from being Cosplayers, as well as acquiring gifts from sponsors, merchandisers, promoters, and retailers. For many Cosplayers who have a pronounced outlay of money for Cosplay, it is tempting to find a way to financially profit at Cosplay.

Participating in the Cosplay is expensive, from the cost of the costume, to travel and hotel expenses, to convention fees. Also, constructing the fantasy character's costume is typically extremely time and resource intensive. While veteran Cosplayers may know ways to cut costs, they still dedicate significant amounts of time to their costumes, fans, and performances. For example, Yaya Han lists hours spent on each costume (on her website), which range from eight to more than thirty hours. Han lists on her website the amount of time she spends on creating her costumes, such as 50 hours for Jellyfish (2015) and 200 hours for Camilla from *Fire Emblem Fates* (2017). Robin Rosenberg's and Andrea Letamendi's research revealed that Cosplayers spend "an average of 40 hours preparing each costume" for not less than US$100 cost for materials for each costume (2013: 16). Eventbrite's 2015 fan survey data shows 70 percent of Cosplayers spend more than US$100 at conventions beyond accommodations, food, parking, and so forth. The same survey indicates that each year 60 percent of Cosplayers attend three or more conventions and 27 percent attend five or more; this is more convention attendance than any other category of fan (Eventbrite 2015a). It is Cosplayers' contention that the "costs" associated with Cosplay are offset by the benefits of the experiences within the subculture, such as social interactions, ephemeral fame, and the joy. Some Cosplayers share inside jokes referring to "Cosplay" as "cost play" because of the considerable financial commitment required for costume construction, hotel lodgings, travel expenses, and convention fees.

Cosplay fandom hierarchy

Michelle McCudden, a fan researcher, suggests that fandoms have "hierarchies" for their members determined by "devotion" (2011: 14), which is demonstrated in the Cosplay fandom by obsession for character accuracy and costume detail. The hierarchy within the Cosplay subculture reflects its structure, which has a central core surrounded by two concentric bands comprised of groups diffusing into each other. The positions of members within the subculture are fluid and flexible; they may move between the core and bands, and even into other fandoms. Costumes are visual indicators of the Cosplay fandom, and the attention to the character's details demonstrates the level of commitment and informs the meritocracy of the fandom.

At the core are Cosplayers dressed as fantastic characters, ranging from first-time novices to veterans with awards, each demanding space and attention with their fantastic and energetic performances and costumes. Consequently, the central core and subsequent bands of the Cosplay subculture hierarchy is malleable and able to expand (and contract) to accommodate the requirements of the Cosplayers. Within the Cosplay core exist factions or subsets of the subculture for genres from which characters were selected, which suggests Cosplayers exist in more than one fandom at the same time. When roleplaying a character, Cosplayers simultaneously exist in at least two fandoms: Cosplay fandom and the character's fandom. Attempting to portray a character with accuracy and consideration for the related storyline within a given genre, the Cosplayer boldly negotiates the fandom from which her character originates. Consequently, audience members (Cosplayers and fans of the character/story being performed) evaluate the Cosplayer's appearance and performance.

The first band radiating out from the core includes fans, Cosplay professionals, fan fiction writers, judges, vendors, and merchandisers. Many individuals from this band exist within the center of the subculture when they assume Cosplayer characters. Eventually celebrity Cosplayers reach status, however, that does not allow them to easily return to being an average Cosplayer. While vendors and merchandisers may not be Cosplayers, judges range from Cosplayers to craftspersons/experts/researchers to illustrators/authors (the creators of the source materials for most Cosplay characters).

Lamerichs accurately asserts that Cosplay is the "embodied practice" of portraying the character accurately with the use of the Cosplayer's body and dress (2011: 4.4). By immersing herself into the characters' backstory, storylines, and appearances, the resulting costumes and performances reflect the Cosplayer's position within the fandom. Furthermore, the physical act of dressing in and wearing the costume and makeup with accessories and props consumes the Cosplayer's body and assists in projecting the desired character (see Figure 2.2).

At the same time, the Cosplayer must position the character within the Cosplay fandom without betraying the expectations of their Cosplay peers (or audience). The appropriate interactions and connections between fandoms are taken for granted until expectations are not met. At times of conflict, the Cosplayer who

Figure 2.2 Gaara is a character from *Naruto* anime series, who wears a giant calabash-shaped gourd covered in symbols and filled with magical sand. The Cosplayer constructed this sizable accessory from paper mache and paint. Photo: Therèsa M. Winge.

caused the offense quickly seeks to resolve the issue usually through humor and continued but careful interactions. There is the rare Cosplayer, however, who utilizes social media to plead her case, in the hopes that fans and peer Cosplayers will respond with support.

Cosplayers share a fan language referred to as "fanspeak," which varies slightly between the reference genre and fandom. Fanspeak is not unique to Cosplayers, and many terms are shared across many fandoms. A "muggle," for example, is a non-magical person according to J. K. Rowling in the *Harry Potter* book series. Cosplayers (and many other fandom members) use "muggle" to refer to any person who lacks imagination or is simply boring and trite. An additional layer of meaning occurs when a Cosplayer roleplays a *Harry Potter* movie character. Additional examples of Cosplay fanspeak are fanac (fan activities), fen (plural for "fan"), flame (insults about someone's costume or performance), OC (original character), and squee or kawaii (cute or adorable). Due to the integration of diverse audiences at fan conventions, fanspeak is both a shared and privileged form of jargon, which keeps conversations private to the fandom subculture(s).

"Headcanon," for example, is the practice of adding to the understood knowledge about a character with new information created by the Cosplayer. A Cosplayer dressed as Raven from the animated television series *Teen Titans* informed me that, because of her shadowy persona on the show, she loves to eat dark chocolate when she is sad. This Cosplayer invented headcanon (i.e., an affection for dark chocolate) about the portrayed character (i.e., Raven), which constructs a personal bond with the character.

In addition, Cosplayers, similar to fans from many fandoms, write fan fiction or fanfic, which are fictional stories written within the tropes of a chosen genre using established and new characters while taking the storyline(s) into new and often unexpected directions. Fanfic also offers possibilities to inspire new, reinterpreted mash-ups and original characters for roleplaying. These reinspired characters have limitations beyond well-known characters, in that, they only exist to the extent as written in the fanfic. Furthermore, writing fanfic offers fans a space to flex and explore their creativity, expand storylines, and sometimes rectify storylines that they feel depart from structures of the genre or the story's established universe.

Individual Cosplayers garner significant benefits from being part of the popular and growing Cosplay fandom. Both online and in person, Cosplayers are greeted by the welcoming social network, which provides support for activities from choosing a character, to designing and constructing a costume, to advising on performances and competitions. In addition, Cosplay functions as a creative outlet for participants from their sketching and designing the appearance, to constructing and customizing the costume, to practicing and performing the character. While the fandom circles around the creative aspects of Cosplay, individually Cosplayers highly value their participation in social networks (Eventbrite 2015a).

Due to the significant role of media attention to Cosplay's growing popularity, models, professional photographers, spectators, and media itself occupy the outermost band. In some subcultures, these people would not be included in the subculture's overall composition, but the influence and interactions of this band can be felt throughout the entire Cosplay fan subculture. Cosplay models, for example, originally occupied the core of the fan subculture. Then, these Cosplayers move to the first band when they become celebrities, and if they become less involved with Cosplayers they will eventually migrate to the outermost band. Accordingly, the second and outermost band contains those who exist at the periphery of the Cosplay fandom, and commonly interact with non-Cosplay fandoms and fans as well as Cosplayers. Security, researchers, and convention organizers commonly exist throughout this band.

Further influencing the hierarchy and structure of the Cosplay subculture are the promoters, researchers, and harassers. These individuals penetrate the fan subculture's structure as judges, panel guests, vendors, or audience members. For this reason, Cosplayers manipulate, limit, expand, and contract the fandom into directions that best suit the collective's goals when interacting with these individuals.

In the case of promoters, they attend conventions to gather knowledge about Cosplayers and disseminate their information. Promoters of Cosplayers and/or Cosplay events shape the fandom scene according to their (financial) needs, and will employ the media and other Cosplayers accordingly. Some Cosplayers find promoters a necessary evil, while others enjoy the media attention they bring despite the hypersexualization they promote, which is one of the issues facing Cosplayers today. All the same, promoters expand the reach of the subculture from fan communities to the mainstream popular culture, where there are additional promotional and merchandising opportunities for financial profit.

Researchers are not new to fan conventions, but as more of them seek interviews and photography sessions with Cosplayers, they create rivalry with the media and fans. Most of these studies are qualitative, meaning the researcher interacts with Cosplayer(s) for interviews and observes their events and interactions with one another. But the very act of researching the fandom adds new elements to the subculture. Accordingly, researchers are changing the fan community by their presence. Also, as researchers disseminate their findings about Cosplayers, they impact the fandom by focusing a reflexive lens on specific aspects of Cosplay. As a result, the new and focused attention from researchers creates opportunities for change within the fandom.

Due to harassers over the last few decades, Cosplayers were rarely seen out on the urban streets (beyond temporarily on those near the convention center where a fan convention is held), which is dissimilar to other contemporary subcultures. Once at the fan convention and in costume, Cosplayers rarely leave the venue, except for the Cosplay parade or occasionally to get food or caffeine. In March 2016, during Sakura-Con in Seattle, Washington, I saw a trail of Cosplayers in costume between the convention center and a nearby coffeehouse and hotel. And, in August 2016, during Gen Con, most Cosplayers in costume only left the convention space to walk to nearby hotels and food trucks across the street, which informally extends the convention area. Outside the convention spaces, Cosplayers are most vulnerable because they are not in a large group and risk pestering and harassment from bullies and other non-empathetic observers. Accordingly, harassers are primarily found physically at fan conventions and virtually on the Internet. In spite of the harassers, both sites attempt to offer Cosplayers refuge from the mainstream gaze (and judgment), and present opportunities to make social connections with other Cosplayers as well as fans from differing but like-minded communities. Safety and protection is not the primary motivation for Cosplayers' preferences for these sites, but it is an added benefit and may become a more significant factor in the Cosplay fandom's future.

Still, harassers infiltrate both the fan convention and Internet websites, and lurk outside convention spaces causing difficulties for Cosplayers. Harassers are significantly impacting more than just the Cosplay fandom subculture. Convention organizers and website moderators can attempt to control unwanted attention and activities. Conventions organizers, for example, are developing protocols for proper ways to interact with Cosplayers (and female-representing attendees) and disseminating that information to all attendees. Along a similar theme, at some conventions, Cosplayers are being turned away or sanctioned if their costume (or clothing) is deemed too revealing. Feedback to the latter is negative because Cosplayers feel it is damaging to the fandom overall, and lacks recognition that many female characters are hypersexualized within their original media. Accordingly, promoters and convention organizers reacting to complaints about harassers inhibit and limit Cosplayers to keep them safe, which complicates their presence at fan conventions.

The convention space provides a socially constructed performance space for Cosplayers and roleplaying. Viewing these costumed characters posing and roleplaying to audience's applause in the convention space, one might assume the Cosplayers are exhibitionists; however, a closer examination reveals that most Cosplayers struggle with their private and public personas and anxieties. In constructed public spaces (conventions or Cosplay event), Cosplayers' personas are somewhat predictable as their character while in public spaces, but outside the fan convention spaces their personas oscillates between Cosplay character and actual identity.

In recent years, Cosplayers are making conscious attempts to bring Cosplay into everyday life by creating original annual events such as International Cosplay Day, and dressing in costumes for already-established holidays, such as Bakeneko in Japan (dressing up as cats) in mid-October, or Krampus (dressing as scary goat/man) around the Christmas holiday. Furthermore, Halloween presents a complicated subject among Cosplayers because of the obvious comparison between the practice of wearing costumes for trick-or-treat in Western culture and the Cosplayers' use of costumes at fan conventions, parties, and events. In the most general sense, the costume is where the similarity ends (see Chapter 5). Several Cosplayers from my research, however, reported wearing Cosplay costumes for Halloween in addition to fan conventions.

The perception of "always being seen" or viewed is a common phenomenon that the Cosplayer experiences in her individual social reality when in costume. In order to better understand this phenomenon, I offer cynosure recursivity or the continued reflection on and adjustment to oneself at the center of attention or admiration where precise representation and meaning necessitates numerous reoccurring performances. In other words, the Cosplayer is reflexive in the focus of the audience's attention, where she or he roleplays a character with repeated executions in order to achieve a successful interpretation.

Individuals behave differently if they believe they are being viewed versus how they behave when they think no one is watching them. Accordingly, the Cosplayer's behaviors, when in costume and performing in public spaces, are intentionally constructed with the constant anticipation of the audience's gaze. Moreover, Cosplayers rehearse portrayals, poses, performances, and roleplay, but are also improvisational when interacting with fans, audience members, and other Cosplayers.

Similar to other fandom research (see Brownie and Graydon 2016; Cherry 2016; Gapps 2009; Jenkins 1992), Cosplayers are also an interpretive, participatory, and performative fan community. Cosplayers value collective experiences with their peers as well as with members of other fan communities. Fan activities once practiced in private and isolation are now very publicly displayed and performed. The Cosplay subculture adjusts accordingly, and even thrives in front of its fan audience and peers. At fan conventions, Cosplay performances are not solely reserved for the official competitions; they also happen spontaneously in hallways, hotel rooms, private parties, and other similar locations.

In recent years, possibly due to the harassment reported by Cosplayers and increased hallway congestion caused by photographing the growing numbers of Cosplay at conventions, there are designated spaces cordoned off for Cosplayers to pose in and for photographers and fans to gather the outside of that space. When inside the Cosplay area, it is understood that fans may take photographs at will, but in all other spaces fans are expected to ask for permission to photograph Cosplayers. As a result, this designated space results in a more respectful environment for Cosplayers, at least within the more public spaces of the fan convention.

The Internet serves the function of extending the Cosplayers' lifestyles beyond the physical spaces of the convention. This is especially beneficial for

Cosplayers living in more rural areas and without peer Cosplayers locally. It provides Cosplayers with a place to display images of posing as their characters and costumes beyond the convention, as well as a space for them to ask for costume and character advice, give/seek feedback, and socialize with peers. In addition, Cosplayers maintain social connections and networks online. The Internet also provides Cosplayers with access to sources for more characters, as well as access to vendors in any part of the world for purchasing costumes, accessories, and props.

The financial commitment for a single character is a significant investment for a Cosplayer. The exact cost of a costume, however, is difficult to assess because there is limited information for the quantifiable components. While fabric and notions for costumes have clear financial value, the time spent on construction and learning new skills are not always calculable. Furthermore, Cosplayers are more likely to discuss time expended and techniques used rather than the money spent on materials. The Cosplayer's financial expenditures continue to grow with fees for attending conventions, travel to and from, and hotels. Accordingly, Cosplayers' display of their characters and related costumes demonstrates conspicuous consumption of both the media where the character originated and the creativity and execution of the costume.

While Cosplayers have few opportunities beyond becoming celebrities, models, or spokespersons to earn money from their Cosplay activities, there are individuals external to the fandom making a profit from Cosplay. Retailers and vendors sell goods to Cosplayers; photographers market images of Cosplayers to fans and Cosplayers; and entrepreneurs produce weapons and other specialized props to vend to Cosplayers. CRI (China Research and Intelligence) reports that global revenue from Cosplay costumes produces US$11.7 billion in annual sales (CRI 2014). According to SoraNews24, Enako stated in a television program that she earned US$3,500 per stage appearance and US$97,763 for two days at Comiket fan convention (Ellard 2016).

Cosplay fandom conventions

Fan conventions exist in all forms and consciously cater to specific fandoms ranging from sports memorabilia to comic book collectors to sci-fi and fantasy enthusiasts to tabletop gamers. Consequently, not all conventions are Cosplay friendly, nor would Cosplayers necessarily be interested in attending conventions marketing to noncompatible fandoms. Each convention has its own personality, if you will, and Cosplayers respond to a convention's characteristics and attributes. Regardless of the financial costs and distance, Cosplayers return enthusiastically to fan conventions that enhance Cosplay experiences, embrace the fandom's members, and foster the subculture's growth and evolution. Cosplayers do not favor conventions that lack supportive infrastructures or overtly limit Cosplay activities. They work with convention organizers to address issues impacting Cosplayers, but they are not beyond using Cosplay's vast numbers to create public forums protesting a change concentrating on systemic concerns.

The fan convention frequently functions as a lens to focus the Cosplay fandom into groups, genres, and specific activities. Within the structure of the fan convention, Cosplayers cease to operate as individuals dressed in costumes, but instead become part of the Cosplay fandom subculture. The creation of this temporary fandom community and geographic space of the convention creates an inside/outside perspective, which further concentrates the costume-clad fandom into a singular entity.

Some Cosplayers plan, design, construct, and practice for an entire year to cosplay one chosen character at a specific convention (or competition), while others plan multiple characters to perform each day of several conventions. Intense levels of dedication and concentration are common traits among Cosplayers, along with the accompanying apprehension, nervousness, and anxiety. The revealing of a new character is a significant occasion in a Cosplayer's tenure. Most Cosplayers return to their favorite genres for character selections.

Conventions and the fan communities they support attract and contribute to the longevity and growing subcultural impact of the Cosplay fandom. These protected fan spaces serve as sanctuary zones for roleplaying, poses, and dialogue contribute to the portrayal of the character for accuracy, humor, fun, and/ or competitions. The fandom, however, expresses concerns that conventions give too much attention to Cosplay celebrities and models over the needs of the average Cosplayer attendees who financially invest in attending conventions and purchasing merchandise.

Cosplay fandom experiences

Cosplayers are drawn to the shared positive experiences within the fandom, especially those spaces created while at a fan convention (and other Cosplay-sanctioned environments), as well as the fandom lifestyles beyond the conventions. Overarching the Cosplayers' experiences are opportunities to socialize with like-minded individuals and share in each other's fan experiences, such as roleplaying, photography, competitions, parties, and parades.

Each year there are new conventions, and established conventions move to new locations to accommodate and meet the growing needs/wants of various fan communities. Most of them include Cosplay activities because of their popularity among attendees. Cosplay events and activities are highly entertaining and attract large audiences, which are beneficial for fan convention organizers and promoters.

The most noteworthy Cosplayer experiences appear to connect to and flow through the costume. Cosplayers share construction tutorials, advice, and support, which constitute a significant amount of online posts. They take photographs documenting the costume design and construction in process and post their steps online for feedback and bragging rights. The costume and its relationship to the character are central to many in-person conversations at conventions.

Lamerichs's suggestion of four elements to Cosplay "fan costumes"—"a narrative, a set of clothing, a play or performance before spectators, and a subject or player" (2011: 1.2)—is a good starting point for understanding Cosplay. I, however, consider the performance and spectators separately because of the distinct roles and their effects on the Cosplay fandom subculture. In addition, Lamerichs's four elements only consider the Cosplayer in the act of Cosplaying for an audience, and neglects acknowledgment of pre- and post-activities where the Cosplayer prepares for and then decompresses from the performance.

Fan prosumption

Brigid Cherry in *Cult Media* discusses when fans handknit garments from their favorite shows, such as *Dr. Who*'s or Harry Potter's scarf and *Firefly*'s Jayne's handknit hat, they wear them as part of their fan dedication to a character (and storyline). In this way, Cherry's research demonstrates fan "prosumption" (production + consumption) (2016: 15–17), which draws from Alvin Toffler's concept of "prosumption" as material objects created by a producer who is also the consumer and also understood as the "prosumer" (1980: 265–88). The act of prosumption is directly connected to the DIY (do it yourself) culture/movement and "participatory culture" in most fandoms as they are utilized within fandoms (Cherry 2016: 15–17).

In most cases, the Cosplayer participates in prosumption because the fandom encourages (if not demands) her or him to construct the majority of the costume, which she or he personally wears for conventions, performances, competitions, photography shoots, and other Cosplay events. The individual Cosplayer is inserted into every aspect of the Cosplay experience. Furthermore, the costume serves as a representation of the Cosplayer's labors, from which members of the fandom and audience members assign value and merit.

Karl Marx argues that the expenses associated with the average labor hours (and raw materials) necessary to manufacture a product determine its value (2009: 133–35; 212–15). The worth of the Cosplay costume, however, is assessed beyond its labor and materials by its contributions to the fandom and sentimental value. Marx addresses this additional value with his concept of fetish[4] value (2009), which reflects the additional values embedded in the performance and fixation with qualities to/for the creator that center around the costume, which is extended to the audience and fans of Cosplay.

John Fiske suggests that fans consume as well as produce culture and closely related cultural capital (1992: 33). Correspondingly, Cosplayers generate their own unique fan culture and capital that resembles other known fandoms. Cosplayers further produce culture with their use of costumes as well as their social networks and theatrical performances adding to the atmosphere of the convention. The fandom's cultural capital is evident in the photographs of the Cosplayer dressed as fictional characters and the material object of the costume shared on social media.

DIY practices (i.e., artworks, handcrafts, fanfic, videos, etc.) are common activities for members of numerous fan subcultures (Cherry 2016: 9; Hellekson and Busse 2006 and 2014). The DIY ethic supports self-reliance and creativity for the production of material items instead of purchasing mass-manufactured and corporate-issued products or services. Fan production (Sullivan 2013) and prosumption (Cherry 2016) are the expected outcomes of the DIY praxis. Moreover, DIY is frequently necessary as a practical option that provides fans with merchandise and products not available or affordable in any other venue. In this way, the Cosplayer customizes costumes unique to her interpretation and creativity of a given character.

The fan participatory culture developed parallel to the DIY culture, which is reflected in the Cosplay fandom (Cherry 2016: 15–18; 25). DIY offers spaces and methods for the democratization within the Cosplay fandom: that is, anyone is welcome to participate in the Cosplay fandom and develop strong design and construction skills to create costumes, props, and other similar objects for portrayals and performances. The DIY skills perfected by Cosplayers are further disseminated via the Internet beyond the fandom to the general public. In this way, the Cosplay fandom is exposed to a broader audience. Subsequently, some Cosplayers also gain notoriety on the merits of their elaborate costumes and exceptional design and construction skills.

The bias of "gendering of crafts" recognized by scholars (Cherry 2016: 25–26; see also Stalp 2007; Stalp and Winge 2008) has not negatively impacted the Cosplay fandom. It appears that being a female-dominant subculture the fandom constructs and encourages a social system that values and assigns merit to crafting skills and outcomes. Accordingly, the fandom values creation skills and well-made costumes, accessories, and props, which extends to makeup and styling.

Furthermore, Fiske (1992) discusses how fans create meanings "semiotic productivity" (37) within the culture they participate in, as well as establish "cultural industries" (30) for the products produced. Fiske draws on Pierre Bourdieu's model in order to outline how popular culture system "distribute[s] its resources unequally" and "promotes and privileges certain cultural tastes and competencies . . . through . . . [an] educational system," which is "not socially and institutionally supported" (1992: 31). Most fandoms reflect portions of Fiske's description with growing distinctions, and Cosplay is no exception. The Cosplay subculture is democratic with its own educational system that promotes the sharing of communal information. Cosplayers attend fan conventions (i.e., the institution) for the purposes of building social networks (i.e., support) (see also Bainbridge and Norris 2013).

David Gauntlett explains that fans utilize social media to "share" their fan objects and details about the "making" of the items (2011: 64–66). In fact, sharing is a crucial component to the Cosplayer community with informal expectations of reciprocity. Cosplayers share beyond the tutorials and short performances posted on the Internet; they also exchange feedback and offer advice and support. The sharing democratizes Cosplay, as all Cosplayers, even celebrities, share similar information for recognition of their efforts from their fans and peers.

Furthermore, building a network of peers, which functions as a support system, is the recognized/rewarded methodology for becoming a successful Cosplayer. Once a new Cosplayer connects with more established veteran Cosplayers, she or he receives and learns by the examples demonstrated through tutorials and even gains support from Cosplay peers through shared common experiences of building skills and creating costumes.

The role of material culture is paramount within the Cosplay fandom. Cosplay dress, including costumes, makeup, wigs, accessories, and props, as well as merchandise and services, contribute to the construction of the fandom's material culture. The handmade costumes, accessories, and props range in quality from glued or taped together to exquisitely detailed execution, which position Cosplayers in intimate contact with the objects of their creation. This intimacy extends to wearing costumes of their beloved characters that contribute to the shared experiences within the fandom.

Katherine Flemming suggests that the contemporary understanding of the fan is more than just a consumer of the material object produced and/or marketed to the fandom (2007: 16). Furthermore, the fan is committed, invested, and sometimes obsessed (financially, socially, and emotionally) to her fandom. Cosplayers, more specifically, may be both consumer and producer, who consciously contribute to the longevity and evolution of the fandom.

Furthermore, the relationship between Cosplayers and their dress (costume) imbues the objects with magickal power and value to the individual and fandom. The power of making and wearing the creative object carries empowerment for the maker/wearer. The value stems from costs associated with buying portions of and time spent assembling the costumes, as well as the sentimental meanings associated with the character and costume.

An additional factor establishing the significance of the material culture of Cosplayers' dress is the nonverbal communication represented in the Cosplay costumes. The Cosplayer's character's story is embedded in the semiotics of the costume and overall appearance. In this way, the character transcends the page or screen to encompass the Cosplayer and by extension add to the collective material identity of the fandom.

Fandom researchers

Researchers have had an increased interest in fandoms in the last few decades, reflecting the acknowledgment of fans within popular culture, such as television series (*The Big Bang Theory* and *Silicon Valley*) and films (*Fanboys* and *Galaxy Quest*), which celebrate fans and genres with strong fan themes and characters. The fan convention further facilitates research because of the high concentration of thousands of fans in a single space including public walkways. Cosplayers are easily recognized in their costumes and known to be friendly to and cooperative with researchers.

Researchers documenting the Cosplay fandom further establish the subculture not only within the greater fandom found at fan conventions. Research on the fandom and the subsequent publications have limited reach but the subject matter grows in popularity and draws in new readers. The exact impact of researchers and their studies on fandoms is not yet known. Researchers, however, are increasingly becoming common spectators and factors at fan conventions. While the resulting studies offer insights into fandoms, they also interrupt and impact the usual fan behaviors, interactions, and environments. The Hawthorne Effect, also known as the Observer Effect, suggests there are benefits and drawbacks to research participants realizing they are being observed (French 1953: 98–135). The researchers' presence modifies behaviors of the fans with whom they interact, the structures of fandoms within convention spaces, and social compositions. Subsequently, researchers are impacting their study's findings each time they interact with members of fandoms.

Qualitative research studies with fans are limited, and even fewer draw on the rich data attainable through ethnographic methodologies. Documenting some fan activity and fandoms, the book *It Happens at Comic-Con: Ethnographic Essays on a Popular Culture Phenomenon* (2014) edited by Ben Boiling and Mathew J. Smith includes several essays that highlight the positions of ethnographic researchers at Comic-Con in San Diego, California. Other scholarly research of fan spaces and activities include but are not limited to Brigid Cherry (2016), Henry Jenkins (1992), Camille Bacon-Smith (1992), and Matt Hills (2014).

Within qualitative research about fandoms, the Cosplay fandom is the focus of only a few studies. Still, researchers, of course, are drawn to Cosplayers because of their dynamic appearances and performances within fandom spaces. Moreover, Cosplayers are outgoing and friendly, which makes for ease of securing research participants and their interviews.

Summary

From the varied sources that inspire them, Cosplayers throw themselves into the challenges associated with their fandom, whether it is creatively solving costuming issues or portraying more complicated characters or writing fan fiction that allows for the introduction of an entirely new heroine. Capturing the essence of their chosen character is the goal of most faithful Cosplayers, who seek to emulate and portray a persona.

Cosplay subculture, perhaps, represents the most complex social structure of all the fandoms because of its reflexivity and inclusivity, as well as because of their significant social media presence. The fandom's hierarchy further illustrates the multifaceted layers of the subculture both inside and outside any Cosplay-focused fandom conventions.

In Chapter 3, I focus on the themes and thematic analysis revealed from Cosplayers' experiences drawn from quotations, observations, and visual analysis. Each theme is individually analyzed and discussed for complexities in order to provide a more accurate representation and a deeper understanding of the Cosplay fandom and the role of dress/costume. The thematic analysis exposes overarching patterns in the Cosplay fandom.

3

IT'S NOT JUST A COSTUME: COSPLAY IS A WAY OF LIFE

Cosplayers are some of the most generous and reflexive research participants with whom I have ever interacted; they were eager to share their experiences inside and outside the fandom subculture. They discussed the psychological, social, emotional, physical, and economic challenges, drawbacks, and benefits associated with being a Cosplayer. Also, Cosplayers reflected on their perceptions about and interactions with other Cosplayers and people closely associated with Cosplayers. My examination of these Cosplayers' experiences revealed ten Cosplay constructs, or themes, each with numerous subthemes.

Cosplay constructs (themes)

The constructs or themes are the essential elements that form the Cosplay experience(s) for Cosplayers (and their fans). Exploring the Cosplay constructs reveals how the Cosplayer's environments are constructed while evolving with its changing and challenging inputs and impacts.

I offer a thematic analysis for the constructs emerging from exploring the experiences of Cosplayers within the Cosplay fandom subculture. The constructs (or themes) are as follows:

- Cosplay Costume (subthemes: Dressing, The Fantastic Body, Crossplay, Designing and Constructing the Costume, and Technology);
- Constructed Representations (subthemes: Character Selection, Genre Rules the World, Archetypes, and Mimetic Fandom);
- Photographs and Videos (subthemes: Documentation, and Exploitation);

- Social Networks and Communities (subthemes: Socializing, Social Media, Belonging and Inclusion, and Fans at the Convention);
- Performativity and Roleplaying (subthemes: Fan Convention Competitions, Masquerades and Parades, and Group Challenges and Activities);
- Creativity (subtheme: Imagination);
- Empowerment and Self-determination (subthemes: Identification, Character Recognition, and Pride and Accomplishments);
- Escapism (subtheme: Cosplay bubble);
- Devotion and Obsession (subthemes: Dedication, and Financial Expenditures and Investments); and
- Fun and Play (subthemes: Humor, Drama, and Parties).

I utilize grounded theory and inductive in combination with deductive analysis for each of these themes. Each theme is individually analyzed and discussed for complexities and patterns in order to provide a more accurate representation and a deeper understanding of Cosplay. The theme and resulting analysis are supported with specific examples and narratives from interviews and collected data. By exploring the constructs or themes revealed within Cosplay experiences, it is possible to understand how Cosplay is far more multidimensional and layered than simply fans dressing in Halloween-style costumes.

Costume makes the superhero: Cosplay costume

Costume Cosplay is a theme of the Cosplay experience because the costume serves many functions as it dresses the Cosplayer in a disguise, an alter ego, and a new identity. The costume is embedded with symbolic and semiotic codes simultaneously representing the Cosplayer, character, and genre, as well as identifying the Cosplayer as a member of a fandom. In this way, the costume both conceals and reveals the multitudes of entangled identities, leaving the Cosplayer to perform according to parameters often established within the visual communication of the costume.

While highly constructed and negotiated, the costume acts as a significant identity marker for the Cosplayer. The character's identity is fantastic and ephemeral, which is intimately enmeshed with the Cosplayer's identity. These constructed and deliberate identities are donned and doffed similar to the Cosplay costume, which carries the visual markers of the character. Accordingly, Gaara from the *Naruto* anime series stated, "I love his style, and what he stands for."

Brownie and Graydon propose that Cosplayers are not necessarily becoming the Other by bringing hero qualities to surface (2016: 121–22), while at the same time stating that the "costume emphasizes otherness" (2016: 42). My research suggests that Cosplayers both emphasize and become the Other with the specific characters they embody by virtue of their costumes and portrayals of characters in the socially constructed environments of conventions or related events. Moreover, the ways race, ethnicity, and size manifest in Cosplay portrayals (costumes and performances) visually communicate the Other.

"Cosplayers . . . find themselves empowered by dressing as a superhero" (Brownie and Graydon 2015: 4). This assessment is also extendable to Cosplayers who dress as any fictional character, because Cosplayers draw on the agency and strength of their assumed personas even when the characters appear diminutive or delicate. Accordingly, one Cosplayer commented, "You feel cooler than you actually are [laughs]." Kadaj from *Final Fantasy VII* stated, "Looks good . . . cool weapon . . . good movie!" One Cosplayer referred to his character's physical appearance by waving his hands across his body and saying, "He's a cool bad guy!" The traits of a given character extend to the Cosplayer through dress, performances, and even subsequent photographs, as well as through other ways Cosplayers consume character portrayals. Furthermore, spectators and fans imprint the Cosplayer with the characters they roleplay.

Cosplayers embody demure to powerful characters when dressed in their costumes, and the act of roleplaying provides further emphasis on the escapism and diversion personified in the character traits and appearance. Milk from the comedy anime *Super Milk Chan* stated, "She is fun to play . . . irreverent!" Even the meekest characters, such as the adolescent and irrelevant Milk, offer the Cosplayer with a disguise from which she or he finds refuge from the realities of everyday life and the chaos of the fan convention (see Plate 3.1).

Rosenberg and Letamendi (2013) offer research that further suggests that Cosplayers wearing a mask, for example, were bolder and less self-conscious (see also Miller and Rowold 1979; Mullen, Migdal, and Rozell 2003). The costume functions as a type of "mask" that the Cosplayer uses to protect the vulnerable self while also possibly emboldening her to roleplay in front of an audience. A first-time Cosplayer shared how she had some fears about cosplaying in front of people, and finally stated, "I like acting like the character and interacting with other people as the character."

Closely related to the costume functioning as a "mask" or disguise, the Cosplayer also experiences agency from taking risks when donning the costume. Segona (original character) shared: "While cosplaying, it is easy to meet folks, fun to talk to people." A female crossplaying Machi, a male drummer, stated: "The best part about Cosplay is the chance to play someone you are not." The costume allows the Cosplayer to negotiate the anxiety of meeting new people by inviting introductions and conversations about the character and its appearance. The costume further functions as a shield between the Cosplayer and any fans, as well as the realities of everyday and fantasy.

Drawing on Joanne Eicher's definition of dress functioning as nonverbal communication (2000), the Cosplay costume reads as nonverbal communication similar to the ways the dress of the original characters the Cosplayers are portraying. Also, further extending earlier discussions from Rauch and Bolton (2010), the costume provides a narrative in which Cosplayers engage the viewer to create a dialogue, redefining the character and Cosplayer within the convention settings.

Dressing

As the Cosplayer dons her character's appearance (costume, makeup, etc.), she practices the act of "becoming" the character. The Cosplayer creates a ritualized process of dressing and applying makeup into detailed steps in a specific order that lead to an intentional, visual transformation. With each additional element of the costume, the Cosplayer's identity is further concealed and suppressed until the character is revealed. In this way, the process of dressing represents a ritual of transforming the person into the fantasy character.

The Cosplayer negotiates her personal identity distinct, and yet combines with the salient identity of the character when in costume and roleplaying. Cosplayers seem to genuinely enjoy these negotiations of identities, as one Cosplayer stated when discussing her excitement for cosplaying, "I get to be someone else for a day!" These negotiations also lead to blended identities, where the Cosplayer assumes aspects of the character's personality outside of roleplaying or the fandom.

The costume has a complex, layered meaning for the Cosplayer: it is often the first iteration of the Cosplayer assuming the character's identity. The superficial representation of the costume and overall appearance contribute significantly to the recognition of a character, which makes its accuracy a paramount concern to the Cosplayer. Furthermore, the costume is meaningful to the ways Cosplayers execute, roleplay, perform, and even become their chosen characters.

The fantastic body

The role of the Cosplayer's body is crucial to the presentation of the costume/ appearance and representation of the character. The human body's natural physical structure is accentuated, revealed, or hidden, and often exploited within the identity of the Cosplay character. If the costume functions as the prologue to the narrative (story) for the Cosplay character, the natural human body serves as the framework from which Cosplayers' performances are incorporated and extended.

The connections between the body and costume further indicate the ways that dress impacts the senses (Roach-Higgins and Eicher 1992). Accordingly, Cosplayers note the weight of the costume on the body: the smells associated with its construction and wear; the feeling of the cloth against the skin causing rashes or soothing actions; and even the sound of rustling or clanging costume pieces. Cosplayers endure the negative impacts on bodily senses, but, instead of modifying the costume, they strive for representative accuracy.

As the Cosplayer embodies the fantasy character, they transform their bodies into otherworldly beings, which liberates them from earthly bonds (even if only through the capacities of the costume, fantasy, and performance). A Cosplayer highlighted these struggles when commenting about the difficulties associated with "trying to make physics-defying costumes stay together all weekend" (Winge 2017). The Cosplay body is a fantastic body as envisioned and executed by embodying the fictional character.

Written on the Cosplayer's body are the genre, the character, and the story. In some cases, the genre is literally written on the skin with a tattoo of a favored character, symbol, or insignia from the Cosplayer's favorite genre. While Cosplayers did not readily speak about their personal body modifications, these types of tattoos were often visible. When observing Cosplay tattoos, it is difficult to determine whether the body modifications are permanent or temporary, which is a testament to the quality and detail of Cosplayers' temporary tattoos (Plate 3.2).

The lived body existing at fan conventions presents challenges both for the fans and the spaces being utilized often in ways they were not originally designed. One Cosplayer commented, "I hate the BO [body odor] smell in the rooms." Fans at conventions are known for not showering or being concerned with hygiene because they are distracted by fan activities and do not want to waste a moment away from the fandom. Thus, conventions post hygiene suggestions, such as posters with reminders about the importance of showering, brushing teeth, and drinking plenty of water. Furthermore, many Cosplayers complained about the heat and perspiration when wearing their costumes, which contributes to the difficulties of managing body and hygiene concerns raised by fans and subsequently convention organizers and staff. One Cosplayer stated, "The worst part about Cosplay is how the costume is so hot and makes me sweat."

Convention spaces are climate controlled, however, it is commonly physically uncomfortable for Cosplayers who may wear multiple layers of clothing/fabrics and heavy costumes. Characters and costumes that require physical effort to wear or perform create additional issues and discomforts for the Cosplayer. While tugging on the layers of his costume, a Cosplayer dressed as Lord Darcia III exclaimed, "It [the costume] is so hot!" Consequently, some Cosplayers create costumes with ease and comfort in mind; Taako from *The Adventure Zone* podcast shared, "I want it [the costume] to be comfortable. I don't want to get hot or have something too heavy that I have to drag around" (see Figure 3.3).

While convention spaces are climate-controlled environments, the air conditioning or heat settings attempt to accommodate many individuals assuming they are wearing single-layer clothing meant for interiors. These preset temperatures are not typically comfortable for Cosplayers wearing costumes and performing. Consequently, these environments contribute to Cosplayers sweating and subsequent body odor issues are all too common at conventions, as previously discussed. The body issues at fan conventions, however, are not solely the concern of Cosplayers.

Figure 3.3 From *Wolf's Rain*, the character Lord Darcia III has the Cosplayer's entire body covered by costume and mask, which is physically uncomfortable during the fan convention. Photo: Therèsa M. Winge.

It is also noteworthy the ways in which the Cosplayer's body occupies space, especially with the increasing fandom numbers that are clumped together in confining and ill-suited convention spaces. Katamari Damacy, a videogame character with a large head spanning more than three feet wide, acknowledged his discomfort about his costumed body in the convention space, "hot costumes and narrow doorways." Many Cosplayers echoed Damacy's complaints about the constrictive spaces at fan conventions, and I noted that many Cosplayers entered and exited rooms sideways to accommodate movement with large weapons, props, and costumes (Winge 2006a) (see Figure 3.4).

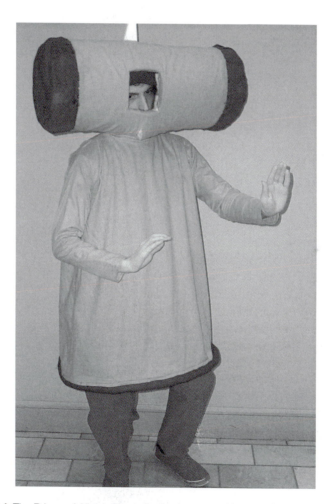

Figure 3.4 The Prince of All the Cosmos, also known as Katamari Damacy, is the primary character in a videogame by the same name. The Cosplayer complained about attempting to move through the convention spaces and the heat inside the costume. Photo: Therèsa M. Winge.

In addition, non-Cosplay fans, artists, and vendors at conventions are quickly becoming annoyed with the space consumed by Cosplayers (and the audience they attract) because cosplaying denies them space or even presence. Specifically, artists and vendors' booths are blocked from view when Cosplayers move through isles in large costumes, and more often Cosplayers are blamed for constriction of the flow of traffic because their fans stop them for pictures or autographs.

In an attempt to address many of these concerns, often the convention areas are usually marked off with tape to indicate the "Cosplayer Area," where Cosplayers are encouraged to gather to give fans access for viewing, photographs, and autographs. While the shared spaces designated for cosplaying attempts to keep Cosplayers safe, they are fraught with new issues. The spaces are often crowded with Cosplayers trying to perform for photographs. The backgrounds are not always suitable for many characters. Cosplayers and fans alike are often confused where the designated Cosplay space is located and what times specific Cosplayers will be present, because these spaces are not clearly marked and non-Cosplayers accidently wander into the designated areas.

The Cosplayers also bemoan the physical strain and weight of their props, weapons, and armor when trying to move within the convention space or to and from their hotel room. Wolfwood, a priest armed with an oversized cross-shaped pistol, stated how he was physically exhausted after "carrying a six and a half foot by three and a half foot wooden cross" through the crowds in convention hallways (see Figure 3.5). Despite the cross being hollow, the prop's size and weight made it challenging to maneuver or even hold upright.

Cosplayers commonly offered discussions around habituating the Cosplayer's body in convention and performance spaces. One Cosplayer summarized her bodily experiences, "Being too hot or too cold in the costume . . . the costume restricting you as in moving, eating, using the restroom . . . having to deal with makeup, hair, or wigs, having to remove my glasses for photos and such when the character doesn't wear glasses." Accordingly, the Cosplayer's body exists as a physical space for negotiations for the character's appearance (and identity). Accommodations and adjustments may be made for the character's appearance where it is required to accurately achieve recognition from audiences.

Subsequently, numerous Cosplayers also expressed how they choose characters because they shared physical attributes, such as hair color or physical build, but did not extend to sex or gender identity. Genjo Sanzo a character from *Saiyuki* stated, "He [the character] quite frankly kicks ass . . . has a fun costume and hair similar to my own." Hair color and style, eye color, and height were mentioned as appreciated shared traits with selected characters. Unfortunately, Cosplayers were unable to distinguish between being attracted to characters who shared physical traits with them or if they loved characters and

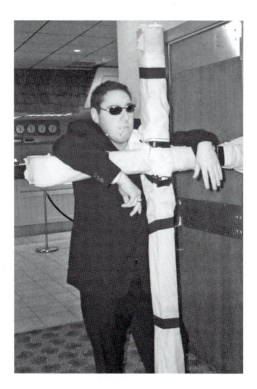

Figure 3.5 Wolfwood, a gunman priest dressed in a black suit, drags a heavy 6'6" × 3' cross through the crowded hallways of the fan convention spaces. Photo: Therèsa M. Winge.

then searched for any similarities that could be capitalized on for the characters' appearances.

Furthermore, the Cosplayer's body is a target for controversy and debate. The Cosplayer's body and costume consume space, as well as their fans who gather around them, which is a point of contention at fan conventions where other fandoms also demand space and attention. When I was interviewing Cosplayers, they discussed additional difficulties such as harassment, representations of race, and body size, with idealism and optimism. Also, the Cosplay body serves to negotiate representations of gender and sex with a type of Cosplay called "crossplay."

Crossplay

"Crossplay" refers to a Cosplayer of one gender who portrays a character of a different gender (Hank 2013; see Figure 3.6 and Plate 3.7). Lamerichs further states that crossplay is the combination of drag and Cosplay, often suggesting parody (2011: 3.5). Crossplay is so common in the Cosplay fandom, yet not frequently discussed among Cosplayers: in fact, the term was created by the mass media. It is noteworthy to acknowledge that crossplay has commonly been practiced since before the Cosplay fandom was given its name, especially when most science-fiction or fantasy characters were male. At contemporary fan conventions, crossplayers include girls, boys, women, and men who dress as, and roleplay as, characters of differing gender.

In my research, I found that Cosplayers are drawn to crossplay for four primary reasons. Cosplayers crossplay to experience being

1   a favorite character (gender does not factor into the choice);
2   a character of a different gender (due to empowerment, challenge, parody, etc.);
3   part of a pair or team (limited membership often requires one or more Cosplayers to portray a character with a differing gender from the Cosplayer);
4   the focus of an intended audience's attention (for reasons of spectacle, humor, fame, etc.).

Donning a character with a different gender allows the Cosplayer to experience agency and/or vulnerability associated with that character's gender. While Cosplay, in general, offers freedom for participants, those who crossplay are further empowered by having a constructed identity and appearance for the Cosplayer, indicative of a deeper understanding for the character's and gender's expected behaviors. A woman cosplaying Superman enjoys the perceived strength and power of being (or representing) a strong male character in a dynamic body-contouring suit, as well as being a superhero. Accordingly, a Cosplayer created a mash-up character that combined a male and female character to capture the best of both. A Cosplayer portraying an original character stated, "Chopper is my favorite character from the series. He's cute and sweet and fun to play. Rukio is my favorite female character from the series. I love her personality and we have similar hair." Cosplaying another gender also creates situations of vulnerability either inherent to the gender or within the persona of the portrayed character.

While predominance of crossplay within the Cosplay fandom may suggest to outsiders that Cosplayers are moving away from the gender binary prevalent in the real world, a deeper examination suggests crossplayers do not carry these dress behaviors to their jobs or into non-fandom activities. In Western culture, heterosexuality is the normative expectation (Butler 1993: 237), where viewers are challenged by anything that does not fit the social contract. Accordingly,

Figure 3.6 A female Cosplayer wears contact lenses, silver wig, and faux leather costume with her constructed foam, tape, and plastic Velvet Nightmare Gunblade weapon to crossplay Yazoo, a male character from *Final Fantasy VII*. Photo: Therèsa M. Winge.

Catherine Thomas's ethnographic study of Cosplayers notes how Cosplayers remarked with ferocity how the practice of crossplay does not suggest sexual or gender orientation (2014: 32). Within the carnivalesque atmosphere of the fan convention and the playful nature of the Cosplayers (Lamerichs 2014: 5), crossplay would be permissible and even celebrated for its entertainment value. When convincing portrayals are not the desired outcome, crossplay can be an effective vehicle for entertainment. Furthermore, Thomas found that men crossplay for "shock value" (including parody), while women crossplay to transform into powerful male characters (2014: 37).

A Cosplayer shared a time when she and a female friend crossplayed as male characters for a competition:

> One year, we did a fake kiss on stage while both of us were dressed as guys. Her as Zoro and me as Luffy, both from the anime *One Piece*. We got a lot of cheers and laughs from the audience along with some "Oh noes." It was a compliment not an insult because it was supposed to be funny.

Another type of crossplay is when a female Cosplayer dresses as a hypersexualized female version of a male character. In 2013, Nicole Marie Jean, a Cosplay celebrity, dressed as Bane from the movie *The Dark Knight Rises* at the Arasia science-fiction convention. Her costume was tight fitting, with high-cut shorts and low-cut top revealing her cleavage. With this type of Cosplay, the Cosplayer is not attempting to portray a male character as a masculine archetype, but instead crossplays the character's gender with amplified erogenous zones.

Resculpting and reshaping the natural human form to the desired physical appearance of a character presents challenges for Cosplayers. Most of the Cosplayers who crossplay are girls/women and they expressed their need to negotiate and manage their bodies in order to play male characters. Cosplayers discussed binding their breasts and padding their clothing to conceal hips or derriere in order to more accurately portray male characters. A female Cosplayer dressed as Gojyo, a male half-demon character from *Saiyuki*, stated her frustration with her own body differing from the character's body by discussing the challenges of "binding my chest and trying to look perfect."

At every convention I attended, I met many crossplayers. Most of the Cosplayers who crossplayed were females dressed as male characters, along with several non-gendered characters, which is not surprising considering the high population of female Cosplayers and the limited amount of female characters. Still, it is difficult to determine who is crossplaying a character without confirmation from the Cosplayer, because many convincing costumes do not betray the gender of the Cosplayer beneath. Machi, from the visual kei band Lareine,[1] presents an interesting example of crossplay because the Cosplayer identified as female while cosplaying a male drummer, who dressed in the band with Lolita styling including long ruby red curly wig, feather headpiece, makeup, and lace and satin Victorian styled dress. As for the reason for crossplaying, Machi stated, "Because he's pretty and a talented drummer." In this example of Cosplay, the female Cosplayer dressed as a male performer who dressed as a stylized female, which suggests the fluidity of gender in the fandom.

Moreover, Cosplayers focus little on who is a crossplayer, unless the portrayal is merit worthy. It seems that the attention given to crossplay began with and continues to be fetishized by the media. This creates difficulties in the fandom, where the media seeks out crossplayers for photographs and stories that become "clickbait" online. These stories further exoticize the Cosplay fandom, which encourages cyclical patterns between Cosplayers and the media.

Designing and constructing the costume

The design and construction of the character's costume present a significant rite of passage into the Cosplay fandom (see Brownie and Graydon 2016: 119). Cosplayers expressed this rite of passage in individual ways reflecting the activities or material culture that manifests significance. Kyo Sohma from *Fruit Baskets* stated, "Finishing my first costume . . . it wasn't perfect but the costume made me a Cosplayer."

Cosplayers design costumes that reflect the appearance of the character rather than considering the physical constraints and demands on the Cosplayer's physical body. Consequently, a costume may place strains on the Cosplayer's body, creating discomfort ranging from mild perspiration to lasting physical pain. The Cosplayer's physical comfort, however, rarely factors into the costume's design and it is certainly not paramount to accuracy.

Cosplayers regularly commented about the burden of "the work" required to design and create the costume and overall appearance of the chosen character. Some Cosplayers lamented about their lack of skills compared to the requirements needed to accurately portray the characters' appearances. One Cosplayer crossplaying Sanzo from *Saiyuki* bemoaned, "The worst part is sewing difficult fabric," while Yojimbo complained that there is "lots of work to do well" when cosplaying.

Closely related to the skills and work necessary to create an accurate and innovative costume, the time required for construction complicates the completion of costumes before a fan convention. Captain Harlock commented, "They [the costumes] take a lot of time to make!" while pointing to detail work on the trim of the costume. Also, a Cosplayer with an original character, Vampire Hunter, expressed, "The work! Because, when you are crunched for time, it's hard to do."

Cosplayers struggle to manage their time and energy between work and/ or school and Cosplay activities. Superfan Cosplayers frequently choose their fandom over other non-fan responsibilities and activities. Accordingly, many Cosplayers "work to play," that is, they live with parents or roommates and only work enough to pay for necessities and Cosplay expenses.

The ways Cosplayers secure the costume varies in specifics, but, in general, costumes are handmade, store-bought, or are a combination of handmade and store-bought. Vash the Stampede from *Trigun* shared his costume process: "I liked the character and I already had on hand most of what was required [for the costume]." Another Cosplayer dressed as Ashley from the *Warioware* videogame series by Nintendo revealed her costume design and construction: securing a dress from a secondhand store but buying orange fabric to construct the hems and headpiece (see Plate 3.8).

Since cosplaying is extremely expensive, Cosplayers save money by reusing elements from past or damaged costumes, incorporating personal items, and shopping at secondhand and surplus stores for supplies. When characters dress in contemporary clothing, Cosplayers may find portions of costumes in their own or a peer's closet. Scavenging past costumes is precarious for Cosplayers because in the process of making a new character's costume they permanently lose the old costume and associated character, to which Cosplayers often become emotionally attached.

Costumes become damaged at conventions in crowded hallways among bustling people with large props and weapons snagging on each other's dress; damages occur from wearing, performing, cleaning, packing, and traveling as well. Damage to costumes ranges from body odor and sweat, to rips and tears, to food and beverage stains. Experienced Cosplayers bring repair kits and cleaning supplies to fan conventions. One Cosplayer shared that her worst Cosplay fear is "when you hear a rip . . . nothing worse." Another Cosplayer shared her frustrations about trying to manage her costumes at conventions, "Ripping my costume . . . gloves not as accurate as would like . . . non-accurate boots."

Subsequently, Cosplayers are forced to find innovative ways to repair their costumes effectively and quickly while at a convention. One Cosplayer described her favorite method of repair: "I hate having costume malfunctions. You have to duct-tape [the costume] to yourself. Pulling off the tape hurts!" Duct tape and superglue were common solutions for costume issues, such as fabric ripping, seams tearing open, and embellishments becoming loose or falling off.

While most Cosplayers I met designed and constructed the majority of their costumes, nearly all purchased some portion of their costumes. Buying wigs, contact lens, weapons, and props are acceptable among Cosplayers because of the technical difficulty in producing quality versions of these items. Cosplayers also strive to learn new construction skills in order to create their own realistic-looking, high-quality prop weapons and accessories.

Technology

Closely associated with purchased portions of Cosplay costumes is the growing position of technology. As a theme, advances in various technologies benefit Cosplayers in the construction of costumes, props, and weapons. The advancement in and availability of contact lenses, for example, allows Cosplayers to achieve the unique eye shapes and colors seen in animation, television, and film. In fact, specific types of contact lenses are marketed to Cosplayers.

Cosplayers expressed their frustration with their attempts to create costumes and weapons that were convincing, but eventually even the most complex technology will be simplified and marketed to the average consumer, making it accessible for Cosplayers. With open-source technologies and software, Cosplayers have access to creating a vast array of fantastic effects similar to those found in videos, movies, cartoons, and literature.

Even the raw materials utilized by Cosplayers have improved in recent years, due in part to the popularity of Cosplay. Yaya Han markets fabrics designed for the needs of Cosplayers, such as satins and tulle to make princess dresses and oil-slick scale fabric for lizard and dragon skins, at Jo-Ann Fabrics. In addition, online companies such as The Ring Lord market shiny scale-style metal tabs to Cosplayers with patterns for them to knit/stitch into structures to resemble dragon scale armor for a custom fit and movement of the body.

Expected technological advancements will eventually allow Cosplayers to achieve feats and attain (super)powers similar to the characters they portray (see Patten 2004; Brownie and Graydon 2016). Even current consumer availability of cutting-edge technology and products allows Cosplayers to achieve costumes and performances not easily achievable or even possible in the past years. Furries' and other anthros' tails may be equipped with Cervo technology to allow movements in designated patterns to create movement, which could be further enhanced with the use of an Arduino application that facilitates programmable motion, illumination, and/or audio incorporated into the costume where applicable. The Cosplayer roleplaying Bane can embed a voice modulator into the facemask to achieve the characters' signature mechanical voice. Electroluminescent wires (known as EL wires) are used to create illumination for TRON, Daft Punk, and Ultron costumes. Goku from *Dragon Ball* became an Internet sensation when the video surfaced of him riding a hover board covered in foam and fiber insulation to create the appearance of him floating on a moving cloud.

Wings are particularly difficult to design, build, and wear because they need to be symmetrical (in most cases) and balanced. Some Cosplayers want their wings to move like the characters' wings, which requires additional technologies and skills to achieve. In 2015, Elmins Cosplay built animatronic wings for his portrayal of the character Aether Wing Kayle from the *League of Legends* videogame, articulated by his custom-built Arduino application. In 2004, for the Schoolgirls and Mobilesuits' Cosplay competition, Heather Luca constructed motorized moving wings for her Steampunk-styled costume.

In addition, Cosplayers are pursuing skill sets and technology that facilitate constructing the costume accurate to fantastic illustrations, CGI (computer generated imagery), and special effects. Recognizing Cosplayers' need for building and construction skill sets, specialized panels are convened at most conventions that Cosplayers attend. At the 2017 Shuto Con, a panel was assembled by Sanddriver Studios to discuss 3D printing and its possible uses within Cosplay costumes. While the panel informed attendees about how to use various technologies to create portions of costumes, it was also a promotional for Sanddriver Studios' costume-making services. The 3D modeling software and printing provides Cosplayers with the means to create precisely designed and lightweight components for weapons, props, and costume details.

Mirror, mirror on the wall: Constructed representations

Constructed Representations reflect the ways Cosplayers construct representations of alter egos and identity(ies) embodied within the characters they roleplay. These costumed representations also present understandings of mediated identities that extend and expand the self. These constructed representations reveal information about character selection, genre, and archetypes, as well as the role of the mimetic fandom. In addition, these representations also reveal the Cosplayer in subtle but detectable ways.

Cosplayers draw on three primary motivations around these constructed representations. First, they share their "love" of the character. Edward Elric from the *Fullmetal Alchemist* stated, "I just really like this character. I also like the bold use of color in the costume!" Another Cosplayer shared, "I love the series, plotline, and the character!" Cosplayers' intense emotions for their chosen characters dictate much of their constructed representations and Cosplay experiences.

Second, Cosplayers acknowledge their excitement about "being someone you're not." Usagi Yojimbo, a rabbit samurai from manga/anime declared, "I like samurai! A lot! I was born in the wrong time! But now, I am a samurai . . . and a rabbit." Cosplayers enthusiastically construct an identity and appearance different from one's own.

Third, "people knowing [the character] who you cosplay." Yazoo from *Final Fantasy VII* stated, "Yazoo is one of three brothers from *Final Fantasy VII* . . . it is a well-known favorite that everyone recognizes. It's elegant, beautiful, and action-packed." Cosplayers value and actively seek out character recognition from fans, audience members, and even passersby.

Character selection

Character selection is drawn from genres that reflect the Cosplayer's deep appreciation, devotion, and even fanaticism or obsession. Cosplayers commonly select their characters with personal connections to fiction and fantasy genres. The process a Cosplayer commonly uses to select an individual character is usually an emotional decision, often without a logical or rational explanation.

In most cases, Cosplayers have a deep affection and even love for their selected characters, which they expressed in a variety of ways. In my research, I observed the painstaking effort put into costumes and appearances, as well as performances that draw on in-depth research and knowledge. I also witnessed many arguments stemming from points of contention regarding specific characters' storylines and/or traits, where Cosplayers defended their character's position with unbridled fervor. These arguments revealed the Cosplayers' devotion to characters and storylines.

Cosplayers consume the character in the original mediated form as a fan, which becomes a form of in/formal research for their eventual Cosplay portrayal and performance. Some Cosplayers also create original characters, which may be inspired by existing characters, popular culture figures, fanfic, or otherwise originating from their imaginations.

Dedicated Cosplayers research their characters through multiple sources whenever possible. They watch portions of animations or live-action movies or videogames over and over again in order to gather minute details about a character's appearance, gestures, poses, dialogue, and storyline(s). Numerous sketches of designs staying true to the character but also allowing aspects of the Cosplayer's personality would need to be incorporated. The final result is composite character that reflects the original media and the Cosplayer.

Cosplayers participate in transmediation by interpreting characters and their storylines from the original mediums into the fandom subculture. Subsequently, Cosplayers become embedded in the media of their character and the character's storyline(s). Comic books, graphic novels, films, and videogames, as visual mediums, provide exceptional guides for character interpretation, costumes, and portrayals for Cosplayers. Consequently, characters from literature without visual references are less common and when Cosplayed often have multiple interpretations. It is also easier to cosplay a character with visual irony or satire when the image of the character is well established for the Cosplayer and audience, such as wearing a smiley-face button on the Dark Knight Batman armor.

Genre rules the world

Cosplayers' love of the character is closely related to their love for a genre, but it is not entirely derived from where the character originated. The genre commonly establishes the character's world and rules for that world, which are useful to a Cosplayer portraying a character in spaces without genre cues or guideposts.

The Prince of All the Cosmos, also known as Katamari Damacy, described his character, "The Prince is a small green man. He rolls a large ball around the earth to collect a material for stars. Nobody had done the costume when I first conceive the idea. I admired the offbeat nature of the [video]game and its rules." The rules established within the genre establish performance boundaries for Cosplayers. Additionally, Cosplayers create rules using headcanon where genre guides do not exist.

Archetypes

Gunnels suggests that the Cosplay character is understood as an "archetype" and the accompanying costume as "fetish" (2009: 4.2). Jungian archetypes were frequently revealed when Cosplayers discuss reasons for selecting their character and shared traits. There are three archetypes popular, or more frequently seen at conventions: Hero/heroine, Anti-hero/Anti-heroine, and Villain/Villainess. These archetypes share many commonalities, which is evident when Cosplayers discuss their favorite and past characters.

The Hero/heroine archetype represents the ideals Cosplayers want to portray and possibly attain, if only temporarily. Haku from *Naruto* shared, "I chose him [the character] because he is a very kind, caring person who felt life was useless without a dream. He sacrificed his life to protect his most important person and his dream." Also, Captain Harlock stated, "I like the classic, older anime heroes. I have cosplayed Moose from *Ranma ½*, Inuyasha, Bram Stroker's Dracula, and [characters from] *Babylon 5*."

The archetype of the Anti-hero/Anti-heroine is an appealing character for the Cosplayer who wants to portray a hero/heroine with a dark side. Captain Harlock described the character as "a 30-plus year old Anti-hero, who opposes the rule of the Machine Men." Anti-heroes, such as Batman or the Punisher, provide Cosplayers with layers of the persona to expose or hide in their portrayal.

The Villain/Villainess archetype shares many similarities with the hero/heroine and Anti-hero/Anti-heroine characters but with evil overtones. Seifer Almasay, from *Final Fantasy VII*, discussed his enthusiasm for roleplaying a villain, "My friends and I Cosplay in groups and not only do I play a good villain but I look the most like him." Roleplaying a villain allows Cosplayers to "act" in ways not necessarily acceptable in the real world, which is empowering and inspirational. The Villain/Villainess necessarily needs a foil, which provides the Cosplayer with opportunities to interact with the hero/heroine Cosplayer.

Mimetic fandom

Cosplay exists as a mimetic fandom (see also Cherry 2016); Cosplayers strive to create exact replicas of characters' appearances and imitate their well-known poses, actions, and dialogue (Brownie and Graydon 2016: 111; Lamerichs 2011: 7). Meticulous research and laborious efforts are poured into recreating live-action facsimiles of fantastic characters and their appearances drawn from source media. The mimetic characteristics of the subculture are enhanced by the roleplaying and audience participation (and suspension of disbelief).

Cosplayers endeavor to achieve character accuracy (on some level, usually appearance) to establish their authenticity with the members of the Cosplay subculture and other fandoms. Most Cosplayers strive to portray characters with precision and creativity; still, there is flexibility as to interpretation of accuracy by peers and even by the Cosplayers themselves. Humorous portrayals offer allowances for certain tolerances in accuracy if it contributes to everyone enjoying the wit, and exceptions are made for mash-up or original characters that do not have a specific point of reference for audience members.

The appearance (including costume, hair, makeup, and props) exists as a mimetic composition, which is necessary for immediate recognition and identification of the character. When observers recognize the character's identity, this represents the successful transition on the part of the Cosplayer. Moreover, by creating exactness and precision in the character's appearance, the Cosplayer is then afforded some latitude in roleplaying.

Also, by giving characters three-dimensional attributes and a life beyond the page (or original existence/media), the Cosplayer is allowed to insert the self into the roleplaying. Accordingly, the Cosplayer frequently extends beyond straightforward mimicking of the fictional character. Frequently, Cosplayers bring characters to life by simply interacting with their audience members, especially with children, who want to believe their favorite character is standing in front of them. Cosplayers also commonly give their characters humorous dialogue and/or actions or performing skits that further the characters' storylines.

Many characters selected by Cosplayers have symbols incorporated into their dress/appearance. Cosplayers not only mimic these symbols, but they also modify them to reflect their own identities connected to their selected characters. The letter "S" on Superman's chest may become a "C" for SuperCosplayer. Mario and Luigi (videogame characters) could have the Cosplayers' initials on their hats instead of the characters' "M" or "L" respectively.

Contrary to the issues with literary personas, the characters from films or television series are associated with specific and often well-known actors, which may limit who feels comfortable roleplaying certain characters (Lamerichs 2011: 4.5). These persons who resemble the actor (dressed as the character), however, are frequently rewarded with compliments as to accuracy, even if the costume is not as accurate. At Gen Con 2016, there were two individual 4th Doctors from *Doctor Who* both roleplayed by older men, but one looked exactly like the actor who played the 4th Doctor, Tom Baker, and he received many compliments on his "costume" especially near the *Doctor Who* merchandise vendor despite his scarf, shirt, and shoes being inaccurate to the character. The other 4th Doctor had a more accurate costume but did not receive the same kind of recognition or compliments, and was even told about the successful portrayal of the other Cosplay Doctor near the same *Doctor Who* vendor's booth. Merits, such as compliments and requests for photographs or autographs, reinforce the Cosplayers who select characters with similar physical traits as themselves.

A picture is worth 140 characters: Photographs and videos

Photographs and videos were revealed in the ways that Cosplayers communicated the importance of how photographs document, celebrate, and capture the Cosplay character (and Cosplayer) in a given place and time, which establishes the Cosplay fandom as image-centric. A thoughtfully designed and well-constructed costume garners attention from fans and peers, assuring requests for photographs and autographs, which are usually disseminated liberally through social media venues, giving the initial experience a second life via its photograph. Consequently, being photographed is an essential component to the Cosplay experience.

Cosplayers are reflexive regarding their photographs, in that the Cosplayer in the photograph is directed and mirrored back to herself, visually suggesting and confronting the relationship between the Cosplayer and the character. Cosplayers continuously consciously think about their outward personas (appearances, costumes, gestures, languages, poses, etc.). Photographs not only function as capturing the fleeting moments of time with friends, fans, and other Cosplayers, they also serve as documentation of specific characters and costumes. Cosplayers take selfies dressed as specific characters and pose with peer Cosplayers and fans to share on social media.

While some photographers snap a quick picture of a Cosplayer, many collaborate with the Cosplayer to capture the character's best features, costume, and pose (see Brownie and Graydon 2016: 116). As conventions institute rules about interacting with Cosplayers (and any persons in costumes), it is foreseeable that in the near future photographers and Cosplayers will enter into informal or formal agreements for all photographs. An alternative possibility is that Cosplay photographs may exclusively be staged and performed with only the surroundings and non-Cosplayers disrupting the authenticity.

In this way, Cosplayers posing for photographs are similar to *tableau vivant* (see also Dunchesne 2005), where costumed reenactors imitate poses from past events or incidents to create a "living picture." Cosplayers are photographed while reenacting their chosen characters' poses or performances from the source media, often well-known scenes or passages of text. An important distinction is how Cosplayers inject themselves into characters, which may be revealed in photographs with subtle expressions, gestures, and costume variances.

The act of posing for a photograph is deliberated and premeditated for the Cosplayer no matter how extemporaneous or candid the pose and expression appears to the observer/fan. Cosplayers practice posing in front of the mirror, as well as performing with friends. Their true moments of spontaneity include other Cosplayers who introduce new factors to the performance. Moreover, the Cosplayer knows that when she is in costume, she is likely to be photographed.

Cosplayers experience ephemeral fame when posing for photos with or giving autographs to their fans, Cosplay celebrities/professionals, and other fandom's celebrities. This temporary fame is renewed when the images of Cosplayers are posted on social media sites. Subsequently, the fame and even temporary celebrity status associated with photographs (and autographs) encourages Cosplay subculture to be image-centric. The photograph itself (even in digital form) functions as a trophy of a successful costume and a celebrated portrayal of a specific character. Cosplayers share these photos with friends, fans, and peer Cosplayers in order to elicit positive feedback and encouragement.

As these photos are circulated and seen on the Internet, the Cosplayer gains notoriety and merits, and their appearance is reviewed for success or failure in achieving character recognition, quality, and accuracy. A photograph of really successful character (i.e., appropriate background, detailed costume, dynamic pose, etc.) quickly circulates through social media channels, which has the potential to attract fans and non-Cosplayers. A controversial costume can also gain Cosplayer notoriety with outcomes dependent on current trends in the Cosplay community.

Circulated images on social media and in print gain their own life in the sense that they are no longer solely the Cosplayer but instead speak to the collaboration between the photographer and Cosplayer. In the Cosplay fandom, images of Cosplayers portraying characters function as fandom social currency both inside and outside the subculture. When these images are placed on social media sites, they serve as documentation, critique forums, and inspiration. In addition, online comments/feedback further imbue Cosplay images (and Cosplayers) with fetishistic and fantastic qualities.

Social media also serves Cosplayers to organize group photography sessions at fan conventions.[2] Specifically and most commonly Facebook announcements and events pages, as well as forums on Cosplay.com, are established for photography opportunities at conventions. Yearly, the major fan conventions include large group photography opportunities for Cosplayers. Groups external to the fan convention organizers, however, usually organize these sessions. The organizers allow breakout sessions for subtheme sessions. Independent groups and companies encourage and even organize these types of photography sessions because of the free publicity for themselves.

In recent years, videos capture more than just still images of the Cosplayer posing in her costume; instead the Cosplayer is shown in motion, moving similar to the character. Cosplayers' performances on video or images in photographs cease to be their property when posted on social media. This stands in stark contrast to Cosplayers being featured in fan videos and music videos, where they maintain ownership over their Cosplay character and alternate identity.

Documentation

Photographs and videos reveal the role of images as recordings of Cosplay characters, costumes, and experiences. Photographs document individual characters and costumes within specific performances and conventions. Cosplayers (and fans) use photographs, especially selfies, similar to anyone who takes pictures to document their relationships and shared moments of time. In addition, fans take pictures of Cosplayers to denote the extraordinary cosplaying appearances within the fandom experience. When images are posted on the Internet within social media and the like, it serves as an archive for photographic documentation.

Audience members (and photographers) "preserve" and document Cosplayers and their characters with photographs (Brownie and Graydon 2016: 116; see Rauch and Bolton 2010). Frequently, these same images also document the fan's position in the fandom (relative to the Cosplayer in the photographs) and interactions with specific Cosplayers. According to Eron Rauch and Christopher Bolton, "Cosplay photography is a form of fanthropology in the sense that it documents fan activities" (2010: 176). They further establish that Cosplayers are highly dependent on the photographers who capture their characters and disseminate the images. (Obviously, photographers are also highly dependent on Cosplayers as a focal point for their photographs.) It should be acknowledged that photographers of Cosplayers are not always interested in documenting the Cosplayers; instead, some photographers are interested in financially profiting from the exotic nature of Cosplay experiences, selling the photographs to various media outlets.

There are different types of Cosplay photographers, and it is not always possible for Cosplayers to tell the difference. Ellen Dorfman, Eron Rauch, and Steve Schofield, for example, are photographers who capture the Cosplayers' experiences with artistic imagery. In addition to fans or other Cosplayers, most professional Cosplay photographers financially profit from photographing Cosplayers and selling the images. To this end, they have high-end cameras and equipment in order to produce high-quality images. There are also artists who photograph Cosplayers who display their photographs online and in galleries. Many Cosplay photographers are Cosplayers or fans of Cosplay, but there are also researchers and the media who photograph Cosplayers for purposes of disseminating information about them beyond the fandom.

Rauch and Bolton (2010) suggest that simply photographing Cosplayers is an act of fanthropology. Instead, I argue that only some photographers participate in fanthropology, while others construct the space and even social setting to assure they can secure images in order to sell Cosplay images for profit and are not interested in knowing more about Cosplayers. In fact, the social context in which photographs are taken is crucial to the nonverbal communication of the still images, but these arranged photo sessions also contribute to the Cosplay environment.

Exploitation

Photographs and videos of Cosplayers are used to exploit the fandom, typically targeted at individual members. The request for a Cosplayer to pose for a photograph and have it circulated invites compliments and criticisms. Still, Cosplayers commonly agree that "the best part of Cosplay is getting pictures taken" and "people asking for your picture." Cosplayers associate having their pictures taken with compliments for their costumes, performances, and related hard work. One Cosplayer stated that her favorite part of Cosplay is "having people take your pictures, telling you that you look good, or people recognizing your character."

The Cosplay subculture is mediated and exploited through professional and amateur photographs and videos that are often disseminated on the Internet without compensation or consideration for the Cosplayer(s). In addition, print media, such as fan magazines and books, featuring Cosplayers primarily prints high-quality color photographs of Cosplayers without context. When the Cosplay subculture is simplified to only "pretty pictures," this oversimplification contributes to the objectification of Cosplayers because it lacks environs, situations, and positionality. Cosplay documentaries represent Cosplayers with more accuracy and contexture but some still exploit the members of the fandom for profit and entertainment.

One Cosplayer dressed as an original character, Barbarian, emphasized the importance of "having people ask to take pictures," which was echoed by many of the Cosplayers in this research study. Accordingly, Cosplayers accommodate and appreciate requests for photographs. Photographs and videos serve as more than acknowledgment for a costume well-made or a successful performance;

visual records also document the progress of construction and completion of the costume, the presentation of a character, a moment in time as a Cosplayer, and offers a self-reflexive examination of the costume/character/Cosplayer.

You gotta have friends: Social networks and communities

The Cosplay fandom serves as a network and community for Cosplayers to socialize with an array of fans and with peers. Cosplayers commonly suggested that they have difficulty making friends or socializing, and Cosplay provides them connections to like-minded persons. Sakura, a Cosplayer, stated that her favorite part about Cosplaying at conventions was "the people that you meet."

The costume affords the Cosplayer a chance to protect their sensitive self inside the fantasy character, which allows for ease of socializing and building social networks. Accordingly, Cosplayers commonly make new friends at conventions, whom they stay in contact with via social media and may only connect with in person at another fan convention. When at fan conventions, Cosplayers also spend time with friends who may or may not be Cosplayers, but are attendees and they share membership in the greater fan community.

The Internet affords Cosplayers opportunities to create virtual communities that suit their individual and group needs. They may belong to an online group for Cosplayers specific to a genre of character, research management, and/or the fandom in general. Cosplayers also use the Internet to connect with and build affiliations with a craftsperson or metalsmith for needed props, weapons, or custom costume manufacturing. Furthermore, the Internet facilitates friendships and intimate relationships outside of the Cosplay environment.

The Cosplay fandom is an organic system, which is in continual transformation as it is continuously exposed to new stimuli, such as new fans, characters, competitions, and critics. Structures and individuals exploiting Cosplayers further impact and modify the fandom in ways members cannot anticipate or control. Consequently, Cosplayers must be resilient and support their intricate social networks in order to sustain the fandom.

Socializing

Cosplayers place significant value on their social interactions with other Cosplayers and other fan communities. These interactions reinforce common bonds and give a sense of belonging to members of the fandom/subculture. In addition, during social interactions with other Cosplayers, they practice roleplaying their character in low-stakes situations and receive valuable feedback on character, costume, and performance.

The social connections and networks stimulated at conventions become incorporated into the larger Cosplay fandom. Accordingly, Cosplayers utilize online resources and contribute to their online fandom communities with interactive games, discussion posts, tutorial videos, and construction progress. Cosplay.com is a popular website for Cosplayers to communicate, share images of Cosplay characters, and ask for advice. At the bottom of an individual's forum post, there is as "signature," a name by which most Cosplayers use to communicate their progress on costumes, array of characters, and/or conventions planning to attend in the coming year.

Beyond friendships, fans also share stories of meeting their significant others at conventions because of shared interests (and proximity). When fans who meet at fan conventions date each other, they often pursue long-distance relationships using the Internet to maintain communications, and may only see each other once a year at the convention (or more if they can afford to attend another convention). Some Cosplayers are so dedicated to their characters and the fandom that they hold their weddings at fan conventions or in themed locations wearing their Cosplay dress (Winge and Eicher 2003).[3]

Social media

The current and future role of social media in the Cosplay fandom subculture cannot be underestimated. Not only do Cosplayers use social media to communicate with one another about their Cosplay activities but they also use it to disseminate and promote their characters and Cosplay skills. Some Cosplayers use the far reach of social media to endorse their craft expertise (construction, weapons, props) and even create a business. Social media allows the Cosplay fandom to flourish in ways not possible before the Internet was available to the public.

Cosplay celebrities and models also utilize social media in addition to their professional websites to communicate with their fans, promote appearances, and share information about characters and charities. Fans have high expectations for Cosplay celebrities and the Cosfamous. Cosplayers demand that the celebrities personally respond to comments and questions on social media. In fact, the popularity of Cosplay celebrities is frequently evaluated based on number of Facebook and/or Twitter followers.

As new types of social media emerge, Cosplayers adopt those platforms that support visual presentations of their characters and provide ways of sharing information with the fandom and Cosplay fans. In this way, Instagram and Tumblr provide an ideal platform for Cosplayers to display their costumes and even any construction in-process images. Currently, the Cosplayers utilize Facebook events for socializing, Instagram for sharing images of characters, and YouTube for videos. Cosplayers have numerous channels on YouTube, where they show new characters and/or offer tutorials for hair, makeup, and styling, as well as costume design and construction.

Belonging and inclusion

Overall, Cosplay communities give the Cosplayer a sense of belonging to something greater than herself as an individual. The social networks and communities created around and within the Cosplay fandom are crucial to Cosplayers. For some Cosplayers, these social connections offer support for designing and constructing costumes and roleplaying, as well as building long-lasting relationships. Cid Highland from *Final Fantasy VII* asserted, "This [Cosplay] is so much fun with friends." Sakura from *Naruto* stated how much she enjoyed attending fan conventions to have "a good time with friends in character costume."

The Cosplay experience continuously reflected the importance of cosplaying with friends. One Cosplayer shared that she rarely cosplayed alone and emphasized the importance of "friends and I wanted to cosplay together." Another Cosplayer suggested that her friend was essential to her successful Cosplay performance: "I have done five Cosplay shows at the Anime Iowa convention. Two on my own, and three with my friend. I get better results as part of a duo with my friend."

As the Cosplayer dons a costume and subsequently the character, she assumes a position within the fandom both from other Cosplayers and fans from other fandoms. Within the Cosplay fandom, there exists the potential for social acceptance and agency. The Cosplay communal experiences construct and sustain the group where Cosplayers experience a sense of belonging and inclusion.

Fans at the convention

At fan conventions, Cosplayers are recognizable in costumes as "Cosplayers," which means they are often mistaken as entertainment for attendees and the general public. Cosplayers, however, are also fans at the convention and want to have some of the same experiences of other attendees, which is rarely possible when dressed in costumes.

Cosplayers interact with other fandoms because their characters are commonly drawn from vast array of genres present at conventions. Some Cosplayers, however, were willing to discuss their marginalization by other fandoms. One Cosplayer commented how she liked "being able to dress as an anime character" but felt other fans just wanted pictures with her, and she wished the anime fans were more accepting of her when she is in costume.

At fan conventions, Cosplayers also dislike managing and sharing spaces with non-Cosplayers, especially those fans who actively verbalize or act on their distaste for costumed fans. One Cosplayer commented, "I hate dealing with the rude comments and actions of non-players." Still, Cosplayers are drawn to fan conventions because they offer the foremost venue for exhibiting costumes and performing characters to receptive audiences. The Cosplayers' presence at fan conventions inserts the Cosplay into the greater fan community, usually in obtrusive ways.

I am just roleplaying my character: Performativity and roleplaying

Cosplayers roleplay (i.e., act, pose, and speak in a manner similar to) the chosen fantasy characters in detailed costumes in public (e.g., hallways and lobby) and private spaces (e.g., hotel rooms) at conventions in addition to masquerades and competitions. This roleplaying ranges from poses with catchphrases to elaborate "plays" with peers, but while roleplaying, the Cosplayer may deviate from the version of the character as portrayed in its source media. Roleplaying requires skills that Cosplayers hone with many hours of practice and feedback from peers. Cosplayers are responsive and quick thinking with impromptu performances in convention and hotel hallways, especially in situational occurrences (i.e., encountering another Cosplayer from the same source material, becoming lost and asking for directions in the convention space, etc.).

Cosplayers assume ownership over the characters they embody, and subsequently lend belief to the part being roleplayed. In this way, Cosplayers participate in "performative consumption" by using the costume with the body to transform an individual into the Cosplay character (Hill 2002: 158). Furthermore, the nonverbal language of the costume and body create the overall appearance of the character that provides visual cues; these cues frequently open spaces for dialogue between Cosplayers and fans.

Cosplayers respond positively to the immediacy of performance (Gunnels 2009), which includes posing for photographs and applause, as well as one-on-one interactions where the audience member engages the Cosplayer on a deeper level about the character and/or costume. The performance of roleplaying a character intertwines the Cosplayer with the media and genre from which the character originated. As individual fans gather, later becoming crowds, Cosplayers' performances and fans' gestures gain momentum. Naruto shared his enthusiasm for performing: "I like acting like the character and interacting with people. They give me energy and my performance is better with more people watching me."

Cosplayers are frequently thought to have ambitions of becoming actors before becoming part of the fandom or even exhibitionists: however, my research suggests that many Cosplayers are fans first who begin by dressing as one of their favorite characters, and, in time, they learn to pose, perform, and roleplay. Accordingly, Taako shared that she "wanted to dress like him [Taako] because I really like him. I don't need to roleplay him . . . not yet, anyways."

Some Cosplayers invest a lot of time, money, and energy into creating their costume and overall appearance, but are not as concerned with roleplay or performance. Other Cosplayers, however, spend lengthy hours preparing and anticipating dressing in costumes, performing and roleplaying for their friends, fans, and audiences. A Cosplayer shared this about her original character: "I created her for roleplaying. I engage in live action roleplaying and I write and draw my own stories."

Cosplayers confess that posing for pictures, competition performances, and hallway roleplaying is exhausting and exhilarating. In fact, roleplaying and performing in front of an audience causes anxiety, not only for the fear of what might go wrong but also from performing in front of large crowds on stage. Yojimbo stated, "The best part of Cosplay is a moment on stage, but the worst part is my wig slipping down while waiting to go on stage!"

Competitions

Conventions almost always include a Cosplay competition and/or masquerade, making Competitions a subtheme of performativity and roleplaying. Participants of Cosplay competitions compete displaying their costume in a variety of poses and/or within a performance relevant to their character. In most Cosplay competitions, Cosplayers are judged on three primary criteria: (1) accuracy of the appearance of the costume to the actual character; (2) construction skills and quality of the costume; and (3) entertainment value of the performance. These criteria, however, are not always clearly outlined for judges or participants.

Commonly, competition judges are usually Cosplay "experts" (i.e., interviewers, bloggers, researchers, costume designers, etc.), celebrity stars from fandom films, and popular Cosplayers. Praise from popular Cosplayers about costume details are valued more than the awards of the competitions prize performance. Their criticisms, however, can impact Cosplayers with positive and negative results. Large competitions usually at sizable fan conventions typically do not allow for judges to individually interact each participant due to time constraints; judges may even be shrouded in darkness to evaluate each Cosplayer or Cosplaying team with anonymity.

The awards in Cosplay competitions include monetary rewards, merchandise, and trophies. More importantly, winning a competition offers bragging rights and the potential to promote a Cosplayer to a more significant position within the greater Cosplay fandom (subculture). Convention promoters and competitions organizers also endorse the winners in order to promote future Cosplay events, which will draw new sponsors and revenue.

Cosplay competitions are more than just a chance to win a trophy and bragging rights. Cosplayers enjoy the challenges of creating the most innovatively accurate costumes and delivering their interpretation of the character within entertaining performances. According to Lauren Orsini, most Cosplayers do not participate in Cosplay competitions but instead they attend fan conventions in costume as an expression of love for their favorite character (2015: 11). My research confirms this assertion but Cosplayers also indicated additional motivations including socializing with friends, shopping for fan merchandise, and dressing in character costumes. Still, their love of the character is a meaningful and often primary motivation for attending fan conventions.

Masquerades and parades

Many fan conventions dedicate one evening to the masquerade (masquerade ball), where Cosplayers display their skills with costumed performances of short skits, often humorous, to entertain sizable audiences from various fan communities. Some masquerades are competitive and offer awards, while others are simply entertaining exhibitions for convention attendees. Masquerades are well attended and the audience actively responds to the performances.

Parades are another way for Cosplayers to display their characters and costumes to large audiences. Masquerades replaced parades at some conventions, but due to the growing popularity of Cosplayers not only at conventions but also in the mainstream, world parades are being reincorporated into conventions again. Cosplay parades are a minimalist means of organization to gather all Cosplayers together in one space for photographs, display of character identities, and entertainment for convention attendees and spectators. Many photographs are circulated on the Internet of hundreds of Cosplayers in groups posed just before or after a fan convention parade.

Dragon Con is a convention that specifically considers Cosplayers in its programming and encourages them to dress in costumes during the day and night because of the entertainment value to the attendees. As early as May 2016, all parade Cosplayers were registered and no others were allowed to participate in the September 2016 Dragon Con Cosplay Parade. Dragon Con also has their masquerade, a competition where Cosplayers compete in teams and daily fan favorites and nightly costume competitions. Dragon Con's commitment to Cosplayers demonstrates the value of this subculture to the greater convention fandoms and promoters. Other conventions are also investing in the Cosplay fandom.

Group challenges and activities

Cosplay challenges are popular among Cosplayers who want to continue Cosplaying beyond the limitations or availability of conventions, hence the subtheme of Group Challenges and Activities. These challenges are conveniently disseminated online (commonly via social media) and focus around a theme or activity, and the challenges may have a charity component to it in order to attract more participants. Cosplayers submit their personas with photographs or videos depending on the specific requirements of the challenge.

GISHWHES (The Greatest International Scavenger Hunt the World Has Ever Seen) holds an annual international scavenger hunt. The scavenger hunt's proceeds are given to a predetermined charity organization. Part of the requirement for this challenge is for individuals and teams to create Cosplay characters and performances focused around a specific theme. For example, in 2015, Jodie Gustafson participated in the GISHWHES scavenger hunt, in which she cosplayed her version of the Donna Reed and June Cleaver characters. Photographs are taken of the Cosplay character and submitted for judging as part of the scavenger hunt (see Plate 3.9). Gustafson discussed her Cosplay experience,

> I have loved playing dress up since I was a little girl and see no reason to stop just because I'm an adult now. I like the creative challenge of using my crafting skills to cobble a costume together out of thrift store finds, dollar store deals, and bits and bobbles from my own home stash. For this costume channeling my inner June Cleaver meant representing the strong women, mostly homemakers, who had a lasting influence on my life. I am wearing my mother's pearls, my grandmother's clip on earrings and broach, and my great aunt's apron, things that I have kept to remember these special women after they passed away.

These types of Cosplay challenges extend the life of the Cosplayer's character beyond conventions. Challenges also offer Cosplayers opportunities to practice their characters, as well as opportunities to imagine new characters, ones that are not necessarily associated with an established storyline. These characters, who are cosplayed in non-convention settings, may also be used for fan conventions and competitions. Cosplayers also use these types of competitions as socializing opportunities with other fans.

Cosplay is the mother of invention: Creativity

A Cosplayer demonstrates creativity when she selects a character, designs the costume, problem solves to construct the costume, and even executes performances. Cosplayers expressed their excitement about being able and encouraged to be creative in the Cosplay fandom. Cosplayers further use creativity in their portrayal of a character with humor, irony, and satire, making original innovations for roleplaying and performances.

The costume and related accessories require Cosplayers to apply creativity and innovation to design, construct, and problem-solve. Early Cosplayers relied on innovation to turn raw materials and repurposed items to create costumes for characters. Some Cosplayers enjoy "the challenge of creativity for creating the costume" (Wolfwood from *Trigun*) because "it is challenging constructing the hard parts of the costume but you feel good when you figure out something new" (Lady from *Devil May Cry 3* videogame).

Imagination

The role of imagination cannot be underestimated in the Cosplayer's performance. It accounts for much of the creativity and innovation found in Cosplayers' costumes and performances. Imagination also manifests in the ingenious ways the Cosplayer spontaneously respond to and interact with audiences. Lady from *Devil May Cry 3* stated, "The best part of Cosplay is using my imagination and turning it into something real."

Cosplayers shared stories about using innovation to repair a costume just before a performance or needing to create an accessory that suits the character but needs to carry a cell phone or medicine. Yazoo from *Final Fantasy VII* stated how she appreciated being able to create "useful accessories to match your costume is a great addition to any Cosplay" (opens her tiny bag to reveal a pocket that held her cellphone and inhaler). This type of creativity and innovation is often unseen and not recognized for the imaginative (and practical) employment. Creativity and imagination are enmeshed into most aspects of the Cosplay experience from the design of the costume through the execution of the performance. Subsequently, these qualities are taken for granted even by the Cosplayers themselves.

With great powers come great agency: Empowerment and self-determination

When Cosplayers discussed the ways costumes and performances made them feel, they also shared how they identify with their chosen characters personality traits, goals and ambitions, and/or physical appearance. Cosplayers value the significance of recognition and awards beyond public acknowledgments, which fosters pride and inspires further accomplishment goals.

When dressed in Costume, the Cosplayers not only imbue the power inherent to the character portrayed; Cosplaying also offers the opportunity for empowerment, agency, and self-determination through the character. A Cosplayer portraying Lady from *Devil May Cry 3* stated, "I really like the [video]game that she comes from and this character especially. She is powerful!" In addition, participating in the Cosplay fandom empowers Cosplayers with agency and confidence that appears to extend beyond the fan convention and the costume. Gojyo shared this about his character: "He is awesome! I would want to be just like him if it is possible."

Identifying with the character

Cosplayers identify with their chosen characters, and even express their desire to be more like the characters they dress like and/or roleplay. According to Orsini, "With Cosplay, you change not only the way others perceive you, but, for a little while, how you perceive yourself" (2015: 229). Cosplayers discussed how they admire their characters, with whom they can identify. Rock Lee, from *Naruto,* stated, "He is self-determined like me. He is always an underdog."

In some cases, Cosplayers acknowledge the physical similarities, which leads to identification with the chosen character. Accordingly, Hyuuga Neji from *Naruto* pointed out how "his [character's] hairstyle is similar to my own and he looks cool." Another Cosplayer, Lord Darcia from *Wolf's Rain*, shared how his height was an advantage: "I get to be tall, dark, and imposing."

Cosplayers' identification with the character also reflects their perceived personalities of themselves and those of their character. Sakura from *Naruto* also stated, "My best friend is the closest fit, personality-wise, from *Naruto*, and I could make a couple with [my] boyfriend being Rock Lee." Comparably, Vampire Hunter stated, "I made this outfit to cosplay my character from *Witch Hunter Robin*. I am like this character who is a cleric. She is in a vampire hunter's union and is the informant in the group."

Character recognition

Cosplayers were deeply offended when their characters were misidentified or were unknown to other fans at conventions. Conversely, they expressed excitement for their character "being recognized" based on their appearance and/or costumes (Winge 2006a). Correspondingly, Cosplayers expressed significant concerns if their character was being recognized, and how distressing it is when fans did not know who they were roleplaying. Sir Integra Wingates from *Hellsing* asserted that "fan recognition is important," while others shared how "it is the worst when people say, 'What are you supposed to be?'" and "people not knowing who you are." Similarly, Seifer Almasy from *Final Fantasy VII* simply stated, "I hate it when people do not know what character you are."

Character recognition or the lack thereof can be motivation for future character selection. Cloud Strife, from *Final Fantasy VII*, expressed frustration with experiences of cosplaying characters not being recognized at past conventions and how it impacted his current character selection: "I wanted to Cosplay Advent Children with friends and wanted to have a really well-known costume for once" (see Plate 3.7).

At the same time, Cosplayers are territorial and assume ownership over their chosen/created character's appearance, portrayal, and its performances. This is a contributing factor to Cosplayers creating OCs and mash-up characters, because it is less likely that anyone at the convention will have the same character. These types of characters, however, will limit how recognizable the character is to fans at conventions and elsewhere.

Cosplayers value other's positive reactions, opinions, and acknowledgments of their characters and subsequent dress and representations. In this way, character recognition becomes validation, as well as positive social affirmations for the Cosplayer. Accordingly, Black Widow from *Avengers* stated, "The best part about Cosplay is people recognizing you, and the hugs."

Pride and accomplishments

Cosplayers express immense pride, accomplishment, and joy in their Cosplay experiences. Many of their self-acknowledged accomplishments center around their costumes and appearances, demonstrating their "pride in having a good costume" and the importance of "making something that you can be proud of" (Winge 2007; 2017). In addition, Cosplayers revel in designing and creating costumes and appearances that garner character recognition from fans. Accordingly, one Cosplayer playing Seifer Almasay from the videogame *Final Fantasy VII* stated how "putting the costume together as close perfect as possible and character recognition." This does not mean, however, that costumes need to be perfectly constructed as long as the key elements of the appearance visually communicate the character's identity.

For this reason, costumes that are not well executed but represent a novice's earnest effort are applauded, while support and assistance are offered for the next costume attempt. Similarly, young Cosplayers who wear mostly purchased costumes but attempt to construct portions of the costume are also rewarded with compliments and encouraged to construct more of their costume next time.

Cosplayers are highly motivated to elicit positive responses for their costumes, characters, and performances. Red Queen from *Alice in Wonderland* shared that she enjoyed "people saying THAT IS SO COOL!" Also, Cosplayers are encouraged by awards given for convention competitions, even when it is their friend who wins. Tony Tony Chopper from *One Piece* and Rukio from *Bleach* (a mash-up character) shared, "Last year my friend and I did a mock fight between my character, who was a ninja, and her character, who was a pirate. People cheered and laughed. My friend even won an award for the costume. I was so proud of her!"

Toto, we're not at the convention anymore: Escapism

Escapism is a meaningful theme of the Cosplay experience. Cosplay functions as escapism for Cosplayers, their fans, and audience members. This escapism creates a Cosplay bubble, where Cosplayers and their performances exist outside the structures of the real world beyond the fandom and convention.

Albeit temporary, Cosplay offers captivating distractions from everyday life. While in costume, Cosplayers embody characters offering fantasy identities and dimensions of daydreaming for themselves and others. The Cosplayer as a fan and performer is experienced both individually and communally within various situations of the fan convention. The fluidity between self and group engages Cosplayers in a cyclical exchange. A Death Eater from *Harry Potter* stated, "I enjoy getting into costume in the spirit of the [Cosplay] event that I attend and love to see what other people create in turn."

Desiring to extend the Cosplay experience beyond the fan convention, Cosplayers find opportunities to dress and possibly roleplay as their fictional characters. Accordingly, a Cosplayer portraying Haku from *Naruto* said, "I Cosplay every year for Halloween and here [at the convention]." Also, the Original Vampire from *The Vampire Diaries* stated, "I also play her when I live action roleplay."

Cosplay bubble

The Cosplay bubble demands suspension of disbelief from both the Cosplayer and observers. Inside the Cosplay bubble, the fantastic occurs where there are transitional spaces between reality and fantasy, which requires the suspension of disbelief (Todorov 1973). In this way, Cosplay's use of fantasy characters and storylines aid in the positive reception from viewers ("playing along"). Consequently, the tropes of fantasy storylines and fantastic characters are alluring to Cosplayers.

Still, Cosplayers grapple with the fantastic qualities of their characters within physical, mundane spaces, such as convention centers and hotel hallways. This is where the Cosplay bubble manifests as a (performance) space for Cosplayers and observers to enjoy the fantasy without the distractions of everyday life. Correspondingly, Link from *The Legend of Zelda* videogame stated, "Here, I get to be who I want to be, not who I have to be . . . and everyone plays along."

The viewer is necessary as the other side of performance. Cosplayers are continuously roleplaying to their audience (and the audience's reactions) while maintaining important traits that connect Cosplayer to character. In the exchange between Cosplayer and audience, "spectators are eager to suspend their disbelief" (Brownie and Graydon 2016: 109) in favor of being swept away to the fantastic world the Cosplayer creates.

It's not just a costume—Cosplay is a way of life: Devotion and obsession

Cosplayers shared their tendencies for deep devotion and some obsession (or at the least intense preoccupation) for their fandom and subculture. Since the Cosplayer may be influenced by multiple sources, she may have numerous points of connections to fandoms that encourage devotion and allowances for obsession. The Cosplayer's devotion to the fandom and the related activities is evident in their level commitment and participation. Hyuuga Neji from *Naruto* stated, "I cosplay anywhere that it is socially acceptable." Moreover, Cosplayers were enthusiastic about being superfans and reveled in "getting other people excited 'cause they love the character too!" (Taako), in order to share their devotion for Cosplay. Some Cosplayers' serious attitudes about Cosplay could be interpreted as an obsession because they treat it as real as anything in their real lives outside of a fan convention. Vampire shared, "This is my first con[vention]. But I Cosplay all of my life in secret."

Cosplay has a facade of being all fun and games, but beneath the surface it churns anxieties, stressors, and headaches. Cosplayers shared the ways they channel even the worst emotions into positive energy for Cosplay. For example, Dracula said, "I use the energy from my fear of being around lots of people to give a really good performance."

Dedication

The Cosplayers I interviewed ranged from novices, who were at their first convention as a Cosplayer, to veterans who had a minimum of fifteen years of experience. Cosplayers' dedication and commitment to the fandom ranged from fans such as Rock Lee, who stated, "I have only been cosplaying for a couple of weeks. This is my first time cosplaying at a convention," to Jiraiya, who stated, "I have been a Cosplayer for five years. I cosplay six to seven times each year."

Cosplayers frequently articulated their dedication in measurements of participation. Sanzo expresses her devotion to Cosplay by how often she dresses in character: "Everyday of every con[vention] I attend." Vergil from the *Devil May Cry 3* videogame noted, "I cosplay as much as possible . . . five or six conventions a year." Hinata calculated, "I have been cosplaying since 2001. I Cosplay as often as possible" (see Plate 3.10).

Some Cosplayers only dress in character the day of the masquerade, parade, and/or competition. This is due in part to lengthy process of dressing in costume and the potential for damaging a costume before competition. Many Cosplayers are extremely devoted to the Cosplay experience and are saddened when it is over. To this end, Dark Vash mourned, "The worst part of Cosplay is when it ends."

Financial expenditures and investments

Cosplayers interviewed shared information about the amount of money spent on costumes alone. These amounts ranged from US$10 to US$800, but most costumes were just under US$100 when the Cosplayers excluded the costs of props or weapons. Only three Cosplayers admitted that their costumes were completely store-bought. Instead, most Cosplayers reported they themselves had constructed their costumes except for the props and weapons, which either had been purchased or were constructed for them by others.

Some Cosplayers even referred to Cosplay as "cost play" and stated "the cost can be prohibitive depending on the costume" (Vash the Stampede from *Trigun*). And, a Klingon from *Star Trek* added, "The worst part about Cosplay is the time and money I have to spend." Still others qualified the expenses as offsetting the Cosplay experience: "I spent about $400 on this cosplay [costume] but [I am] willing to spend thousands . . . not all at once of course" (Vampire Hunter).

Cosplayers strategize approaches to contend with the financial cost of the costume. One Cosplayer stated, "I self-designed my costume but I bought some materials and things I took apart from Goodwill" (mash-up character from Tony Tony Chopper from *One Piece* and Rukio from *Bleach*). Cosplayers often use secondhand items for materials, structures, and details because used items are more affordable than new items.

My research suggests purchased costumes are not as valued within the fandom, and rarely rewarded with awards or recognition from Cosplay competitions. Also, there are correlations between the cost of raw materials and time invested in creating costumes, winning competitions, and achieving recognition of the characters. That is, costumes with raw materials costing over

US$100 and involving numerous hours of construction tend to secure the most awards in competitions. Whether the costume is made or purchased, however, have little connection to Cosplayers' satisfaction. Their positive experiences directly related to costumes include performing for an audience, being recognized as the character, and posing for photographs.

Have fun! Fun and play

There is a good-humored message of "Have Fun! Don't be a Dick!" found as a motto on convention posters, and even as one of the "rules" at Cosplay events and competitions. The idea behind the motto/rule is that Cosplay should exist as a "fun" and "playful" space, and that no one should take it (or themselves) too seriously, even during stressful situations.

Cosplay is about having enjoyment and being playful, and most Cosplayers embrace this philosophy with great enthusiasm. Despite the highly competitive nature of Cosplay competitions, Cosplayers are encouraged to make merry and good-naturedly engage others and peers. Hinata from *Naruto* exclaimed, "I love dressing up in costumes with my friends and having fun!"

The fandom actively encourages and engages in play and make-believe by assuming characters and performances. Some Cosplayers even suggested that without a playful spirit, characters would be dull and listless on the stage: "If you aren't having fun, no one is having fun!" (Red Queen from *Alice in Wonderland*).

Humor

Humor is an important factor in Cosplay, it surfaces in Cosplayers' costumes and performances. Even serious characters benefit from humorous skits and improvisational performances. Accordingly, Yojimbo expressed, "I do this to have fun and laugh! Everyone likes a funny Cosplay."

Cosplayers utilize humor in their performances as a vehicle to share their multidimensional characters and engage audience more fully. Laughter also releases tensions and insecurities that the Cosplayer may be experiencing in connection with public performances. The humor is often self-effacing, which has the ability to render fictional characters as real individuals with flaws and failings.

Drama

While most of the Cosplayers I interviewed enjoyed having fun, others drew attention to the negative aspects of Cosplay. One Cosplayer bemoaned,

"The worst part about Cosplay is the drama." Drama was commonly described as Cosplayers "gossiping," being "mean," "not having fun," and being "bad" or not doing it "right." An additional type of drama that Cosplayers contend with is harassment from outsiders that takes shape as sexual harassment, bullying, and assault.

Cosplayers claim they are not causing drama themselves, but instead it is caused by others. Kadaj from *Final Fantasy VII* declared, "I really dislike bad Cosplayers!" Cosplayers define a "bad Cosplayer" differently depending on the criteria they prioritize in their own Cosplay experiences. For some, "bad" reflects criticisms about the costume, while others use "bad" to refer to poor humor, sloppy performance, or even awkward social interactions.

There are some Cosplayers who cause drama when they offer harsh criticism to Cosplayers whom they perceive do not Cosplay "right." Cid Highland from *Final Fantasy VII* noted that the worst part of Cosplay is how some "people looked terrible," suggesting the Cosplayer did not care enough for their selected character to spend time and money on their costume. This critique became so commonly known that the retail store Hot Topic released a T-shirt with the printed message: "Cosplay: Do it right or not at all." Unable to recognize this sentiment originated in the fandom, Cosplayers used social media to reject the T-shirt and message printed on it. Consequently, Hot Topic eventually withdrew the T-shirt from sale (Orsini 2015).

Parties

Some Cosplayers choose to host parties where Cosplayers and fans are invited to socialize in costume and character at and beyond the convention. Cosplay parties typically take place in hotel rooms at fan conventions. Generally, these parties are open to anyone, but are heavily populated by Cosplayers. These parties commonly have a theme encouraging and generating specific types of characters or genres. Parties are excellent venues for to present new, original, controversial, or mash-up characters in a safer, smaller environment than at fan conventions.

The Cosplay experience

During my research, Cosplayers shared their Cosplay experiences with fervent enthusiasm. Emerging from the research, including field notes, interviews, and photographs, were interconnected constructs or themes and subthemes reflecting the Cosplayers' experiences, which formed within the Cosplay fandom. While the Cosplay experience spans themes of Cosplay Costume to the Fun and

Play, the following attempts to reveal the Cosplay experience by highlighting the themes and subthemes discovered in this research. (In Chapter 6, I explore the Cosplayer experience extending from this Cosplay experience as gleaned from themes and subthemes.)

Reinforcing the focus of this research, the Cosplay Costume is the most commonly discussed theme among Cosplayers and is even a topic of discussion for fans from other fandoms. Cosplayers explained in detail their processes for Designing and Constructing the Costume, and some even shared the importance of Technology in the costume execution or depicting fantastic abilities. They also described the laborious process of Dressing in costumes and the needed perfection when applying makeup in order to create the Fantastic Body. In addition, the individual costume design and construction accommodates Cosplayers who want to Crossplay.

Cosplayers invest substantial amounts of time and energy into creating their Constructed Representations of self and character. Individual Cosplayers communicated their deep love of their respective characters by sharing intimate details about their Character Selection and the character's position within the Genre Rules the World. As members of a Mimetic Fandom, Cosplayers portray the Archetypes inherent to fantastic characters.

The importance of Photographs and Videos for the Cosplay fandom became evident when fans interrupted my research interviews numerous times to take photographs with and of their favorite character or Cosplayer. Photographs and Videos function as visual currency and merit for the members. These visual representations serve as Documentation across an array of socially constructed moments and mementos of characters, costumes, performances, events, and relationships. Unfortunately, there is always the risk of Exploitation, but Cosplayers do not seem dismayed and readily pose for pictures for and with almost anyone.

The members of the Cosplay fandom construct Social Networks and Communities as natural extensions of the activities associated with cosplaying and as ways of coping and supporting each other while navigating the fandoms as Fans at the Convention. In the Cosplayers' quest for Belonging and Inclusion, they overcome anxieties and pressures to socialize and perform with and for other Cosplayers as well as for the strangers. The use of social media facilitates this construction, support, and maintenance of social connections.

Cosplayers demonstrated the captivating qualities of Performativity and Roleplaying for the fandom and audience members. Not all Cosplayers participate in Fan Convention Competitions, but most will walk in the Masquerades and Parades, which draw large crowds at fan conventions. The latter also allows the Cosplay fandom to demonstrate their significant number of members. In addition to these highly publicized Cosplay events, which are often organized by the fan convention, there are smaller Group Challenges and Activities that solidify relationships in tighter social groups but also provide Cosplayers with another venue for their character performances or chance to compete in new and creative ways.

Cosplayers utilize Creativity when conceiving their costumes, performances, and character interactions. They share stories of using innovation and their imaginations to repair a costume, cover for someone who forgot her lines, and design and construct lightweight weapon props that visually appear hefty and ominous.

Cosplayers demonstrated Empowerment and Self-determination more than they were able to talk about it specifically. They shared stories about how they were Identifying with the Character, as well as successfully dressing and roleplaying so that observers have Character Recognition. They beamed with Pride for their Accomplishments with their character, the costume, and for the fandom overall.

The Cosplay fandom's activities function as Escapism for Cosplayers and their audiences. Their formal and informal performances create the Cosplay bubble, where fantastic characters give live-action performances that may expand to encompass audience members. Inside the bubble, the real world blurs in favor of the surreal realm of fantasy characters, friendships, belonging, and recognition.

Cosplayers expressed their devotion to the Cosplay fandom through their love of the character and costumed performances; superfans are proud of their Devotion and Obsession with Cosplay. Most Cosplayers demonstrated a significant level of Dedication to the fandom, which was secondary only to their Commitment to their characters, as well as performances and costumes as key components to the portrayal of given characters. Their Devotion (and Obsession for some) is evident in the Financial Expenditures and Investments.

The importance of Fun and Play to the Cosplay fandom was reinforced with the Cosplayers' sense of Humor and playful nature in their interactions and performances, as well as with the Cosplay motto: "Have Fun, Don't Be a Dick!" As with any dynamic social system, Cosplayers noted the ways that Drama occurs and their distaste for it, even when they may also contribute to it.

The Cosplay experience is commonly thought to begin when the Cosplayer is in costume and performing at the fan convention, however, that perspective lacks grounding in everyday life. The Cosplayer shapes and forms the experience in individual ways, which contribute to the composition and structure of the fandom. In turn, the Cosplay fandom reflects the Cosplay experience through the complexities of the social structures with their drawbacks and benefits.

Summary

Cosplayer experiences are reflected in the constructs/themes and subthemes, which further established a deeper understanding of the Cosplay fandom.

The narratives along with observations and interactions revealed that the Cosplayers' experiences are deeply connected to their dress/costumes, which are reinforced by social interactions, images of Cosplayers, performances, and fun.

Cosplayers innovatively construct costumes and props, apply intricate makeup, and style elaborate wigs to recreate or create fantastic characters. In Chapter 4, I examine the significance of the Cosplay costume. I discuss the allure of common Cosplay genres, leading to character selection and construction of complex and elaborate costumes. With an intentional focus on costumes, dress, and appearances, Chapter 4 will explore costume as fetish, fashion, and material culture. The costume facilitates socializing and roleplaying because it disguises the self and permits the character to be revealed. I also examine how the costume (and appearance) is intertwined into all of the Cosplayer's experiences by exploring the themes revealed during this research study.

4

DRESSING THE PART

Cosplayers are closely associated with performance and roleplaying, in that members of this subculture "stay in character" or perform as their designated character when dressed accordingly. With each additional element of the costume the Cosplayer dons, the more complete the transformation is into the fantastic character. Cosplayers tend to select fantastic characters from genres that offer extraordinary storylines. Why choose to portray the ordinary character Serena when Sailor Moon offers similar mundane qualities but with magical powers? Of course, some Cosplayers enjoy the challenge of portraying more than one related character at a time, such as transforming from Diana Prince to Wonder Woman.

The Cosplayer profoundly relies on the visual (nonverbal) cues communicated with the character's costume (i.e., dress and appearance). To this end, they dedicate copious amounts of time, efforts, and resources to constructing their costumes in a detailed manner; styling hair or purchasing and styling wigs; and securing or constructing any accessories, props, or weapons. The role of the Cosplayer's dress returns to the genre, storyline, and character while also moving the Cosplayer forward and establishes her identity. Spawning from similar sources are costumes that become fashion and fashion that resembles costumes.

Cosplay genres

The primary Cosplay fandom's genres are the broad categories without clear boundaries from which Cosplayers select characters. The genres commonly portrayed by Cosplayers are science fiction, anime and manga, comic book's and graphic novel's heroes/heroines and Villains/Villainesses, mechs/robots, and horror creatures. While less common, depending on convention and time period are the controversial genres such as Furry and World War II Nazi. In the last two decades, Steampunk characters are common sights at fan conventions, and are commonly fan-created characters.

Cosplay primarily draws on two large genres: science fiction and fantasy, with subgenres and closely related genres including superheroes/superheroines, Steampunk, and anime/manga. The most popular ways Cosplayers consume these genres are by watching movies and cartoons; reading manga, graphic novels, and comic books; and playing videogames. From this fairly passive consumption, Cosplayers extract details about their chosen characters, whom they shape into their vision. Costumes, including wigs, makeup, and props, are crucial to visually communicating the essence of the character to audience members.

Science fiction

It should be acknowledged that the genre of science fiction, or "sci-fi" for short, is one of the earliest examples of fantastic storylines, which inspired fans to dress like and roleplay their favorite characters. Science-fiction characters provide Cosplayers with opportunities to become out-of-this-world beings with abilities and disabilities beyond those of normal human existence. Moreover, these characters exist as malleable organisms, who are embedded in fertile storylines ideal for roleplay because they mirror reality while at the same time offering extraordinary fantasy and escapism.

Cosplayers are also drawn to the science-fiction genre because it offers multifaceted characters within complex storylines, such as Darth Vader from *Star Wars*, the Borg from *Star Trek*, and even the Tardis or Daleks from *Dr. Who*. In a similar manner to the ways the television series *Star Trek* from the 1960s and the *Star Wars* movies from the 1970s introduced the public to the genre of science fiction, the science-fiction genre has created lifelong fans. In the following years, writers expanded the genre within comic books and attracted diverse audiences. As the public is exposed to these fantastic characters, fans seek out ways to gain a richer understanding of the characters, such as purchasing merchandise, reading comic books and graphic novels, playing videogames, writing fanfic, and cosplaying their favorite characters.

Cosplaying science-fiction characters usually presents physical challenges that Cosplayers need to resolve with creativity and innovative technologies. Non-humanoid aliens, for example, usually need prosthetics, makeup, and/or props to create their otherworldly appearances. Consider an Andorian from *Star Trek* who needs blue skin makeup and antenna, while the Xenomorph, also known as the Alien, is significantly more difficult to cosplay with its enormous, elongated helmet-like head, articulated whip-like tail, and long spindly limbs. Some Cosplayers welcome the challenge of creating these types of costumes because their overall success is often determined by the spectacle of the costume more than the performance.

These types of characters have additional practical appeal as well. Since science-fiction characters may exist outside the bounds of binary gender, such as the Founders from *Star Trek: Deep Space Nine* and Vorc from *Farscape*, it is possible for these characters to be universally portrayed by any Cosplayers. The Tardis or a Dalek, for example, are not dependent on gender, race, ethnicity, or body type because of the rigidity and uniform robotic structure of the costume. Cosplayers design and build costumes to accommodate the human form underneath, while also outwardly portraying the fictional character.

The science-fiction genre endures as a popular category for Cosplayers to select characters. In fact, this genre may be the largest and most popular among fans because it regularly encompasses other genres, such as superhero/superheroine and supervillain/supervillainess and anime/manga. The continued popularity of movie franchises, such as *Star Wars* and *Star Trek*, inspire and fuel fans' interests with diverse and captivating characters and storylines. Cosplayers bring these characters to life at conventions and other Cosplay events for fans to interact.

Superhero/superheroine and supervillain/supervillainess

The archetypes of Hero/Heroine and Villain/Villainess have numerous things in common, not completely surprising with comparable tragic backstories that commonly include a binary decision to be "good" or "bad." Still, these characters are appealing to Cosplayers because they also offer complexities and three-dimensional traits, and are frequently written and illustrated as more dualistic than simply binary.

Drawing on Jungian archetypes, it is possible to understand how the "Hero" has the potential to be good or bad depending on interacting factors and the "Shadow" archetype (Jung 1992). Their similarities in dress are undeniable. Some superheroes/superheroines are even mistaken for Villains/Villainesses, such as Batman or the Lone Ranger whose masks visually communicate their possible criminal status. In these characters' storylines it is common to find individuals commenting about how these "heroes" are in fact "criminals" because their masks visually suggest they have something to hide.

While there are numerous male heroes and villains in Western comic books and graphic novels for Cosplayers from which to choose, finding female heroines and villainesses is significantly more challenging. In fact, even finding female comic book or graphic novel characters who are not in need of rescue and offer strong characteristics are limited. Cosplaying heroines, villainesses, and many other female-representing characters leads to spirited and lively discussions among

Cosplayers regarding the limited number of strong leading female characters to portray. Moreover, they lament about the lack of female characters who are not presented as sex objects in the source media. Sexy heroines and villainesses tend to reflect extreme traits drawn from Western ideals of female beauty and hegemonic tropes, which consequently limits who is able to accurately portray these characters wearing extremely revealing and/or body-contouring costumes in the Cosplay fandom.

Frequently, these heroes (and many villains) are most recognizable by their strong silhouettes (commonly based on upside-down triangle—across the broad shoulders down to the pelvis and back up to shoulder). Villains who do not resemble heroes tend to be tall, lean, and angular in their physical appearance, and dress in dark and ominous hues. Even with body supplements, these types of physiques limit those who are able to cosplay heroes or villains convincingly. Other anime, comic book, and graphic novel heroes and villains, however, are the most popular characters for Cosplayers at fan conventions.

Due to the fantastic elements of the Superhero/Superheroine or Supervillain/Supervillainess archetypes, their appearance results in failure because it is an "impossible object" (or illusion) that cannot be achieved in the real world (Chabon: 2008: 17; see also Brownie and Graydon 2016). Steven Gapps further notes how some Cosplayers live lifestyles that allow them to more accurately represent the physical appearance of the character(s) they portray (2009: 98) without truly being the character. While some pursue strict nutrition and exercise regimes to achieve a fantasy body, others wanting to roleplay similar characters adjust the costume to fit their natural body and add padding or paint the costume to visually suggest muscle definition. Still, other Cosplayers wear the costume and roleplay the character regardless of the differing and respective body shapes or sizes.

At the same time, heroines and villainesses tend to be hypersexualized, nearly without exception. While these female characters do not necessarily have overaccentuated muscles and triangular frames (similar to male heroic characters), they frequently have oversized busts, extremely narrow waists, and curvy hips. Achieving these types of extreme physical attributes are challenging feats for most Cosplayers, as they would be for most people.

Comic book and graphic novel heroines frequently include Wonder Woman, Barb Wire, Storm (see Plate 4.1), and Batgirl; villainesses commonly include Catwoman, Mystique, Poison Ivy, and Circe. Most heroines' and villainesses' physiques reflect the natural human body, which is noteworthy in the areas of the body recognizable as Western erogenous zones that are enhanced to create hypersexualized beings. Since many of these female characters are illustrated with hypersexualized physical attributes, Cosplayers often feel compelled to enhance areas of their body (breasts and hips) and/or decrease other areas of their body (waist). Many of these enhancements are usually temporary, but some Cosplayers pursue permanent breast/pectoral, buttock, calf, and bicep enhancements.

Fans are commonly stereotyped as being out-of-shape, preferring to sit and watch instead of being physically engaged: however, this does not accurately reflect the range of body types and activity levels of Cosplayers. Many Cosplayers will diet, exercise, or even use extreme methods attempting to achieve a physique similar to their chosen character. Frequently Cosplayers comment to friends online and in person about achieving a specific weight or size so their new costumes will fit for another competition, or a new character's body type is achievable for an upcoming fan convention.

Zarya from the *Overwatch* videogame or She-Hulk from Marvel Comics are sometimes considered too masculine for female Cosplayers because of their pronounced muscular structures; these female characters are also difficult to roleplay for the same reasons. While some males crossplay these characters because their natural physiques lend themselves to play physically well-developed muscular characters, females take on the challenge because it is empowering to roleplay such a physically strong character. The characters with notable muscular bodies may be ideal choices for Cosplayers who bodybuild to maintain a muscular form, but individual character selections may also conflict with body type.

Instead, female Cosplayers may choose to portray male characters with well-defined muscular form or to conceal the female body under padded costumes. The females who crossplay male characters to reverse the associated visual messages and sexualize males in the same way female characters are portrayed in media. This, of course, also eroticizes the Cosplayer wearing the costume, which is then under scrutiny from inside and outside the fandom.

The Hero/Heroine or Villain/Villainess characters with body types that do not resemble the human form or have physical dimensions beyond (or less than) the human body typically have a basic frame from which to attach additional arms or legs or even a second head. Consider the superhero Hawkman with his feathered wings or the villain Dr. Octopus, also known as Otto Octavius, with his mechanical tentacles. Comic book and graphic novel Heroes/Heroines and Villains/Villainesses who utilize the human body as framework offer Cosplayers a frame from which to be Captain America or Scarecrow, but it is a greater challenge to portray Carnage, and even more difficult to cosplay Nightcrawler or Clayface, who have many non-human features. These are more challenging characters for Cosplayers to portray, such as the heroine Susan Storm from the *Fantastic Four* comic books while she activates her superpower of invisibility, and the villainess Callisto from the *X-Men* comic books, with her multitude of tentacles where her arms would be. While prosthetics assist in achieving otherworldly forms and adds extra limbs, Cosplayers struggle with the physical demands of the added weight and discomfort associated with additional elements. At Comic-Con in New York in 2015, there was a movie-realistic Ironman dressed in Hulkbuster armor, which was an enormous shell standing 9.5 feet tall and weighing ninety-five pounds, which totally encased its Cosplayer, Thomas DePetrillo.

Many of the classic comic books and graphic novels from Western culture feature heroes and heroines in primary colors (red and blue) with accents of metal (e.g., yellow or gold). The traditional Superman wears the hues of red and blue color-blocked with accents of gold. These colors visually communicate strength and power. Consequently, today's superheroes still make use of heroic primary colors for their costumes/dress, while supervillains commonly wear a black hue to visually communicate their sinister and evil traits within the storyline. Superheroes/superheroines and supervillainesses have more range in the hues of their uniforms based on established characters.

Captain America and Wonder Woman wear red, white, and blue—patriotic colors—and symbols of stars and stripes representing the United States. As superheroes emerge who have connections to other countries or cultures, their costumes may reflect their origins. *Burka Avenger* is a Pakistani comic book, for example, created by Haroon. Reflecting the issues associated with extremists closing girls' schools in Pakistan, the *Burka Avenger* features Jiya, a schoolteacher by day and the Burka Avenger heroine by night. Jiya, a Muslim woman, does not wear her burka while teaching; instead, she wears it as the Burka Avenger when she fights for education for girls. This type of female character is rare because she is non-Western and does not wear a costume that reveals her body's shape. Jiya is diminutive, intelligent, and has a deep connection to her community; she shares more commonalities to Japanese heroines, such as Princess Mononoke, Kiki, and Sen (Chihiro Ogino) from Hayao Miyazake and Studio Ghibli, rather than her Western counterparts from Marvel Comics, DC, and Dark Horse Comics.

Even within the fantastic uniform of the superhero, aspects of the individual Cosplayer's personality are incorporated, assuring that each Cosplay costume is unique. This is equally true for superhero teams who wear specific assigned uniforms, as individual members modify their dress to reflect the self usually in a minute or subtle way. In a similar manner, the Cosplayers interject themselves into the chosen character, which is commonly revealed within their costume details. From monograms to iconic articles, Cosplayers incorporate symbols of their identity into their costumes that are read as nonverbal and semiotic communications.

While crossplayers portray characters of the opposite gender that commonly typify respective gendered traits, some male Cosplayers may crossplay muscular female characters and vice versa. In this case, these Cosplayers may also be able to capitalize on their own muscular physiques instead of relying on padding or prosthetics to portray physically fit or hypermasculine body. These examples, however, are more rare than those crossplay examples that typify gender stereotypes.

Cosplayers over thirty years of age are limited in source characters of similar age and body types from which to choose. A few exceptions include characters such as villainess Granny Goodness (from Jack Kirby's *New Gods*) who is an older female character with wavy gray hair, and hero Professor Xavier (from *X-Men*) who is not only elderly but relies on a wheelchair for mobility. Older Cosplayers, however, may adapt characters of differing ages, often with a sense of humor, to their differing aged bodies (see Plate 4.2). For example, an older Cosplayer exaggerates her portrayal of an elderly Wonder Woman with sagging breasts, long gray hair, and adds a cane as a prop.

Some Cosplayers confront the stereotypes associated with many comic book and graphic novel heroines and villainesses by not allowing the limitations of the illustrated body types to define the characters they select to roleplay. Not only do Cosplayers re-conceive these characters but they also create original female characters, who offer more empowered roles with masculine physical traits and costume elements. Or, they demarcate an established character in a new way that speaks to current social positions of females. Still other Cosplayers use humorous skits in competitions and social circles to address the narrowly defined roles for female characters.

Sidekicks

It is not always superheroes/superheroines or supervillains/supervillainesses chosen for Cosplay characters; sidekicks (and secondary characters) often provide Cosplayers with rich character attributes. Sidekicks are not always well defined in the storyline of the source media, thus offering more latitude in roleplaying and Cosplaying. For the adventurous Cosplayer, the sidekick offers unexplored territory for roleplay and character development.

The sidekick's position next to the Hero/Heroine or Villains/Villainesses is well suited for two friends who want to Cosplay together. Cosplayers who want to Cosplay in pairs may choose companion characters, such as siblings (e.g., Wonder Twins from the *Justice League*), romantic interest (e.g., Sailor Moon and Tuxedo Mask from *Sailor Moon*), and hero/heroine and Villain/Villainess (e.g., Batman and Poison Ivy). Similarly, a group of friends who want to cosplay together may select characters from a team to roleplay, even if not everyone is personally drawn to her specific character (see Lamerich 2014). Characters may be assigned to individual team members according to costume elements or physical characteristics, such as hair color or length because hair is difficult to match without the appropriate wig or hairpiece.

Most Western female heroines and villainesses, such as Wonder Woman or Poison Ivy, do not typically have sidekicks per se, but instead some of these heroic

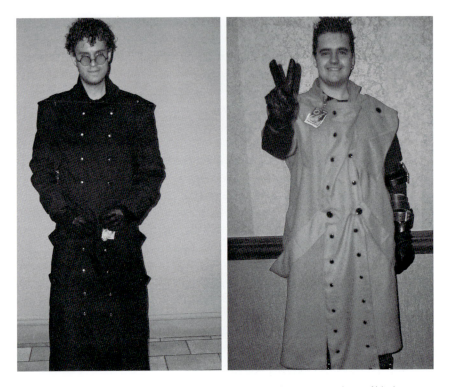

Figure 4.3 Two Cosplayers portray similar but distinct character versions of Vash as Dark Vash and Vash the Stampede from *Trigun*. Photo: Therèsa M. Winge.

women may have henchmen or act as part of a team, such as Storm as part of the X-Men team or Dr. Girlfriend and her Murderous Moppets (Tim-Tom and Kevin) from *The Venture Brothers* cartoon. This gives Cosplayers options of portraying an individual character and/or being part of a larger group/team of Cosplayers.

Sidekicks (and henchmen/women) must be distinct in their dress to be recognizable without their linked superhero/supervillain. At the 2016 Gen Con, the villain Monarch from *The Venture Brothers* cartoon was nowhere in sight, but twelve of his henchmen (members of the Fluttering Horde or Minions of the Mighty Monarch) flanked the hallway (Winge 2016). Their costumes were similar with yellow and black colors with crisp wings on their backs, but distinct in that each costume revealed its handmade uniqueness. Conversely, the sidekick can function as further recognition for identifying the superhero/superheroine or Villain/Villainess cosplayed, where friends who roleplay the hero and sidekick together assure that the fans will engage the Cosplayer team as recognizable and cohesive characters.

Sidekicks also inhabit storylines that evolve with the character presenting the Cosplayer with opportunities to roleplay mash-up or multiple versions of the same character. Within (and associated with) the Batman franchise, for example, Robin is Batman's ward and sidekick in fighting crime in Gotham City. While most sidekicks do not have storylines beyond the hero/heroine, Robin, however, eventually leaves Batman and transforms himself from a sidekick into a superhero (Nightwing and later Red Robin) (see Figure 4.3).

Similar to Robin, some sidekicks are eventually as famous as the main character they accompany. Consider Doctor Watson, who has in his own right to fame but is still the sidekick to Sherlock Holmes from Sir Arthur Conan Doyle's detective literary series. Moreover, with the success of the *Sherlock Holmes* movies (2009; 2011) and television series *Sherlock* (2010–present) and *Elementary* (2012–present), Doctor Watson is a well-known sidekick who adventures and investigates without his more-widely known teammate.

While sidekicks are not the most popular characters among Cosplayers, these lesser-known characters are needed and provide opportunities for Cosplayers to practice and expand their roleplaying skills. Roleplaying sidekicks offer Cosplayers a low-risk opportunity to imprint and integrate their own personality and identity with a recognizable character but who is less developed as primary character or more likely to be two-dimensional in the source media.

Anime and manga

Anime and manga offer dynamic characters with vibrant hues and exquisite details, rich with personality flaws and potentials, and embedded in highly imaginative storylines. The complexities of anime and manga characters are appealing to Cosplayers because they often defy genres or typical character tropes commonly employed in Western culture's comics or cartoons. Anime and manga characters are challenging to Cosplay because of their fantastic qualities, such as dynamic hairstyles that defy gravity, clothing constructed of saturated hues, magical accessories, and exaggerated physiques.

Early in Cosplay history, science-fiction characters were overwhelmingly popular and commonly seen at conventions. Since the 1990s, however, Japanese anime and manga characters are some of the most popular Cosplay characters regardless of the convention. Lunning suggests that *shojo* manga and anime (comics and cartoons made for girl and young women audiences) with its "alluring" illustrations of large-eyed girls and empowering storylines attracted females to want to cosplay anime/manga characters (2011: 72–77).

While this proposition accounts for some of the popularity for certain character types within the fandom, it ignores manga's and anime's contributions of storylines and genres beyond shojo and even characters that clearly contrast with the schoolgirl archetype, such as mechs and animal characters. I further argue that anime and manga's greatest contribution to fan culture is three-dimensional, well-developed female characters who are powerful yet vulnerable, embedded in seductively illustrated stories grounded in real life that inspire and torture the reader/viewer. These storylines resonate with fans worldwide, who identify with the characters; of course, Cosplayers are attracted to roleplay these types of characters. In addition, the ways these stories are illustrated with captivating figures positioned in epic backgrounds while often animated in gorgeous hues cannot be underestimated in Western audiences' and Cosplayers' attraction to the media.

A strong competitor for inspirational characters from the manga and anime characters is when a new Hollywood movie or series is released, such as *America: The First Avenger* (2011); *Star Wars: The Force Awakens* (2015); and *Deadpool* (2016), where Captain America, Kylo Ren and Rey, and Deadpool, respectively, became popular characters among some Cosplayers directly after the movie's release. The only anime films that compete with these types of Hollywood blockbusters come from Hayao Miyazaki and Studio Ghibli. Characters from *My Neighbor Totoro* (1988), *Princess Mononoke* (1997), *Spirited Away* (2001), and *Howl's Moving Castle* (2004) are iconic and routinely cosplayed at fan conventions. While characters from blockbuster movies and popular TV series are popular Cosplay characters in the years directly following their release, most are seen less and less at conventions over time.

There are some well-known anime/manga characters, such as Naruto (see Figure 4.4) and Sailor Moon, who are commonly seen at most conventions. Despite numerous Naruto characters attending the same fan conventions at one time, Cosplayers continue to don these popular characters because they enjoy the camaraderie of recognizing like-minded fans who also appreciate the same character. There were, however, several Cosplayers who expressed a dislike for other Cosplayers dressed similar to their chosen character. Cosplayers even made negative comments if the other Cosplayers were not dressed the same at that moment, suggesting rivalries existing between Cosplayers beyond organized competitions based almost entirely on appearances.

When fans recognize the character based on its appearance (i.e., costume, styling, makeup, etc.), this recognition permits the Cosplayer to take liberties with performance. Especially with characters who have iconic appearances, the Cosplayer may take greater risks within the performances and perhaps the costumes by interjecting their own personalities into the characters. Character traits may be exaggerated for humor, or flaws may be exploited for the sake of the performance.

Cosplayers also enjoy challenging themselves to discover lesser-known or the newest anime and manga in order to be the first or only person to cosplay a specific character. While fans may not readily recognize this new character, if the costume and overall appearance are intriguing and/or dynamic, there is the potential for the audience to engage the Cosplayer for more information about

Figure 4.4 Naruto Uzumaki, from the *Naruto* series, is a common anime/manga character seen at fan conventions. The Cosplayer is demonstrating one of Naruto's signature poses. Photo: Therèsa M. Winge.

the unknown or secondary character. Moreover, the Cosplayer has the potential to "own" the character and establish its interpretation within the fandom.

Kawaii is a Japanese concept that describes products, animals, and people as cute but with endearing vulnerabilities, which is a common trait for many anime and manga characters. The popularity of anime and manga has led to many fans around the world to embrace kawaii, and seek to interject that brand of cute into everything. Official fan merchandise is also designed with kawaii styles in the shape of *chibi* versions (i.e., head and eyes larger in proportion to much shorter and slighter body) of superheroes, aliens, and robot figures.

The kawaii-ification of characters extends to fans' interpretations of characters. Not surprisingly, Cosplayers are attracted to the kawaii aspects of anime and manga characters. Subsequently, they reimagine their Cosplay characters, who may have no connection to anime/manga, as big-eyed, cute character with dynamic hue-saturated hair, exaggerated limbs, and fragile features. In this way, anime and manga impact the Cosplay subculture beyond the ways the genre manifests itself within the fandom as specific characters.

As previously suggested, the genre of anime/manga is intricately intertwined with the contemporary Cosplay fandom. Currently, anime/manga and Cosplay have a mutually beneficial relationship that interplays and interacts off each other's popularity with symbiotic results. The relationship between Cosplay and anime/manga is so paramount that individuals outside of the fandom commonly assume that all Cosplay is inspired by anime/manga, or Cosplay is an activity primarily practiced in Japan.

Punk genre

The Punk subculture's ideology and aesthetics are co-opted within science-fiction and fantasy storylines to construct provocative characters in dystopian environments. Accordingly, the Punk genre in these contexts commonly explores a futuristic reality that shares similarities with contemporary society, where characters experience extraordinary plight and challenges within dystopian storylines. Many subgenres of Punk are combined with science fiction, including (but are not limited to) biopunk, cyberpunk, dieselpunk, splatterpunk, steampunk, and stitchpunk.

The Punk genre and its subgenres are captivating to Cosplayers that they not only assume characters from various forms of media, but they frequently create original characters within the subgenre. Some may even assume related lifestyles beyond those exhibited during the fan convention. Still, the scenarios surrounding these original characters often reflect the environments established in Punk subcultures.

Steampunk genre and fandom

In a 1987 letter to *Locus* magazine, K. W. Jeter, an author of cyberpunk novels, references the term "Steampunk" for the first time in a way that connected the science-fiction genre to a new subgenre that is based on steam technology and other Victorian era originating elements (Jeter 1987). While H. G. Wells's and especially Jules Verne's literary works inspire the steampunk genre, William Gibson and Bruce Sterling's book *The Difference Engine* (1990) popularized Steampunk as a literary form for mainstream culture, contributing to the development of the Steampunk subculture. Accordingly, the Steampunk genre is situated in a fictional, alternate reality where the world is reenvisioned as embracing the steam engine (instead of petroleum engines) and nineteenth-century American West and British Victorian era styles and tropes, often referred to as the "neo-Victorian era."

Matthew Sweet claims that, in *Inventing the Victorians* (2001), North American writers envisioned and wrote about the Victorian era culture commonly used as a framework for the Steampunk genre. The associated literary characters are three-dimensional, rich with flaws and talents that lend themselves to complex storylines. Over the last few decades, the Steampunk genre has expanded beyond literature to anime (*Steamboy* and *Steam Detectives*), films (*Wild Wild West* and *The League of Extraordinary Gentlemen*), and television series (*The Adventures of Brisco County Jr.*, *Copper*, and *Ripper Street*).

Steampunk, however, is limited when exploring female characters, but as authors challenge hegemonic notions of women in a neo-Victorian setting it expands the genre. Sarah Water, for example, challenges the genre by considering class conflicts, feminism, and sexuality in her books *Tipping the Velvet* (1998), *Affinity* (1999), and *Finger Smith* (2002). In addition, Steampunk films and television series are further expanding the roles for women characters, such as Rebecca Fogg who was a fashionable Steampunk heroine in the TV series *The Secret Adventures of Jules Verne* (2000) with more action scenes than her male counterparts. Fogg's Victorian-style skirts, corsets, and even undergarments frequently transformed to assist her in scaling a wall, skydiving from a dirigible, or sword fighting with villains.

Steampunk Cosplayers portray literary, anime, film, and television series' characters while they also invent original and mash-up characters that follow the tropes and trappings of the genre. The Steampunk genre is popular among Cosplayers because established media and fanfic do not only inspire intriguing characters but they also can create original ones. Subsequently, the genre inspires numerous original characters who are closely associated with the portraying Cosplayer.

The popularity of Steampunk and Cosplayer's interest in designing Steampunk characters created a demand for more information about the fandom subculture, especially its dress. Cosplayer, designer, costumer, and Steampunk enthusiast, Samantha Crossland wrote and illustrated *Steampunk & Cosplay Fashion Design & Illustration* (2015), which is primarily an illustration text that also makes strong connections between Cosplay and Steampunk. The text explores the Steampunk subgenre as it is frequently utilized by Cosplayers, as well as commonly used as materials and silhouettes. Samantha Crossland's illustrated text and others like it function as resources to develop drawing/sketching skills in addition to literature that Cosplayers use for illustrating and designing costumes.

Cosplayers create "neo-Victorian" versions of characters, who are infused with Steampunk genre elements. Steampunk costumes tend to include distressed brown, rust, tan, and black fabrics fashioned into nineteenth-century silhouettes with modern features, accessorized with leather satchels, cog and gear details, brass metal buckles and leather straps, decorative leather or fabric top hats, metal and leather helmets, ornate walking sticks, and goggles (see Plate 4.5). These costumes are expensive and time consuming to create. Female characters' dress tends to restrict movements for Cosplayers, which may be why some females adopt male dress but do not crossplay as male characters.

Fans of Steampunk enjoy extending the lives of their Cosplay characters outside the convention and even incorporate elements of the subgenre into their lifestyles. Subsequently, the Steampunk genre has developed into the steampunk subculture: this subculture has implications and expectations for its members beyond those of Cosplayers. Unlike many genres, steampunk fans create significant spaces for the groups to exist beyond the fan convention. Accordingly, Steampunk fans create and join themed formalized groups, as well as organize Steampunk-themed conventions. The DIODES—Dioscurian Imperial Order of Dreamers, Engineers, and Scientists—is a Steampunk group in Minnesota that is part of a larger fandom group, the Geek Partnership Society. DIODES conducts itself as a social group, who meet for larger events several times a year to explore the worlds of Steampunk with friends, as well as to support collaborative efforts.

Steampunk is one of the most popular of the subgenres of punk and science fiction among Cosplayers. Still, Cyberpunk and Stitchpunk characters are seen at fan conventions. Stitchpunk, for example, has ragdoll-style characters with human traits. Stitchpunk was inspired by the animated movie 9 (2009): Cosplayers dressed as the ragdoll 9 character carrying a light bulb on the end of stick at fan conventions; the costume required the Cosplayer be completely stitched inside the fabric.

Overall, the array of Punk subgenres appeals to Cosplayers because they offer diverse frameworks with common threads in science fiction from which original, three-dimensional characters are developed and roleplayed. Cosplayers portraying Punk-style characters are purported to completely immerse themselves into these characters. It is considered a significant Cosplay achievement to create a character, who is both fun and visually interesting while also reflecting a dystopian storyline.

Furry fandom

Furries, or Fur Kin, exist in their own Furry fandom or Furdom (Furrydom) and subculture, as well as within the Cosplay subculture (albeit their position within the greater fandom community is highly controversial). Its members are known for dressing as fictional characters, who possess a combination of human and animal characteristics. Furries portray anthropomorphic animal-human hybrid characters in faux-fur costumes commonly standing on two legs (instead of four). A Furry persona is referred to as a "fursona." While some Furries identify as Cosplayers, many are reluctant to align with the Cosplay fandom.

The Furry subculture has been the focus of blog posts, magazine articles, television series, and music videos. MTV, for example, featured Furries on one of the episodes for the *Sex2K* series when they aired the documentary *Plushies and Furries* (2001). Then, in 2003, *CSI: Crime Scene Investigation* was inspired by MTV's airing of the documentary and focused an episode on Furries titled "Fur and Loathing." In 2005, the musician Moby released the music video for the song *Beautiful*, which exclusively featured Furries in human situations. Subsequently, Furries are a highly fetishized and satirized subculture in popular media.

The Furry subculture is highly organized and developed online communities, which offer socializing venues, thematic online games, and discussion resources. There is a Wikifur site that features information about the Furry subculture. This fandom, however, is sensationalized within the media and has exotic lore even among convention fandoms. Subsequently, as the Furry fandom is exploited by the media, and convention fandoms scrutinized them skeptically.

In the documentary *Fursonas* (2016), individuals who identify as Furries are interviewed but the film depicts the entire subculture in a sensational manner. The media also exploits the Furdom by suggesting it is a subculture for sexual deviants. While some Furries participate in sexual or intimate activities while wearing their fursuit, the subculture claims it is not the norm anymore than any other fandom.

Similar to Steampunks, Furries extend their characters into their lifestyles resulting in themed groups and conventions. There are several Furry-focused conventions, such as Califur, a Furdom convention started in 2004 and held in California (califur.org); the Midwest Furfest Chicago, started in 2000 (furfest.org); and AnthroCon started in 1997, which claims to be the largest Furry convention in the world (anthrocon.org).

Furries portray commonly original characters not necessarily found in a specific storyline, but may be inspired by fantasy characters and storylines, such as Cheetara from the *Thundercats* cartoon and Pink Panther from the *Pink Panther* cartoons, as well. There are Furry character generators online to assist fans in creating original characters. Furries are sometimes confused with Bronies (fans of the *My Little Pony*; the term blends "bro" and "ponies") and other anthropomorph fandoms that include animal costumes as significant components. While Bronies can be part of the Furry subculture, the converse may not always be possible. The distinctions between the anthropomorphic fandoms are sometimes difficult to determine for outsiders.

Closely related to Furries are *Gijinka* but distinctly different.[1] "Gijinka" is a Japanese term meaning "humanization" or "anthropomorphism of anything non-human," and in regard to Cosplay the term refers to humanizing animal traits from specific characters (Winge 2017). In addition, the resulting Gijinka characters must have qualities of *moe*, which is a concept from Japanese popular culture, and refers to anything that causes the viewer to feel affection and even attraction for an object. To achieve a Gijinka character closely fitting with Furry Cosplay, Cosplayers might transform animal wings into human arms, ears into a helmet with projections on top, and depict large animal eyes to attain qualities of moe. When showing or performing these characters at conventions, Cosplayers may have the stuffed animal character with them to show what moe qualities they are emulating on the stuffed animal to authenticate the cosplaying transformation.

The costume is crucial to the successful transition from human to Furry, as well as character maintenance. Furries often conceal large portions, if not all, of their bodies beneath a fursuit made from faux fur, complete with animal-specific ears and tail, in order to achieve the desired appearances. Some Furries, however, especially newcomers to the subcultures, may choose to wear a minimal costume of tail and ears on a headband. While wearing the Furry costume, the subculture member is supported by fellow subculture members to make sounds and speak similar to the animal being portrayed and mimic the animal's actions, such as swishing the tail or cleaning oneself with tongue and paw. The combination of faux fur, vocal exchanges, and gestures create a scenario rich with potential for fetishisms and exploitation.

Many fans interested in being a Furry start by simply carrying stuffed animals as their first foray into the Furry fandom. Constructing clothing to accompany the fursona is not commonly as complicated as creating a fursuit, and is often unnecessary depending on the character. Clothing and accessories specific to the character may be worn over or in addition to the fursuit. Fursuits are incredibly difficult to make with any level of quality due to materials and construction issues in fitting to/over the human body. The Madefuryou brand fursuits are well known among Furries. In 2016, many Furries wearing the Madefuryou brand were invited to be photographed in a collective group wearing their fursuits, which was later disseminated on social media by the company and Furries.

Videogames

Videogames appropriate from all common fan genres, offering a wide array of characters ranging from adorable monsters to conflicted superheroes to magical children. While storylines are often limited to the confines of the game (i.e., rules, avatars, levels, and environments), Cosplayers may also develop characters from related fanfic or develop an individualized storyline beyond the videogame.

Videogames avatars or characters inspired by anime and manga are extremely popular with Cosplayers. Currently, many videogame avatars are illustrated to resemble anime/manga characters, such as Kitana and Shaman King. *Final Fantasy* videogame characters are popular among Cosplayers, with Cloud Strife being one of the most popular characters, as Cosplayers enjoy creating, carrying, and performing with the Buster Sword (an enormous broadsword [see Plate 3.7]).

As new videogames are introduced, Cosplayers adopt the associated new avatars as characters for roleplay at conventions. Despite the success of recently released movies, books, or videogames, Cosplayers still appreciate the classics. Classic videogame characters seen at conventions include Zelda and Link, Chung Lee from *Street Fighter*, Sonic the Hedgehog, and Mario Brothers. While these characters are not as popular as those from more contemporary videogames, the classic videogame characters are well known by fans of all ages and the nostalgia encourages interactions between Cosplayers and audiences.

Videogame gear and weapons lure Cosplayers because of their extraordinary sizes and dynamic appearances. Cloud Strife's Buster Sword is estimated to be five to six feet long, which is difficult to manage for its size and weight. The Lady character from *Devil May Cry 3* (see Plate 4.6) and Spartan Sniper from *Halo* both wield large weapons, which pose challenges for Cosplayers in terms of construction and management at a convention.

The *Borderlands* videogame is a science-fiction space western, first-person shooter that inspires popular Cosplay characters such as Mad Moxxi, Maya the Siren, and Gaige the Mechromancer. *Borderlands* appeals to numerous Cosplayers because the videogame showcases numerous female characters with diversity in size, anthropomorphic characters, and even children characters. In addition, this videogame offers developed storylines, which Cosplayers can exploit for performances.

With the release of the recent movie *Assassin's Creed* (2016), Ezio Auditore da Firenze, from the *Assassin's Creed* videogame, is seen as a Cosplay character more at fan conventions. This character is a middle-aged man, which is appealing to some Cosplayers who want an "age appropriate" character who also has a dynamic appearance and traits. Still, the character is portrayed by Cosplayers of all ages.

In recent years, the videogame *Minecraft* has inspired characters with pixelated appearances. Steve and Alex (i.e., player avatar skins) are popular characters who are often riding a pig (large stuffed animal) or accompanied by Creepers, Zombie Pigman, or Enderman. Due to the rigid pixelated square shapes that comprise the shapes of the characters, there are numerous video tutorials about how to construct costumes from soda and beer cardboard boxes. As a result, the Cosplayer has stiff movements and smaller range of motion but is highly recognizable as being inspired from *Minecraft*.

Videogames whose target audience is primarily males refer to dressing the avatar in "gear" instead of "dress," "costume," or "clothing" (Brownie 2015: 145). This term is used within the Cosplay fandom selectively. Primarily male roleplaying videogame avatars/characters referred to their costumes as "gear," while very few females referenced portions of their costumes, but usually indicating weapons as "gear." Still, most Cosplayers regardless of gender or gender roleplayed referred to their dress as the "costume."

Popular culture

Characters drawn from the popular culture are also well loved by Cosplayers. Orsini suggests that characters draw from popular culture "are often subject to vigorous personalization" because the characters are so well known (2015: 178). I also suggest that since popular culture is everywhere while still consumed on an individual level through unique perspectives, these characters lend themselves to both ubiquitous recognitions when interpreted through the Cosplay portrayal.

Television series, movies, music videos, and literature are frequently the sources for pop culture "characters," such as Buffy and Angel, Hulk Hogan, King Arthur, or zombies. Cosplayers are also attracted to iconic pop culture celebrities, such as Elvis Presley, "Weird" Al Yankovic, and the Spice Girls. Creative Cosplayers are also inspired to create mash-up characters using pop culture figures because they are so recognizable. Pee Wee (Herman) Munster, for example, is a mash-up of television characters of Pee Wee Herman and Herman Munster, who has the chosen appearance and traits that the Cosplayer customized and styled.

Transmedia storytelling and characters

Many of the characters that Cosplayers are drawn to roleplay tend to exist within transmedia or multiple media platforms. The characters in transmedia storytelling are distinguishable by differing appearances in subsequent versions. Consider the many versions of the well-known characters Harley Quinn and the Joker, originating with DC comics. Harley Quinn's appearance and even some traits vary from comic book to cartoon. This is also true for the Joker, who from the early *Batman* comic books varies slightly from the *Batman* television series but differs greatly in *The Dark Knight* movie as played by Heath Ledger. Both Harley Quinn and Joker wear unique dress and appearances in *Suicide Squad* (2016), particular to this storyline. Moreover, each subsequent mediated iteration of the character contributes to the greater narrative in which they embody. At conventions, Cosplayers dressed as versions of the same character from different storylines take advantage of photographing and cosplaying opportunities.

Accordingly, the Cosplayer designs the character's overall appearance by selecting one of the versions or by combining the preferred traits from any of the incarnations that best suit her needs and desired identity. The resulting Cosplay character represents the Cosplayer's connection to the character. Furthermore, the performance reflects the version(s) selected as well as the Cosplayer's perception. Subsequently, the act of Cosplay further presents and extends the character as a transmedia object.

The Internet allows Cosplayers to experience characters in a wide array of media formats, including game tutorials, podcasts, radio shows, and web comics. These formats inspire Cosplayers characters even if they lack visuals. In those cases, Cosplayers may create their own versions of the characters or rely on fan art or fan videos to inspire characters and costumes. Online radio shows, such as "1918," "Welcome to Night Vale," "Archive 81," and "Space Casey," inspire Cosplayers to create steampunk and science-fiction characters from audio sources.

Tisha Turk offers the concept "horizontal metalepsis" to explain the bridging of the source material and the new text created from fan production (2011: 96), which is useful in understanding the ways that Cosplayers utilize source media for fan production of costumes and performances. Horizontal metalepsis is also closely connected to transmedia in this way, as Cosplayers utilize transmedia storytelling in order to roleplay and portray characters who traverse genres and storylines from fantasy into real life. The story contextualizes the character and defines the character's world. The narrative and character as interpreted by the Cosplayer, while slightly modified, exist across medias extending into the fandom worlds.

Cosplay characters

Cosplayers are inspired to portray the characters from animation, comic books, graphic novels, films, literature, and even videogames. Character selection is commonly based on a Cosplayer's personal identification with a given character, but it also may include other factors such as physical traits or having a "cool" and/or "challenging to reproduce" weapon or prop. Groups of friends who want to Cosplay together select a team of characters to roleplay.

In addition to personal motivations for selections, Cosplay friends and peer frequently influence character selection, especially for the first-time Cosplayers. Fans may be convinced to Cosplay for the first time in order to help their friends who need another team member to Cosplay a specific fictional team.[2] These types of characters often complete a team or group, which clearly benefits their peers but it also gives the new Cosplayer the experience of dressing and performing, all with support and guidance from friends and peers.

The Cosplayer researches her selected character for dialect, poses, gestures, and dress/costume in order to give an accurate portrayal. Closely reviewing, memorizing, and understanding the character's storyline is also crucial.

Cosplayers are always improvising storylines but they typically remain true to the character as it is portrayed within its original source media. In fact, when Cosplayers add information to the established canon of a character, the new information is known as a "headcanon."

While researching the character, the Cosplayer is also acquiring information about the related storyline(s) and genre(s). This building of knowledge that each fan undertakes nurtures the Cosplay fandom by infusing it with new inputs and stimuli. As new people join the Cosplay fandom, the knowledge base increases, which ensures the longevity of the fan subculture. Subsequently, Cosplayers analyze characters carefully in order to design and build costumes and accessories with detailed precision. All aspects of the Cosplay costume are carefully constructed to transform the mundane corporeal body into a fantastic vessel for the Cosplayer to embody.

The allure of comic books, web comics, or graphic novels, for instance, includes the compelling graphics, high-concept plots, and dynamic characters. Comic books, however, simultaneously occupy a place in popular and low culture. Furthering its mass appeal are the storylines that often parallel real life with allegories and similes to reach diverse audiences. In recent years, some writers challenge the stereotypes often associated with comic books by including diverse characters and storylines that reflect the sociopolitical complications of global society.

An additional example of the allure of these visual mediums is how comic books and graphic novels inspire live-action movies, which brings a verisimilitude to the characters. *Kick-Ass* (2010) is a movie about how everyday people become heroes and heroines to defeat the bad guys terrorizing their city. Since most characters in animation, comic books, movies, and videogames are firmly positioned as an archetype, the everyday comic book heroes or heroines both defy and fulfill the Jungian archetypes, such as the Hero (e.g., Superman), Anti-hero (e.g., Batman), Maiden (e.g., Snow White), Trickster (e.g., Joker), and Villain (e.g., Cruella de Vil).

Within the Cosplay fan community, no individual person has exclusive ownership portrayal over a specific character, nor is a Cosplayer regulated by the fandom to portray any single (or multiple) character(s) from a specific genre. Frequently there are more than one Batman, Superman, and Wonder Woman at any individual convention. However, within smaller social groups of Cosplayers there is more communication preventing unintentional duplication.

Within some genres there are well-known rivalries, such as Marvel Comics versus DC, and *Star Trek* versus *Star Wars*, which are often exploited to demonstrate fan pride. These rivalries, however, offer opportunities for entertainment, fun, and photographs for Cosplayers. In Orlando, Florida, at the 2016 MegaCon, Zachare Sylvestre organized and secured photographs of a large gathering of Marvel characters on one side of a staircase and DC characters on the other side, posed as rivals. At the same convention, a Marvel photoshoot for Cosplayers and fans was also organized. The two photoshoots were scheduled so as not to have conflicts for fans participating.

In recent years, Cosplayers have been creating new original characters but still fit within a specific genre or even creating mash-up characters from two or more existing characters and/or genres. The development of these original characters provides Cosplayers with agency and empowerment. These characters, however, are not without their drawbacks, such as a lack of character recognition and difficulty with designing the appearance.

From Japanese anime and manga, Cosplayers often portray magical girls (Napier 2000), such as Sailor Moon or Sakura Kinomoto, who possess magical powers and may have magical objects and animal familiars. Frequently, these magical girls are teenagers, who have burgeoning sexuality similar to their magical powers, and are heroines in training. They are commonly dressed in schoolgirl uniforms or children's clothing. Another type of magical girl is the one who communes with nature and/or is spiritual. In the 1997 anime film produced by Studio Ghibli, *Princess Mononoke*, San is one such character who was raised by wolves and seeks to protect the forest. The 2017 Shuto Con's theme was magical girls, which manifested in the year's advertisements and many Cosplayers dressed as Sailor Moon and Sailor Scouts, Cardcaptor Sakura, and Princess Tutu.

Figure 4.7 This collage of images documents the process of using Worbla to make Ashley's buckles for her shoes. Photo: Therèsa M. Winge.

Finally, mechs from anime/manga are seen at conventions constructed from materials ranging from cardboard and duct tape to Worbla[3] and epoxies (see Figure 4.7). Mech and robotic characters that do not resemble the natural human form are further difficult to Cosplay beyond the demands of the costumes because the Cosplayer's face is often obscured, making it challenging to communicate emotions or even deliver dialogue.

Mash-up characters

Cosplayers produce original characters by combining two or more established characters, such as Elvis Stormtrooper (Elvis Presley and a Stormtrooper from *Star Wars*) and Iron Tin Man (Iron Man from *Iron Man* and the Tin Man from *The Wizard of Oz*). Mash-up characters usually have humor or puns in their name, such as Peewee Herman Munster or Finding Captain Nemo. The most successful mash-up portrayals are inspired by two or more well-known characters with recognizable aspects of their appearances, which encourages fans to guess correctly at the linkages.

Princess Leia, Boba Fett, Darth Vader, and Luke Skywalker are popular characters from the *Star Wars* franchise and are often combined with other characters from disparate genres to create mash-ups, such as Pimp Vader and Elvis Skywalker. Zombies are another popular character type that is easily combined with other characters, such as Zombie and the Beast and Martian Zombie Hunter. Also, Disney princesses are popular characters to mash-up with characters with traits not commonly found in the source materials, such as mash-ups Snow White Boba Fett (seen at 2015 Star Wars Celebration convention) and Zombie Disney Princesses (seen at 2008 Dragon Con).

Numerous online forum threads (discussions) are dedicated to Cosplayers sharing ideas for mash-up characters with suggestions for possible names and costume ideas. There are also Pinterest, Tumblr, and fan art websites dedicated to illustrating imagined and actual Cosplay mash-up characters. Cosplayers enjoy creating mash-up characters with recognizable features that fans can identify, and fans enjoy the puzzle of determining the identities of the individual characters. Cosplayers demonstrate merit within the fandom when they succeed at portraying a balanced character with recognizable traits.

Original characters (OC)

Cosplayers are enthused to create their own original characters (OCs) to roleplay. These characters emerge from a variety of sources, such as mash-ups, fanfic, and their imaginations. An original character needs a story from which the

Cosplayer draws information for roleplay and guideposts establishing parameters and limitations, which then become the character's "world." Subsequently, Cosplayers and their friends create (written or oral) stories for their original characters to exist within, from which Cosplayers may draw on for roleplaying.

Understanding the common genres provide a deeper understanding for Cosplayers' experiences with their selected character and roleplaying. These genres further contribute to and at times limit the diversity of the Cosplay fandom while also reflecting common themes that lead to character selection. Furthermore, character selection and related genres, as well as the identity the Cosplayer wishes to project, are primarily accomplished through dress and appearance.

Dress and appearance

The sartorial interactions with the body create the visual language for the Cosplay character, which projects the fandom into fan convention spaces. In this way, Cosplayers appear to be visually dominating and quickly growing in population at fan conventions, but their presence is also creating both positive and negative feedback from inside and outside the fandom. The Cosplayers' appearance is highly debated, fashioned, and envied; it is essential to the immediate recognition of characters and the nonverbal communication embedded in their dress/costume. When discussing Cosplayers' appearances it is important to acknowledge it is not just the clothing but also anything that contributes to the production of the overall appearance of the Cosplayer, from clothing to makeup to prosthetics to props to weapons. I draw on specific examples from my research to explore the Cosplay dress and appearance.

The body

The Cosplayer's body plays an integral role in achieving an accurate character portrayal, but also has the potential to be an area of contention and conflict. Cosplayers, for example, who are not the same height, weight, race, species, and/or gender as their selected character may go to extreme lengths to achieve accuracy in portrayal. These discrepancies between reality and fantasy have led to face-to-face and online debates usually focused on three primary topics: weight, race, and gender.

Baudrillard celebrates the human body as the "finest consumer object," arguing that consumers are active participants within a social system where consumption is supported (1998: 129). The Cosplayer's body is hyperstylized when designed to be a fantastic or otherworldly character for performance. Transforming the human body into a fantastic body is an immense undertaking, which requires Cosplayers' surrendering to the process of transformation. The Cosplayer's body is concealed, revealed, constricted, restricted, expanded, and/ or enhanced in the process of becoming a fantastic character.

The act of dressing is an example of Bourdieu's *habitus*: "patterns of behavior enacted through and upon the body" (2014: 18). In this way, Cosplayers develop ritualize dressing practices in order to transform into their chosen characters. When Cosplayers produce online tutorials, these rituals are performed in front of a camera in order to visually communicate to other Cosplayers how to repeat the process/transformation.

Commonly, superheroes and supervillains exist in fantastic realms with superpowers and enhanced abilities with their bodies frequently resembling the human form. The comic book and graphic novel hero, for example, commonly has an athletic body clad in a body-clinging spandex uniform or costume suggesting the extraordinary superhuman strength and abilities within. Subsequently, Cosplayers who choose these types of characters often utilize prosthetic body suits that enhance the physical form under a spandex costume that holds body supplements in place.

Consider superheroes such as Batman or Superman, who for most Cosplayers would require muscle pads or a padded Lycra suit to create their "ripped" abdominal, bulging biceps, and slab-like pectoral muscles. Brownie and Graydon suggest padding the (superhero) costume to compensate for lacking body creates fuzzy and unclear boundaries between costume and body (2016: 115). Cosplayers seem to enjoy the blurring of boundaries between self and character identities and dress.

The role of the costume, including clothing, makeup, prosthetics, wig or hairstyle, and accessories and props, is paramount in successfully cosplaying a character. Originally, Cosplayers constructed, sewed, or manufactured their own costumes. In recent years, there are numerous resources online and even brick-and-mortar stores. Many Cosplayers, however, create most portions of their costumes in order to maintain control over the final details, as well as to enjoy the creative process.

Cosplayers reported how the most difficult characters to research and portray are those written about in a single work of literature. Without visual references, the Cosplayer relies completely on the written descriptions that exist of the character and appearance, as well as on any fan art that exists. Characters drawn from written text pose unique challenges because the reader determines the exact details of the costume and appearance of the character overall. Costumes created for characters from videogames, movies, or cartoons/anime already possess visual references but pose their own challenges. A common issue for Cosplayers is how to successfully recreate a character drawn in two-dimensional space, such as in a comic book, into three-dimensional space, as costume, makeup, and other styling details.

The costume

Cosplayers are critical of their peers who purchase their entire costume instead of constructing it from raw materials. The exception is the purchasing of items that are essential to the character's appearance but either requires advanced skills to create, such as weapons or high-quality items (e.g., contact lens and wigs). Purchased or constructed, the Cosplayer's costume is a significant expense of time and money. Cosplayers participate in active consumption instead of passive; that is, they (as fans) consume products from their favorite genres and even incorporate some artifacts into their Cosplay costume.

Cosplayers' intricately constructed costumes, precisely applied makeup, and carefully practiced moves are displays of their conspicuous consumption of character, storyline, and genre. The presentation of the Cosplayer's detailed appearance and costume, accompanied with exaggerated movements and poses in the main hallways of the convention, is similar to Veblen's account of women displaying their father's and/or husband's wealth while walking the boulevard (1899). The more details expressed in a Cosplayer's portrayal indicate a "richer" consumption of that character.

Some Cosplayers expressed a love for designing and making the costume perfect despite how frustrating and tedious the process. They analyze the character from every angle in various media in order to design a perfect costume and appearance. They enjoy picking out the perfect fabric even if it is difficult to cut and sew. They agonize over the stitching, gluing, and molding of every detail of the costume. Multiple versions of portions of the costume may be constructed to assure it meets the Cosplayers' criteria ranging from accuracy to comfort to performance.

The corset is another article of dress that may be purchased instead of constructed because of the difficulties with making and fitting it with quality. Many Steampunk characters wear corsets because this article of undergarment was common for eighteenth-century women's dress: however, Cosplayers tend to wear these corsets on the outside of their garments, which has become the standard for the Steampunk style for women and men. In addition, the corset is a ubiquitous portion of Steampunk fashion. The popularity of the Steampunk genre, the recent release of *Cinderella* (2015), and cult television series *Penny Dreadful* (2014–16) has contributed to the corsets' comeback with Cosplayers and even within portions of mainstream dress. In 2015, fashion designers Stella McCartney, Riccardo Tisci for Givenchy, and Sarah Burton for McQueen featured contemporary corsets in their collections.

Costume as fashion

Bainbridge and Norris (2009) and Brownie and Graydon (2016) suggest the Cosplay fandom functions within a system similar to the mainstream fashion system including "built-in obsolesce" (2016: 113). These assessments are accurate in that fashion is not possible without the ability to change, and Cosplayers readily embrace novel and innovative interpretations of characters. Unfortunately, the notion of "built-in obsolesce" does not account for individual Cosplayer's attraction to unpopular or out-of-date characters.

Cosplay does not function as fashion as it as commonly understood; instead, this assessment is only accurate in so far as there are trends and new interest in genres and characters often associated with a recently released movie, literature, or television series. Fans, however, are likely to hold on to their favorite character from a film or book, for example, far beyond its popularity in the general public. In essence, what makes fans and fandoms so unique is their devotion for a particular genre and/or character.

Furthermore, Cosplayers secure characters from a wide range of sources that are not always contemporary and may never have been popular. They also choose characters for ironic and satirical reasons, and acknowledge that no character becomes obsolescent. It is unlikely that a fashion system is an apt comparison to the "trends" witnessed in Cosplay. While it is true that some characters enjoy popularity reflecting a recent book or movie, for example, the "popular" characters are highly dependent on the type of convention, geographic location, makeup of the attendees, and even current fan movements.

Brownie and Graydon argue that wearing the vintage Adam West's Batman costume is not favorable or fashionable for Cosplayers (2016: 113), for example. This is not accurate because there are many reasons to Cosplay this 1960's version of Batman, such as nostalgia, appreciation for kitsch, and the Cosplayer physically resembles this specific version. In fact, there is a cache associated with roleplaying a character that establishes a depth of knowledge for a genre or a deep appreciation for the history of the character within the genre or storyline.

Official merchandise is licensed products, such as T-shirts, action figures, and/ or replicas of weapons, which feature images, logos, and symbols supporting the release of films, television series, graphic novels, and the like. As more official merchandise expands into clothing, there are portions of costumes more readily available to Cosplayers and the general public. These types of merchandise function as pseudo-costumes for any fan, which is worn to fan conventions and in everyday life.

In addition, mainstream and fan fashions sold in mass markets inspired by fantasy and science fiction carry encoded visual messages that communicate an understanding of characters, storylines, and genres while challenging norms for dress and/or visually communicating fan status. These types of fashions appeal to a larger audience than official merchandise because it can be interpreted as casual fan status. As fan fashions are disseminated within mainstream markets, there is the potential to grow the fan base for given characters or genres.

Fashion as costume

With the recent popularity of superhero movies and graphic novels, dressing as a fan has become more fashionable. "Geek fashion" or being "fashionably geek" are terms used to describe individuals who dress with a fashionable fan flare. Typically, fans wear official merchandise that highlights their personal fan preference and affection for a superhero/superheroine, cartoon character, or story elements (i.e., landscapes, technology, and alien cultures). While official fan merchandise is frequently seen as a fan T-shirt and easily incorporated into everyday dress, others take greater fashion risks by wearing character belt buckles and hats.

Still, within the subset of fans who wear official merchandise are those who utilize portions of Cosplay costumes within their daily dress or supplement the Cosplay costume with portions of official merchandise. "The Fashionably Geek" website, for example, features Cosplayers dressed as characters to sell merchandise that would appeal to the general fan and Cosplayer. Consider these two types of fan T-shirts: a T-shirt that shows the Batman emblem across the chest and a T-shirt with an illustration of the Batman emblem across muscular chest and abs with his utility belt drawn around the waist. Both T-shirts are fan dress; however, the latter is Cosplay fashion inspired by the actual Batman costume and may be worn as part of a Cosplay costume.

Incorporating portions of the Cosplay costume into everyday dress is a way for Cosplayers to assume their Cosplay character identities while existing in the real world (i.e., outside of fan conventions). Fun Suits are menswear inspired by Marvel and DC comics superheroes and villains that resemble Western menswear business and dress suits (Weberstyle 2016). There are three categories of Fun Suit: secret identity, alter ego, and authentic, which suggest levels of fan commitment (Weberstyle 2016). Additional fan fashions include stuffed animal backpacks, hats with ears, mittens resembling animal paws, and superhero/villain socks with capes, which share linkages with Cosplay costumes and have a market in Cosplay and other fandoms.

Costume as material culture

Material objects are necessary to make the fandom real and tangible to those who participate in fan activities, events, and conventions (Woo 2014: 1.3). An important part of the material culture of many fandoms exists as official merchandise and the ways it is incorporated into the fandom. The material culture of the Cosplay fandom, however, is best understood through the Cosplayers' creative costumes as material artifacts.

The material nature of costumes, in general, is problematic, and Cosplayers are often novices to the construction and maintenance of costumes. The difficulties with costumes are sometime visually evident even within live-action movies or TV series, such as *Star Trek: The Next Generation* (1987–94). In this series, the costume issues included uncomfortable material, which quickly acquired and retained body odors (Birch 2013). And fans will recall Captain Jean Luc Picard adjusting his bodice when rising from a seated position, and how Counselor Dianna Troy's costume changed dramatically from one season to the next. In addition, the challenges of transitioning animation costumes into reality, as seen in the animated costume of Arthur from *The Tick* cartoons (1994–96) to the later live-action Arthur from *The Tick* TV series (2001–02).

Cosplayers experience similar problems with the design and construction of their costumes. Finding the fabric that is correct in hue(s) usually dictates subsequent decisions. Stretchy fabric is usually preferred for form-fitting costumes. Unfortunately, knit and stretch fabrics are among the most difficult to sew, especially for novice sewers. Comfort is often sacrificed in favor of visual and physical qualities that match with the character's description. Even safety is sometime sacrificed. The superhero/superheroine super-suit costume designer Edna Mode, from the animated movie *The Incredibles* (2004), absolutely refuses to create any more capes for superheroes/superheroines because of the inherent dangers in wearing them. This warning is borne out by Cosplayers who trip over or choke themselves when accidentally sitting on their capes at fan conventions.

Costume maintenance and repairs present real challenges that few Cosplayers have the experience or skills to manage. At the 2016 Gen Con convention, an attendee was dressed as an OC cartoonish tailor, carrying a sewer's kit while holding up a large sign reading "Cosplay Costume Repairs." While the tailor's intention was clearly humorous, the reality of maintaining Cosplay costumes is more than satire. Suggestions are shared between Cosplayers such as using one's own spit to remove a pinprick of blood from cloth or how grading and clipping can eliminate bulk around a curved seam. Cosplayers are careful not to smear makeup on the neckline of costume when getting dressed as the character. Still, corner tears in cloth are difficult to repair and sometimes the costume repair is so severe that the Cosplayer chooses to retire the costume (and character) rather than try to mend it.

On online Cosplay forums, entire threads are dedicated to discussions about not wanting to discard or sell character costumes, even the ones no longer worn. Cosplayers discussed closets overflowing with past costumes, and some even scavenge old costumes for new character costumes. The costume represents not only the time and effort invested in its construction but also the emotional and psychological ties for the Cosplayer as well.

Costume as fetish

The Cosplay character's costume or even the suggestion of costume with a prop or accessory functions as "fetish" for the Cosplayer (and others) (Gunnels 2009: 4.2). Drawing on Marx's concept of a fetish as being imbued with a type of magick, the costume transforms the Cosplayer into a fantasy character for themselves and audience. Moreover, the Cosplay costume holds its fetishistic magick even before the Cosplayer dons it.

The mask is not always a disguise for the Cosplayer. This is the flaw in the study by Rosenberg and Letmaendi (2013), where they assumed a mask had to function as a cover or disguise for the face. In fantasy tropes, however, an accessory or minor change in appearance can function as a "mask" for one's real/alternate identity and is an extension of the fantasy. The costume acts as a mask (for the self) but encourages the Cosplayer to be more revealed and empowered.

A basic item of dress from everyday life, such as eyeglasses, holds a complex role when included or excluded from the Cosplay costume. Characters who wear eyeglasses are assessed to be smart or intellectual, and the act of removing glasses suggests a certain sexual allure. Some characters require eyeglasses as part of their costume, and the lack of glasses communicates another side of their character's persona. The minor change of appearance that reveals the superhero is fodder for the Cosplayer's performance. Superman's disguise of eyeglasses and a business suit produces Clark Kent. Humorous skits are performed around the meager mask of dark-rimmed glasses and how nobody can surmise that Clark Kent is actually Superman and vice versa.

In 2003, *Newtype USA* published the article "What Happened to the Glasses?!" which emphasized the importance of eyeglasses for a female character (Newtype 2003). The author is concerned with the integrity of the characters who were once drawn with eyeglasses but were more recently drawn without glasses. The article further asserts that female characters establish traits of intelligence and cleverness visually with the use of eyeglasses. Eyeglasses are a powerful dress item, in that they provide the heroine or villainess with a means of transforming from a meek and mousy character into a superheroine or a sexualized being. Diana Prince, for example, removes her glasses when transforming into her superheroine persona of Wonder Woman.

Making costumes

In the years before Cosplay had a formal name, Cosplayers were forced to rely on their own skills and creativity to produce their costumes because mass-produced costumes, such as those for Halloween, were not suitable to portray fantasy characters for conventions. In fact, many less popular characters were even not available at costume retailers. Subsequently, Cosplayers embraced the DIY culture without realizing that they were at the forefront of a movement. Designing and constructing costumes requires skills not commonplace to many Cosplayers. Sharing skills and mentoring one another is key to the structure of the Cosplay subculture. Cosplayers teach each other sartorial skills, such as drafting patterns, sewing, embroidery, tailoring, and armor construction, in order to create thoughtful fantasy character costumes. They also share ways of styling hair or wigs and makeup in order to help each complete the overall appearance of the character (see Figure 4.8).

This sharing of skills and resources is a common feature of the DIY culture. Cosplayers produce video tutorials to post on YouTube and other social media sites that support videos. For example, Cosplayers have created video tutorials about how to create helmets, armor, and bracers. There are also costume

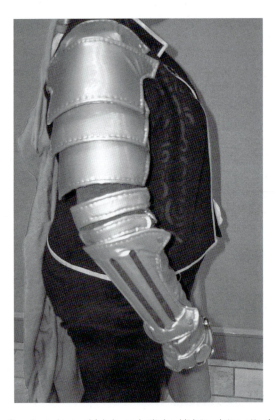

Figure 4.8 The Cosplayer layered fabric and stitched it into plates attached with rivets for arm and chest armor used by the character Edward Elric from *Fullmetal Alchemist*. Photo: Therèsa M. Winge.

designers available for hire prior to and during conventions to create custom Cosplay costumes and make alterations and repairs.

The construction of a costume (or any garment worn on the body) is commonly seen as gendered works of labor (see Stalp 2015): females are traditionally associated with the domestic skills needed to construct (sew) the costume (clothing). And, as Cosplay is female dominant, the fandom is laced with stereotypical feminine acts, such as sewing and embroidery. Brownie and Graydon argue that male Cosplayers may reject these acts because the superheroes they idolize complain about costume construction (2016: 118–20). Despite these assumptions, male Cosplayers are learning and participating in the practices of costume construction.

In addition, when Cosplayers design and construct their costume, it is a form of reenactment similar to the fantasy characters who created their own costume to hide their true identity. Spiderman is seen, in the comic books and movies, creating his own costume and lamenting about the difficulties of sewing (see also Brownie and Graydon 2016: 119). In the movie *Kick-Ass* (2010), when Dave Lizewski needs to conceal his identity while fighting crime, he creates a green jumpsuit (from a wetsuit) with great difficulties. All the materials are purchasable, adding verisimilitude to the storyline of Dave being able to create his own superhero costume.

Acknowledging the work and efforts the Cosplayer dedicates to creating a body and an appearance for a designated character, Lamerich introduces the concept "aesthetic practices" (2011: 5.5), and Brownie and Graydon introduce "aesthetic labor" (2016: 115). These concepts reflect Marxist concepts/theories of labor (2009), where Cosplayers function as producers of aesthetic outcomes consumed by fans.

Cosplayers strive to create costumes that reflect characters with precision while acknowledging the Cosplayer's personality and perspective on the character. The DIY customization of the costume allows for interjection of portions of the Cosplayer's personality into the character. The early necessity of handmade costumes made by individual Cosplayers established the precedent for exceptional details and qualities of customization. Today, store-bought costumes rarely reflect the details of the character's appearance nor incorporate the Cosplayer into the costume. Subsequently, DIY costumes are valued above those purchased or even above official merchandise.

Lamerichs suggests that the very act of constructing one's own costume provides the Cosplayer with a chance to engage in informal competitions with peers (2011: 5). Accordingly, Cosplayers and fans at conventions informally review costumes, which results in complements and critiques to the Cosplayers or secret gossip. Cosplayers recount every effort used to design and construct their costumes in anticipation of admiration and suggestions for more efficient or elaborate methods.

Costume as storytelling

The costume is essential to the Cosplayer's storytelling as it nonverbally communicates information about the character and perhaps even the character's position in the storyline (Eicher 2000).[4] The costume is the first iteration of the story and roleplaying: its presentation suggests many things about the character and her or his current position relative to the storyline prior to posing or performing.

It is rare that an entire costume for a specific character is purchased premade. Subsequently, Cosplayers need to be extremely resourceful. The Cosplayers develop construction skills by watching instructional videos, reading books, and taking classes, as well as by seeking individuals who offer specialized skills and equipment for welding or weapon construction. The truly "crafty" Cosplayers improvise techniques for construction when the needed item does not exist in the "real world." It is considered a point of pride to be self-reliant and resourceful enough to create a costume and persona without purchasing elements or hiring craftpersons. Accordingly, Cosplayers take classes in welding, metalsmithing, and woodworking in order to craft their characters' weapons and props, as well as armor and shields.

Consequently, established businesses now find it very profitable to market materials for Cosplay costumes to Cosplayers. Jo-ann Fabric stores in North America, for example, now sell Cosplay fabrics, notions, and patterns endorsed by well-known Cosplayer Yaya Han with the tagline "Be the Character." Additionally, Yaya Han's and other Cosplay costume patterns are for sale at McCall's, directly marketed for Cosplayers with some licensed characters. Simplicity Patterns features a corset foundation as part of their Effy Sews Cosplay patterns, and joined with LoriAnn Costume Designs to create Doctor Who and DC villain costume patterns. McCall's launched a blog-style website called "Cosplayer" with tutorials that show how to use their patterns to create Cosplay characters, along with interviews, news, and a Cosplay lifestyle blog.

Cosplayers' hairstyles frequently rely on wigs because characters' hair hues and styles are not easily achievable with a real person's hair. For those who don different costumes/characters during one convention, for example, wigs are more practical than modifying the Cosplayers' natural hair three or four times in as many days. Wigs also allow Cosplayers to retain their natural hair color and style so as not to disrupt their lives when not participating in the fandom (see Figure 4.9).

Prosthetics are artificial body parts or skin that cover portions of the natural body to create an otherworldly or fantastic appearance. Nonirritating dermis-bonding agents are used to adhere the prosthetics to the desired area(s) of the body. Prosthetics may be purchased or made from a kit used in theatre or movie productions in order to accurately portray aspects of a character not usually occurring on the Cosplayer's body. Prosthetics include, but are not limited to,

Figure 4.9 The Cosplayer used a wig from another character costume and restyled it for Jiraiya from *Naruto*. Photo: Therèsa M. Winge.

the following: pointed ears (e.g., Tinker Bell, Mr. Spock), tail (e.g., Nightcrawler, Felicia), prominent muscles (e.g., Superman, Captain America), fangs (e.g., Inuyasha, Dracula), contact lenses (e.g., Sabertooth, Yazoo), and horns (e.g., Hellboy, Maleficent). Many Cosplayers require more than one prosthetic to portray a chosen character accurately, such as Nightcrawler from the *X-Men* franchise, who needs fangs, pointed ears, modified hands and feet, and a tail, as well as blue body paint and hair, in order to be recognizable.

Cosmetics, such as eye shadow, foundation, blush, lipstick, and eyeliner, and body paint play important roles in transforming skin color or adding accents to facial or body details. Cosmetics and/or body paint may be used to blend the Cosplayer's skin hue onto the prosthetic for verisimilitude into the overall appearance. Cosplayers prefer to use cosmetics and body paint common to theatre or film productions for its quality, durability, and dramatic effects. Cosplayers hire makeup artists to achieve complex appearances, or teach themselves by practicing with Internet tutorials to apply their own cosmetics and/or body paint.

Accessories complete the Cosplay costume and appearance, as well as being essential to visually communicating the chosen character. Without her jeweled hair ties atop, her pigtails, her jeweled gold tiara, and her Moon Stick (or Cutie Moon Rod), Sailor Moon may be mistaken for a schoolgirl or a magical girl from most anime/manga. Accessories with magical powers, such as the Chibi wand from the *Sailor Moon* anime and Princess Hilda's staff from *The Legend of Zelda* videogame, may actually be constructed to play music, release glitter, or light up to simulate an enchanted appearance. Some accessories are necessary to identify the character. Without his signature black cape with red satin lining, white mask, and black top hat, Tuxedo Mask from *Sailor Moon*, for example, might be mistaken for James Bond or the Black Butler.

Weapons are more complicated to create than most other items of dress for the Cosplayer. The weapons need to visually appear to be constructed from heavy materials but must be lightweight in order for the Cosplayer to easily carry it (and incapable of hurting anyone). Tutorials online to make weapons of an array of materials are foam, plastic, nylon, rubber, latex, and adhesives. Weapons, such as Cloud Strife's Buster Sword from the *Final Fantasy VII* videogame (see Plate 3.7) and Thor's hammer from the *Avengers* movies, are allowed at conventions only if the armaments comply with the convention's safety guidelines/rules.

Conventions developed rules about replica weapons that resemble known weapons and anything that might be dangerous to other attendees. While some conventions ban all weapons, most allow weapons as long as blades and guns are sheathed or holstered so they cannot be used to injure or threaten anyone. Inside most convention spaces, at the time of checking-in, include a process of attaching "peace bonds" (cords or zip ties) to weapons, even replica ones, to ensure that they cannot be drawn or removed from the costume for safety reasons. Consequently, photographs of weapons in action must be taken outside of the convention spaces (see Plate 4.10).

Costumes that transition from one look to another allows the Cosplayer to portray more than one aspect or persona of a character. Cosplayers enjoy the challenge of the costume and traversing the personality and identity changes of the character. Transforming costumes, such as mermaid to girl/princess or unkempt cleaning stepsister to princess, are popular with audience members and best captured on video.

While at conventions, I overheard veteran Cosplayers offer unsolicited but intentionally helpful advice to beginning Cosplayers (sometimes referred to as "newbies") about how to better their costume or their character for a more convincing or humorous portrayal (Winge 2017). The more experienced

Cosplayers suggest places to shop, effective ways to apply makeup, websites for online sewing tutorials, and even craftspersons for hire at the convention. New Cosplayers are usually very receptive to the advice and improve their character's costume for subsequent conventions. This is noteworthy because while Cosplayers are part of the same fandom, many will compete against one another in the masquerade and for attention from convention attendees. Perhaps the successful portrayal of a character benefits the fandom more than individual recognition or success. Still, it should be noted that some Cosplayers do participate for fun and for the "love" of the character and do not seek to achieve perfection in the costume or character nor media attention.

Purchasing Cosplay

Since value is assigned to designing and production of the Cosplay costume, purchased costumes are devalued and discouraged throughout the fandom. Purchasing a ready-made costume for Cosplay purposes is only acceptable or tolerated for children (and the rare, usually also very young newbies). Portion of the costume, however, are acceptable to be purchased and modified with regularity, such as wigs that are cut and styled according to the characters' appearances. Merit is primarily gained with the DIY sensibility within the Cosplay fandom.

There are limited brick-and-mortar stores that carry Cosplay supplies beyond Halloween-style costumes. Subsequently, costumes, wigs, accessories, and even weapons are frequently purchased at online stores, such as Etsy, eBay, and EZCosplay.com. In addition, raw materials are secured at both hardware and surplus stores to build or repurpose for use with the desired costume.

Consequently, official merchandise plays a complicated position within the Cosplay character costume and fandom. The use of merchandise is permissible if it is appropriate to the remainder of the costume (see Figure 4.4: head band is official fan merchandise). That "appropriateness," however, is a moving target determined by how well the official merchandise is incorporated, without dominating the costume. It is difficult to even incorporate some official merchandise that demonstrates fan status into a costume; a superhero T-shirt does not complete the costume even if the Cosplayer is wearing the Lycra leotard with it.

Also, official merchandise must not be anachronistic or out of sync with the overall disposition of the costume. Consider the versions of Batman cowls over the decades, which shapes range from limp cloth masks with pointed ears on top to molded vinyl or plastic, and colors ranged from black to purple to multicolored. The era of the Batman character to be portrayed determines the cowl selected and determines the rest of the costume. The cowl completes Batman's costume, and is often a purchased portion of the Cosplay costume because of its difficulty to construct with high quality. Cosplayers appreciate even a poorly constructed cowl for the efforts used to produce this complex costume detail.

Ritual of dressing in costume

The act of dressing is a ritual, which is heightened when dressing in costume for Cosplay. As the Cosplayer dresses, it highlights the ritual stages of transforming from fan to fantastic character. The Cosplayer's dressing process reflects the three ritual phases: separation, liminality, and incorporation (Turner 1996). I had the opportunity to join a few individual Cosplayers preparing to attend a fan convention and witness the ritual of dressing in character.

In the separation phase, the Cosplayer removes their everyday clothing and mentally separates from the real world preparing to enter the fantasy realm of her character, and eventually the fandom and even the convention spaces. Undressing happens in private until the Cosplayer reaches her foundation garments, where she chooses which garments will remain, if any, before preparing to dress as the character. The everyday clothing is typically placed in a secure location, such as a suitcase or duffle bag, and placed where it is easy to retrieve when convention concludes.

As the Cosplayer begins dressing in the costume, she enters the liminal transition: she is *becoming* the character. Each time she enters into the bathroom to add a new layer or portion of the costume, the Cosplayer as an individual disappears and more of the character is revealed. The liminal phase may last for numerous hours because of the lengthy process of transforming from everyday to fantasy. Some Cosplayers even linger in the liminal phase because it is filled with anticipation and excitement without the anxiety and judgment of an audience (see Figure 4.11).

Once the Cosplayer is dressed in the costume and finalizes the appearance, she incorporates the character into the self with posing and roleplaying. Cosplayers acting and performing as the character solidify the character's persona beyond the costume and appearance. During the incorporation phase, the Cosplayer assumes the fantasy character's identity, submerging the Cosplayer's everyday identity.

The transformation from everyday life to fantasy character is not complete until the hero dons the costume (Brownie and Graydon 2016: 119). Fans dressing in costumes function as a form of "ritual identification" (Bainbridge and Norris 2009: 7), where the Cosplayer is associated with a specific character within a given space, time, and dress. Furthermore, the initial time a Cosplayer dresses as a character serves as a rite of passage (van Gennep 1960), which can be experienced again to a lesser degree with each new character donned by the

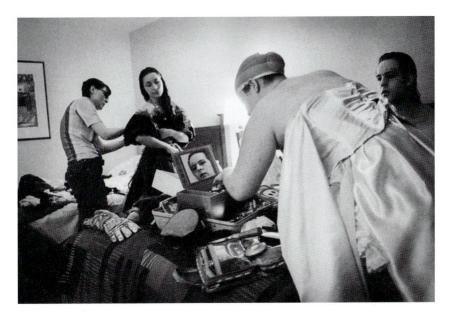

Figure 4.11 Photographer Eron Rauch documented the *Paradise Kiss* Cosplayers in the midst of "con crunch"—finishing their elaborate costumes throughout the night—who ultimately missed the 2002 Anime Central convention Cosplay competition by fifteen minutes. Photo: Eron Rauch.

Cosplayer. The ritual process, however, is experienced each time a Cosplayer dresses in a character's costume.

Fan conventions in costume

Attending a fan convention in costume has both inclusive and exclusive experiences. Some fans, who do not identify as Cosplayers, may demonstrate affection for a character and/or genre by donning portion of a character's dress or official merchandise. This type of character acknowledgment and adoration is understood at fan conventions, even if there are individual disagreements about choices. Robert Rodgers, the proprietor of Limited Edition Comics & Collectables in Cedar Falls, Iowa, purchased an official *Star Wars*' Darth Vader costume, which he wears for promotional, charity, and entertainment purposes (Winge 2017). Rodgers does not identify himself as a Cosplayer, as he states, "I do not consider myself a Cosplayer. I costume; I don't play." Accordingly, Robert primarily wears his costume to various events and only recently began wearing the costume to fan conventions. Cosplayers, however, experience the convention differently than most fans/attendees because of their immersion into the fantasy character.

Cosplayers may encounter difficulties enjoying fan conventions because of continued interruptions for photographs and inquires about costumes and characters. By extension of the Cosplayers, their costumes create an ephemeral connection between the observers and the character. The costumed Cosplayer functions as notification for the observers that a performance is about to happen. At the same time, observers are essential to the Cosplay fandom because they provide recognition of the character and validation for the Cosplayer. While in costume, Cosplayers encounter challenges when trying to experience fan conventions similar to other attendees. They address these challenges in numerous ways, and are assisted by convention rules and designated Cosplay locations for poses and photographs. There is no ideal scenario for Cosplayers, however, to attend fan conventions dressed in costumes and be treated similar to other attendees.

In addition to fan conventions, Cosplayers seek to extend the experience by participating in or hold Cosplaying events. To this end, they dress as their characters for parties, karaoke, and even for Halloween, as well as participate in Cosplay charity events, such as members of the 501st Legion, an international *Star Wars* fan group, who regularly host Cosplay and non-Cosplay charity events while dressed in costume. Furthermore, it is becoming more prevalent for Cosplayers to wear portions of a Cosplay costume and everyday dress together. This type of dress often includes official merchandise because it suggests fan loyalty and not necessarily a Cosplay identity.

Cosplay authenticity

In a media-saturated culture, "authenticity" is ubiquitous; it is applied to absolutely everything and everyone to a point that it lacks meaning. Contemporary Western society struggles with establishing something truly real, as anything not fitting neatly into an established genre or category is judged harshly for its authenticity or lack thereof. This disposition makes it difficult to appreciate anything new or evolving that does not resemble something already known. The subculture's visual culture contributes to its authenticity, where individuals follow unwritten guidelines to create a homogenous group that differentiate themselves from the mainstream (Muggleton 2000: 20–22; Winge 2012: 5; 116).

Cosplay fandom authenticity must be understood beyond its mimetic existence because Cosplayers need to be considered within the fandom's experiences. Authenticity within the Cosplay fandom navigates fan identity and the Cosplayer's identity, with reality continuously encroaching on fantasy bubble. Cosplayers negotiate these anachronistic or incongruous trials, such as the need for a cell phone and an inhaler, with creativity and innovation.

Brownie and Graydon suggest that fan "authenticity" can be purchased in the form of official merchandise when dressing in costume (2016: 114); however, my research suggests that official merchandise has a limited role within the Cosplay fandom. Cosplayers attempt to create accurate character representations with original design and construction instead of purchasing premade costumes or official merchandise. This creative original fan production (Cherry 2016: 24; Hills 2014: 2.17) asserts the authentic character of the fandom.

Further asserting the fandom's authenticity, Cosplayers costume themselves to roleplay fantastic characters and by extension create fantasy realms that envelope more than just Cosplayers. Still, there are moments that pierce the fantasy bubble, where reality bleeds through, continuously altering the fantasy and forcing the Cosplayer to adapt rapidly to meet the demands of her peers and audience. Improvisation is necessary because reality is continuously breaking into the bubble created by the Cosplayer at the convention. While mimetic, the Cosplay fandom and Cosplayers demonstrate authenticity in their genuine love of their characters and subsequent portrayals.

Summary

Cosplayers utilize costumes, prosthetics, makeup, and props innovatively to create fantastic characters inspired from animation, books, graphic novels, television, movies, and videogames. Dedicated Cosplayers creatively solve costuming issues and complications arising from portraying complex characters. The role of the Cosplay costume is the vehicle for ritual and transformation for the Cosplayer, which represents the genre, storyline, and character. Resulting fan fashions play significant roles both inside and outside the Cosplay fandom.

Cosplayers' individual and shared experiences construct the unique structure of the Cosplay fandom. The Cosplayer's costume and overall appearance constitutes the fandom's visual identity. The authenticity of the fandom is evident in its original costume design and construction, as well as in fandom's incorporation into the larger fan community.

As a female-dominant fan subculture, the Cosplay fandom is a dynamic system with creative approaches to issues. In Chapter 5, I introduce the issues and crises facing Cosplayers and the ways the fandom is coping and working to find solutions.

5
GIRL POWER TO THE RESCUE

When Cosplaying, Cosplayers are such happy, positive, and friendly individuals who, when gathered together in groups, cannot help but entertain each other and anyone watching with their antics, satires, and performances. Initially, it was difficult to comprehend how this enthusiastic fandom with members always smiling and laughing could have issues or be harassed by outsiders. Unfortunately, despite the subculture being inclusive, Cosplayers contend with exploitation, conflicts, discrimination, and harassment regularly. Still, the Cosplay subculture is a vibrant, organic system and, as a fandom, is resilient. With the introduction of each new stimulus, the system evolves in dynamic and at times unexpected ways.

The Cosplay fandom is a female-dominant subculture, which is a unique structure and power dynamic for a Western subculture. Subsequently, this subculture suffers the same vulnerabilities and discriminations commonly faced by girls and women in Western and global society. This unique composition of the fandom, however, allows members to approach crises and issues with distinctive and innovative solutions. I highlight specific issues that Cosplayers contend with at fan conventions, on social media, and within the real world because of their affiliation in the Cosplay fan subculture. The unique composition of this subculture, being primary female Cosplayers, could reveal new approaches to solving issues facing the fandom. Is "girl power" the answer to these crises and challenges facing the Cosplay fandom?

Dirty little secret

Cosplay may be the most highly visible fan activity with its media coverage, online presence, convention performances, and photos; still, being a Cosplayer is a secret identity for some, and, for many more, Cosplay activities are dirty little secrets. Some Cosplayers make great efforts to conceal their Cosplay activities and expenses, despite their performances at conventions and images shared on social media. Cosplayers shared with me their fears of certain friends or family members discovering the amount of time or money they spend on Cosplay costume, conventions, and activities. For some, even the Cosplayer identity must be kept hidden. Said one Cosplayer: "Cosplay is my dirty little secret."

Since Cosplay (and attending conventions) requires a significant financial commitment, some Cosplayers prefer not to share that they participate in Cosplay activities or at least not provide outsiders with the exact costs. Also, costumes frequently cost more than US$100, especially when considering all of the expenses related to the costume including makeup, wigs, and props/accessories. Furthermore, there are additional expenses associated with attending fan conventions, including travel, conventions, hotel rooms, and the like. Subsequently, Cosplayers confessed not being willing to disclose or even conceal the amount of money they spend for Cosplay with family or friends not involved in the fandom.

In addition, Cosplay is a time-intensive activity that requires lengthy periods of effort designing and constructing costumes and practicing makeup and styling. Moreover, they rehearse endless hours posing and performing scenarios. Even travel to and from as well as attending fan conventions necessitates substantial time commitments. In more recent years, Cosplayers dedicate hours to posting images and videos on social media. With these significant time commitments, Cosplayers may neglect anything that is not part of the Cosplay lifestyle, resulting in conflicts with family and limiting intimate relationships with anyone who is not a Cosplayer.

Subsequently, Cosplayers may experience conflicts with family and friends who have concerns about the amount of money and time they spend on Cosplay but still tend to remain active in the fandom regardless of the complaints. Accordingly, some Cosplayers choose to hide or downplay their Cosplay activities and expenses instead of coping with the potential conflicts or possible confrontations. For some Cosplayers, this reluctance also means creating alternative Cosplay identities for social media to maintain their secret fandom lifestyle (similar to a superhero adopting a secret identity to maintain a normal social life).

Still, some Cosplayers, similar to fans from other fandoms, may develop an obsession with an aspect of Cosplay or Cosplay overall. Most Cosplayers expressed deep devotion for Cosplay, but some discussed their "obsession" and "preoccupation" with the fandom. Cosplayers further shared specifics about their Cosplay obsessions related to their chosen characters and related storylines: costume design and construction and/or competitions and conventions. Subsequently, the Cosplay identity, for some, is associated with a certain amount of shame because the fandom is associated with labels like "geeks," "nerds" or "obsession," and general misunderstandings about fandoms. Accordingly, participating in the Cosplay fandom has the potential to be a social liability.

Some Cosplayers find it offensive when outsiders refer to Cosplay as a "hobby" because Cosplayers consider it a far more significant aspect to their lifestyle than a simply leisure activity. One Cosplayer explained his disdain for people who label Cosplay as a "hobby" by comparing it to being an athlete:

If I were a baseball player or marathon runner, no one would say it was a hobby. Cosplay takes a lot of skill, time, and money . . . and dedication. Not a hobby!

Cosplayers commonly discuss their Cosplay activities and being part of the fandom as a lifestyle. Being a Cosplayer does have the potential to become an all-consuming identity that demands a significant commitment. As a lifestyle, Cosplay reflects the fandom's and individual's behaviors, values, preferences, and attitudes. The Cosplay lifestyle constructs social structures in which Cosplayers find and negotiate social positions, as well as a framework for understanding the fandom's ideology, material culture, and actions.

The Cosplay lifestyle is meaningful and idiosyncratic from other fandoms, and stands distinct from everyday reality. Cosplayers construct their *fantastic* existence within the fandom from characters and costumes to relationships and support networks. The lifestyle extends from the fandom and Cosplay experiences, revealed from the themes and constructs discussed in Chapter 3.

Women's work

Cosplay is inherently connected with girls and women beyond the fact that it is a female-dominant fandom. Some portions of Cosplay are stereotypically associated with women (sewing and styling), while others are assumed particularly difficult for women (e.g., welding or swordplay). Moreover, within the fandom, women are embracing the sewing machine, power tools, and weapons equally.

It is expected that the Cosplay costume designed and created by the Cosplayer results in most Cosplayers sewing and constructing at least portions of their costumes, which also results in financial savings. While "sewing" is one of the most frequent complaints from nearly all Cosplayers, most are also truly proud of their sewing achievements. "Sewing is women's work? You bet it is!" boasted a Cosplayer (Winge 2017). Both men and women shared feelings of "accomplishment" and "success" for their improvements in sewing skills.

Innovation and creativity are essential when creating a costume that only exists as a two-dimensional drawing or written description in literature. From a more practical perspective, building a costume frequently extends beyond simple sewing skills to complex rigid construction techniques, which may require power tools and associated skills as well as extensive knowledge of materials. In addition to building costumes, Cosplayers learn to style hair/wigs and apply makeup appropriate for their characters.

The costume praxis is empowering for anyone who acquires new skills and knowledge to use tools in order to create costumes for their beloved characters. The skills (sewing, embroidery, knitting, and the like) commonly needed to create Cosplay costumes are assumed to be inherent to all girls and women, while at the same time considered exceptional skills for boys and men to exhibit. Within the fandom, many misogynistic stereotypes are projected on Cosplay girls and women, but these assumptions are being addressed directly or broken down by the attempt to hold all Cosplayers to equal standards.

The thriving success of the Cosplay fandom is due in part to the prioritization of self-constructed precise and detailed costumes, and also the fandom's willingness to share and learn difficult skill sets in order to produce an accurate costume. Community building happens through sharing and mentoring members of the fandom in design, construction, and performance. Cosplayers share across the fandom regardless of subcultural status (novices share with veterans and vice versa). The fandom's dominant female presence creates a social structure that encourages sharing knowledge because the female guidance democratizes the fandom for everyone.[1]

Furthermore, more experienced Cosplayers rolemodel behaviors for new Cosplayers by embracing and promoting skill sets that range from sewing to styling to welding to mechanical assembly, as well as by demonstrating the social structure expected in the fandom. In addition, by posting their accomplishments as documented in images and videos on social media platforms, Cosplayers gain agency and empowerment within the subculture. Cosplayers thrive on the acknowledgments recognizing their merit for character costumes and performances.

Halloween versus Cosplay

Halloween is a contentious topic among Cosplayers because of the continued confusion between the two activities. Specifically, Cosplay exists distinct from Halloween, and Cosplayers are easily angered at the confusion: "Cosplay is not for Halloween!" was a response from a Cosplayer when discussing the subject. Halloween is an American holiday that is annually celebrated on October 31, where children dress in costumes and go "trick-or-treating," that is, going door to door and demanding candy, with the expectations that mischief will occur if not given treats. While adults do not typically take part in this holiday other than to escort children, there are exceptions such as college campuses, where adult students dress in costumes for the Halloween week/end to go out drinking and partying.

Cosplayers also contribute to the confusion between the two activities because they sometimes wear their Cosplay characters' costumes for Halloween. Since Cosplay costumes are expensive and may include weapons or dangerous props, these costumes are not always suitable for Halloween, whose celebrations do not share the similar rules and precautions common at conventions. Frequently, Cosplay costumes are designed and constructed to include even minute details of the character's appearance and Cosplayer's personality; Halloween costumes are regularly lacking such minutia.

The confusion stems from the similarity of both Cosplayers and Halloween participants wearing costumes, but that is where the parallel ends and Cosplayers quickly point out the distinctions. While some Cosplayers may wear their characters' costumes for Halloween, other facets of Cosplay do not manifest, such as performances and posing for photographs. Cosplayers' specific criticisms of Halloween participants include lack of dedication to characters, poor-quality costumes, and absence of performances.

Additional concerns associated with the confusion between Cosplay and Halloween proliferate from the overly sexualized costumes found at fan conventions and those used on Halloween night on nearly any college campus. Halloween costumes marketed to and worn by women tend to use minimal fabric and expose erogenous zones in order to eroticize costumed women (Lennon, Zheng, and Fatnassi 2016). In contrast, Cosplay costumes for female characters are revealing due to two factors: (1) characters are illustrated in body-revealing dress, and (2) Cosplayers alter the costume to be more body-revealing or accent erogenous zones. While dressing in revealing costumes for Halloween or Cosplay is not an invitation for sexual harassment, the costume is used as an excuse by the harassers.

Most Cosplayers maintain that Cosplay is not a Halloween activity, and they do not want to be confused with trick-or-treaters. Still, they acknowledge that the superficial similarities of wearing costumes continue to be confusing for outsiders, as well as the misunderstandings Cosplayers invite by wearing character costumes to Halloween activities. Further contributing to the confusion is the way the mass media represents Cosplay costumes as purely exotic versions of Halloween participants.

Exoticization and exploitation

The Cosplay fandom encounters exploitation at every turn, and many Cosplayers are not prepared for the sudden and overwhelming attention. In the convention environment, Cosplayers can quickly become the center of attention with multiple demands and distractions. As Cosplayers participate in online activities, they further expose themselves for exploitation and harassment.

Sometimes, even the individual members of the fandom unintentionally exploit each other and themselves. Cosplayers share images of themselves and others online, which not only bring validation and positive feedback for a given character and/or costume but may also bring harassment and exoticization. In addition, once the images are made public, they are removed from the context of the fandom. This is particularly true because of the predominance of cameras in cell phones, smart phones, and other similar handheld electronic devices, when everyone is potentially a photographer instantly linked to the Internet. Accordingly, Eron Rauch, a Cosplay photographer, shared with me:

> When digital cameras came into wide use, it changed the relationship between the Cosplayer and convention goer. It made this weird power dynamic, since most Cosplayers were women, and suddenly you had huge mobs of these sketchy dudes aggressively "documenting" them every time they were in public. (See Figure 5.1)

Figure 5.1 Two Cosplayers portraying Cammy and Chun-Li from *Street Fighter* videogame being photographed just outside the convention space by fans at the 2003 Anime Central convention. Photo: Eron Rauch.

The media commonly exploit Cosplayers for news reports, Internet posts, and magazine articles. Provocative or sensational images of Cosplayers are the primary objective for many photographers who are not part of the Cosplay fandom or greater fan community found at fan conventions. Frequently, these images are used as clickbait for online content or sold for distribution without consent of the Cosplayer.

Cosplayers also face more malicious forms of exploitation. The company 2imagesolutions created body pillows from Cosplayer images and sold them online. The body pillows featured the entire front and back of the Cosplayer in costume. Cosplayers had signed releases for their images to be posted to the photographer's website; however, they did not give permission for the creation and production of products to be sold. The Cosplayers featured on the pillows and their fans demanded the company to stop selling the pillows. The company eventually complied with the requests and withdrew the pillows from the open market (Woerner 2013).

For many years, Richard T. Bui, an American photographer, allegedly propositioned Cosplayers to pose nude for photographs (Williams 2015). Dani Phantom, a Cosplayer, reported the photographer, after which additional Cosplayers came forward with similar accusations (Williams 2015). Consequently, there was backlash online that resulted in victim blaming, which, in turn, discourages Cosplayers from reporting these types of incidents.

Even some of the Cosplay fandom photographers capitalize from the exploitation and exoticization of Cosplayers. Those within the subculture frequently disseminate their photographs in books and online sites, from which they may earn a profit (but is not shared with the Cosplayers in the photographs). For most Cosplayers this arrangement appears equitable because images of them dressed in costumes are now in a book or on a website that celebrates their Cosplay character and efforts.

Photographers commonly approach Cosplayers with various requests, and Cosplayers nearly always agree to their requests. In fact, when I asked Cosplayers to take their pictures for this research to document and reference their costumes, I was frequently given permission before I could even share why. While I offered Cosplayers a nominal compensation for their time and photographs, most requests for images of Cosplayers have no compensation and Cosplayers usually ask for a way to obtain copies of the images.

The exploitation of Cosplayers is not likely to end easily because it is financially profitable and even supported to some degree by the fandom. Cosplayers continue to place themselves at risk because most of the fandom's exploitation happens in connection to photographs and the fandom is image-centric. The rapidly growing popularity of the subculture further problematizes the potential for exploitation.

Conflicted bodies and identities

The body is complicated, sexualized, and often ritualized within the Cosplay subculture. Once formalized as a Cosplay body, the body becomes a space for critiqued activities, representations, and portrayals with far-reaching consequences. Cosplayers are evaluated not only for character accuracy but also for comparable body type, and eye, hair, and skin color. While wigs and contact lenses change hair and eye hues respectively for the selected character, body type and skin pigment are more challenging and contentious to alter to the physical attributes of the portrayed character.

Many Cosplayers modify and enhance their natural bodies to create idealized forms of fantastic proportions and features illustrated in the inspirational works of fiction. Cosplayers have endless choices for transforming their bodies provided they have access and financial resources. They utilize cosmetics, prosthetics, waist cinchers, exercise, diet, and supplements, but when the body modifications require significant changes not available with these non-invasive methods, some Cosplayers resort to surgery. In this research study, several Cosplayers discussed other Cosplayers having surgery to enlarge breasts, pectorals, and calves or to reduce waist or thighs, but no one admitted having surgery themselves.

While plastic surgery does not appear to be commonplace to the fandom, some Cosplayers feel it necessary to modify the shape and form of their bodies in more permanent ways to achieve a more precise physical depiction of the character. Breast enhancements are commonly debated and criticized body modifications among Cosplayers. Most notably, Cosplay celebrities, because of their public appearances and media presence, are continually critiqued for their bodies. Breast enhancements for Cosplay models are critiqued negatively and are used as a jumping-off platform for further critiques about participation in the fandom, convention attendance, and costume construction. Yaya Han's body, for example, has been the topic of critique; most debated is whether or not she had breast enhancements. While Cosplayers are criticized for not having achieved correct proportions, they are further censured when they seek out surgery to resolve the issues.

Body shaming has become an important issue in the Cosplay fandom that is negatively impacting the subculture (and other fandoms) in significant ways. In most instances, both female and male Cosplayers evaluate primarily female Cosplayers more harshly than their male counterparts (except in situations where males crossplay female characters). Several satirical memes and comics have been created suggesting that large males can portray characters without criticism but females are held to higher and different physical standards. This is further emphasized by the nature of the female characters, who are written, drawn, and acted with extraordinary bodies.

There is a distinct difference how females "of size" (i.e., larger body types) are treated compared to males with similar body types. This situation has additional complications for Cosplayers, as Cosplayers of size are demanding space within the fandom and recognition for their representations of Cosplay characters. These Cosplayers are not limiting themselves to playing characters similar to their body size. Instead, they are choosing characters in a similar manner to other Cosplayers—because of their love of the character.

For the average Cosplayer, the attention from fans and media is flattering at first but eventually presents difficulties for individual fans and even those in close proximity. Sanzo stated how "the positive recognitions of the effort and attention is good thing," but there are times when "it is too much attention and I just want to be away from everyone."

There are very few characters of size, which leaves larger Cosplayers with challenges when seeking characters of similar body frame to portray. Audience members, fans, and even other Cosplayers may even criticize an individual Cosplayer for selecting and portraying a character smaller than her body size. The criticisms and even bullying (mostly online) lead some Cosplayers to take drastic measures to modify their bodies. Even after drastic diets or cosmetic surgeries, these same Cosplayers still experience some type of body shaming.

Still, from these criticisms the Cosplay fandom has responded with activism in the form of a body-positive movement called "Cospositive." This new philosophy attempted to support Cosplayers of size and was quickly adopted into the fandom: however, in practice discrimination continues from both inside and outside the fandom. Criticisms focused on Cosplayers with body sizes different from characters primarily occur online, but it also happens at fan conventions as observers comment about the Cosplayer's appearance or size. Rhapsody Artajo is a plus-size Cosplayer and an activist for Cosplayers of size. Her character range is vast and she does not hesitate to assume characters regardless of their size. Her social media reflects her activist position with the fandom.

Race and ethnicity is another area of contention in the Cosplay fandom. While hair, eye, and skin pigments are rather easily modified to match nearly any character, it is the latter that collides with racial and ethnic divides. Some Cosplayers challenge the contemporary social constructs and roleplay black characters by using cosmetics and body paint to modify their skin color. They are met with questions and concerns about their use of blackface. Further complicating this situation is the fact that there are few characters of color, forcing people of color to select characters not in their natural skin color, or to use cosmetics to temporarily modify their skin color.

Blackface is more acceptable in some places in the world because those individual cultures have not been impacted by repercussions of slavery. In the United States, however, the use of makeup to darken skin triggers negative reactions from viewers because of historic connections to the use of blackface in minstrel shows, as well as the remaining tensions connected to slavery and the current marginalized positions of minorities. In recent years, skin lightening has also come under criticism because it preferences one skin tone over another. Some Cosplayers, however, defend using makeup to darken or lighten skin because it attains character accuracy; others promote roleplaying characters of any race or ethnicity with the Cosplayer's natural skin tones.

The role of identity politics among Cosplayers manifests itself as marginalization happens when persons are evaluated based on the race and ethnicity reflected in the character's skin pigment. Cosplayers created/adopted the acronym of POC for "players (or persons) of color" in order to engage in the discussion of identities (i.e., characters, Cosplayers, etc.) within the fandom, as well as shorthanding acknowledgments for Cosplayers accomplishments as POC (Winge 2017). The genre of Steampunk, for example, presents further complications for African American Cosplayers in that the fandom is positioned in an era of colonialism. Accordingly, some Cosplayers speak out against the Steampunk subculture. When POC Cosplayers pursue roles within the Steampunk fandom, it interrupts the expected identity politics and redefines the fantasy timeline.

Cosplay is negotiating racial tensions in both who is *allowed* to roleplay specific characters and the races represented within original sources. The diverse and inclusive nature of the Cosplay fandom precludes that there are players of color in the fandom, but the limitations of most source materials are skewed toward characters of European descent. Even among Japanese anime and manga characters, popular sources for Cosplay characters are frequently drawn with exaggerated and accentuated Western features. Currently, a Cosplayer of color is able to roleplay any character regardless of race, while other Cosplayers are discouraged (via peer pressure and harassment) from playing a character that is illustrated (or described) with darker skin.

Addressing this issue, African American Cosplayers are confronting stereotypes by donning characters of any race or ethnicity and promoting them on the Internet. There is a Tumblr site called cosplayingwhileblack, which features African American Cosplayers dressed as their favorite characters. On this blog, there are primarily images of Cosplay characters, ranging from Spock from *Star Trek* to Harry from *Harry Potter* to Linda and Tina from *Bob's Burgers*. The costumes and portrayal of characters on a brown body challenges the status quo and composes opportunities for more diversity within the fandom.

These portrayals and the demand for characters that reflect and represent the fandom's inclusivity may even encourage the creation of more diverse characters. More agile to respond to fandom's requests than large companies, independent artists are introducing more diversity of characters. A comic book artist and promoter of minority characters, Andre Batts created the comic book *Dreadlocks* series featuring African American characters within compelling storylines. These and other independent comics and graphic novels offer more diverse characters for Cosplayers to roleplay.

Similarly and frequently related, it is also controversial in the fandom for Cosplayers to roleplay characters of color if not of their ethnicity or race. It is considered insensitive despite the Cosplayer's love or intense emotions for the character. Despite these concerns, some Cosplayers roleplay characters differing from their ethnicity or race, either because they challenge the notions of racism in favor of "love of character" or are naive to the controversy. Characters challenging the norm tend to face harassment in person and online.

The complexities of roleplaying characters of races that differ from the Cosplayer's natural skin pigment (not necessarily reflecting the Cosplayer's actual ethnicity or race) manifest in conflicts and complicated discourses. One side argues that out of respect for POC Cosplayers and the limited characters of color (COC) that only COC should be roleplayed by POC (Winge 2017). The other side argues their love for a character is respectful and thus defies being roleplayed by someone of the same skin pigment (Winge 2017).

For a fandom that advocates tolerance and fun, this issue is straining relationships and forcing Cosplayers to confront notions of identity politics. Subsequently, the fandom found ways to recognize and celebrate Cosplayers of color. On Facebook, the "International Cosplay Day" page features Cosplayers dressed as their favorite characters as well as Cosplay activism and events. Additionally, in 2017, the International Cosplay Day movement featured African American Cosplayers each day of February for African American History Month or Black History Month.

In 2017, the inaugural year for the Indigenous Comic-Con took place in Albuquerque, New Mexico. The convention featured twenty Native American guests, including Eugene Braverock, actor from *Wonder Woman* (2017) and Renee Dejo, game designer from *Blood Quantum*. The convention's website posted rules for Cosplayers' dress that reflected the organizers' desire for a more culturally sensitive fan space (indigenouscomiccon.com).

Disabilities with abilities

Cosplayers with special needs for mobility or physical accommodations, limitations, and/or service animals select their characters for the same reasons given by the fandom overall—they love the characters. Still, some Cosplayers with special needs or physical limitations want to roleplay characters who resemble them physically, similarly to Cosplayers who select characters because of comparable hair color or body build. Accordingly, a blind Cosplayer may choose to portray Daredevil from Marvel Comics or Toph Beifong from the TV animated series *Avatar: The Last Airbender*, while a wheelchair-bound Cosplayer may choose to portray Professor Xavier of X-Men fame, and a Cosplayer who wants to incorporate her amputation could select to roleplay the Black Knight from *Monty Python and the Holy Grail*.

Cosplayers enjoy using their natural attributes to more accurately portray a character with similar physical limitations, but disabilities are not necessarily factors when selecting a Cosplay character. In 2016, at the Fan Expo in Vancouver, a disabled Cosplayer portrayed a zombie Spiderman (from the Marvel Zombies comic book series) while using a wheelchair, which was not part of the costume. The Cosplayer used her unique physical form and custom-made and distressed costume to visually communicate zombie bites and wounds marks incorporating her missing legs. When requested for photographs, the Cosplayer threw herself onto the floor and struck a predatory pose, creating a more compelling portrayal to the delighted gasps of fans.

Also, Amanda Knightly, for example, uses the Cosplay pseudonym "Misa on Wheels" at conventions and on social media (Orsini 2012). Misa roleplays anime characters from her wheelchair for the love of the characters despite any physical limitation. Furthermore, the Internet affords Misa infinite social contacts and ways to interact with the Cosplay fandom, as well as a platform to inform people about Cosplaying with physical limitations. Misa regularly posts pictures of her Cosplay characters as activism for persons with physical limitations on Facebook and Twitter for her 46,000+ followers. Misa stated on Facebook:

> Cosplay is getting to be more corrupt as it becomes more mainstream. It's becoming more about looking like a Victoria's Secret model and being bullied if you don't. I, for one, am tired of it. Cosplayers are being told, verbally or otherwise, that they need to look a certain way to do what they love. Cosplay is not a beauty contest. Society has done enough harm to the issue of body image. Let's keep it out of the cosplay community. (Knightly, November 6, 2013)

Furthermore, Cosplayers with physical limitations, disabilities, and/or service animals contend with additional issues with their every movement throughout convention spaces and accessing the vendor and artist spaces, which may be prohibitive or challenging in overly crowded spaces. This is further complicated by Cosplay costumes that become entangled in wheelchair components or extend beyond the person that protrude and knock into people and furniture. Accordingly, fan convention organizers are torn between accommodating fans by creating wider walkways between booths and tables or squeezing more vendors into the limited space available.

Service animals present additional concerns at conventions because of the large crowds, possibility of injuries, and distractions from people who want to treat the animals as pets. While all fan conventions are required to allow service animals according to Title II and Title III by the Americans with Disabilities Act (ADA 2009), organizers insist that attendees register all service animals with the convention and wear their service animal identification. Cosplayers with service animals may cleverly costume them and incorporate their helpers into the overall character(s) portrayals. Costuming service animals is commonly discouraged in public spaces and even forbidden at some conventions because of the confusion it causes for people who do not realize the animal is working.

Family affair

The social constructs from the real world continually invade and inform fandoms and their conventions. Most notable are the ways that more and more families are attending conventions, specifically the ways children impact the Cosplay fandom. Children assume Cosplayers are the actual individuals they know from television programs, films, and cartoons. Some parents assume Cosplayers are entertainer babysitters because of the ways they roleplay and interact with children. Cosplayers comment on social media about how this is "unfair" and "dangerous."

Not surprisingly, families who want to participate in Cosplay activities are finding ways for their children to be incorporated into Cosplay teams. As families have children, they embrace characters of family based teams, such as the families from *The Incredibles* and *Bob's Burgers*, who are becoming more prevalent at fan conventions and Cosplay competitions. Families also group together characters from an individual storyline into family style units, such as Captain America, Captain Marvel, Black Widow, and Hulk from Marvel's *The Avengers* franchise. Furthermore, families have their small children portray diminutive characters, such as Blossom, Bubbles, and Buttercup from *The Powerpuff Girls* cartoons, and R2D2, Ewoks, and miniaturized versions of other characters from the *Star Wars* movies (see Plate 5.2).

Not all younger fans attending conventions, however, are part of Cosplay families or even come with family who are part of a fandom. As younger Cosplayers attend conventions with their parents who are nonfans, there are additional expectations for all fans. Cosplayers, specifically, are being asked to design and dress in more modest costumes in order to create a comfortable atmosphere for families with children. Source media, however, continues to illustrate and represent female characters with hypersexualized physical features and body-revealing clothing. Consequently, there is a growing tension for Cosplayers who wish to accurately portray these types of characters in conventions while there are also families in attendance.

At Gen Con 2017, most of the teams competing in the Costume Competition were families, and several even included babies or toddlers dressed as characters. The audience responded positively to the inclusion of children with audible comments of "Aaw!" and "Ooo!" The children's costumes were designed and constructed with the same detail as the older team members' costumes, which suggests the level of dedication to every character in the team.

Cosplay identities

The social mores constructed external to the fandom demand that Cosplayers continuously respond appropriately. The fandom, however, is made up of many individuals with differing social positions and ideologies, making it difficult to create a single cogent path forward. This keeps the fandom in a dynamic state of flux, which has drawbacks and benefits to the Cosplay fan subcultural system. The Cosplay fan subculture strives to accommodate the most diverse members of the fandom, hoping this will assure that the more mainstream members will be accommodated too.

Cosplayers exist as conflicted beings because they "live" in more than one fandom concurrently. Consider a Cosplayer dressed in a blue *Star Trek* shirt with pointed ears roleplaying Mr. Spock; she exists as a Cosplayer and a Trekkie (*Star Trek* fan) simultaneously. Similarly, someone cosplaying Sailor Moon is both a Cosplayer and an anime fan. The latter example adding to the confusion of the Cosplayer's identity is the association with anime/manga. Since many of the Cosplay fandom's favorite characters are anime characters, it is not surprising that all Cosplayers are assumed to be anime fans.

While Cosplayers may appear to be socially agile and even confident in their performances of fantastic characters, they often express feelings of anxiety and social awkwardness. Some Cosplayers prefer to perform in hallways and small social groups instead of competing on a stage in front of hundreds of audience members. Cosplayers use humor to combat performance anxieties and bond with audience members over shared knowledge and laughter. Accompanied by friends while socializing also helps nervous Cosplayers deal with social awkwardness and anxiety issues. The sense of belonging to the fandom contributes to the experience *being* within the fan subculture. Group experiences affirm belonging, as well as confirm *being* a Cosplayer.

As a Cosplayer programs her character's dress (i.e., body modifications and supplements), external evaluations exert controls over her body resulting in alterations within designated parameters for the given characters and desired outcomes (see Stone 1962/1995). This feedback loop of program-and-review produces a conflicted Cosplayer body with multiple identities continually seeking perfection and resolution but never fully achieving either. Moreover, this feedback may contribute to a Cosplayer choosing future characters.

Frenchy Lunning argues that Cosplay is sexualized and gendered, connecting it to Freudian constructs of "feminine narcissism" (2011: 75). She further suggests that since the fan subculture is primarily young women who are "acculturated within the confines of the male gaze—and consequently positioned as 'objects'" (2011: 76). The Cosplayer when dressed in the costume becomes a fantasy object and by extension the object of consumption, which manifests when audiences recognize the characters or ask for photographs and autographs.

Subsequently, female-representing Cosplayers and characters further struggle with internal and external conflicts regarding the fan body/bodies and identity/identities. At a practical level, the female characters' bodies are then more difficult to achieve with accuracy because of their unnatural body proportions (extremely tapered waists, exaggerated breasts and hips). The Cosplayer's body is hypersexualized within hegemonic structures, genres, and storylines, and is further subjugated through the male gaze, especially at fan conventions that have primarily male attendees.

Some convention organizers attempt to deal with harassment by directing their attention at female Cosplayers and their costumes. They ask all Cosplayers to meet certain dress codes, but these codes primarily impact females and female-representing characters. If Cosplayers do not comply with costumes deemed too revealing, they are asked to change their costume or leave the convention space. This action shifts the responsibility onto the Cosplayer and assumes that dress influences other's behaviors and absolves them of responsibilities. Dress research, however, suggests that dress has no significant bearing on negative or aggressive behaviors toward the wearers (Lennon, Lennon, and Johnson 1995).

When purchasing tickets for fan conventions, it is common to also receive notifications about the convention's rules/guidelines, such as unacceptable/acceptable behaviors and dress, as well as related sanctions for violations while in attendance. When picking up convention badges onsite, attendees find the rules posted again in most of the convention literature and even posted on very large posters or banners near the entrances and exits. Purchasing tickets for the fan convention is considered an agreement to follow the rules/guidelines for the given convention.

The Cosplay fandom consists of primarily of fans who identify as females (65 percent), while at any given fan convention the attendees are about equal between men and women with 2 percent reporting nonbinary (Eventbrite 2015a). Since most fandoms are male dominant, the Cosplay subculture exists in a unique composition. It also poses complications and issues for the fandom because of the marginalized positions of females in most cultures. The unique composition of this fandom also positions girls and women in a powerful locus to effect change and foster a supportive environment that all fandoms can benefit from at conventions.

Female Cosplayers occupy powerful and controversial positions within the Cosplay subculture, situated within the larger fan community. Female Cosplayers are challenging the status quo and demanding equality and safety for everyone, which is impacting all fans by redefining fandom spaces. Fan convention organizers, for example, are responding to these demands by changing policies and rules to address the safety of Cosplayers and convention attendees overall.

While most Cosplayers promote tolerance and attempt to improve their circumstances, these issues are complex and offer no simple solutions. As previously stated, fan convention organizers and staff attempt to address the changing fandom landscape by instituting new rules/guidelines. Some Cosplayers speculate that the new rules may make conventions safer, while others find the rules too oppressive and believe that they may limit creativity in characters and costumes. Furthermore, some Cosplayers suspect convention organizers add new rules/guidelines not to protect the Cosplayers but because organizers fear the loss of potential financial gains associated with the Cosplay fandom.

Males in the Cosplay fandom

Unlike most Western subcultures and fandoms, Cosplay is primarily composed of females with a female-dominant culture. While the members of the fandom do not easily acknowledge the significance of women over men in the fan subculture, it has female attributes, strengths, and weaknesses that are evident. As the male Cosplayers' population grows, the fandom is vulnerable to changes that reflect the new demographics.

There are numerous expectations of members in the Cosplay fandom that are contrary to stereotypical male roles and activities in Western society, even within fandoms. Sewing is still not a common masculine activity and was a common complaint from male Cosplayers. Male Cosplayers also contend with stereotypical notions about wearing makeup and styling hair/wigs. Even dressing in costumes may confront hegemonic notions about male heterosexuality.

Accordingly, Brownie and Graydon suggest that male Cosplayers may assert their maleness through character choice and the use of fandom jargon, such as using "gear" instead of "costume," which the latter is more common in the fandom (2016: 111). My research, however, suggests that male Cosplayers adopt the language of the fandom and choose to roleplay a wide range of characters. Some males attempt to establish their position in the fandom by creating exceptional costumes, precise makeup, and perfect performances in order to avoid criticism.

There are unwritten and rarely spoken of rules for crossplay and associated aesthetics. In addition, expectations for males and females differ significantly. Females crossplaying male characters are permitted at any level of accuracy for costume and appearance. Males crossplaying as female characters, however, are regularly ridiculed both inside and outside the fandom. Some Cosplayers commented that if a male wants to crossplay a female, his appearance must be "flawless" or he is likely to be mocked (Winge 2017). Some Cosplayers find these judgments "unfair" and "too harsh" compared to commentary about female-to-male crossplay. But are these judgments imbalanced? In a female space, girls and women define the standards and ideals. Moreover, their understanding of the female aesthetic expected from males may expect perfection, which is not achievable but this double standard is found in other subcultures. Male subculture members, for example, commonly criticized females for not having the correct aesthetic or ideology needed to be a given subculture (LeBlanc 1999). Consequently, some male Cosplayers crossplay female characters with humor; they portray female characters with hilarious roleplaying and costumes. Sailor Bubba, for example, dresses similar to Sailor Moon by a large hirsute man with a beard wearing a schoolgirl uniform and blonde wig; and, Wonder Wobear dresses similar to Wonder Woman also by a large hirsute man with a beard (see Plate 5.3).

The male presence in the fandom seems appreciated and wanted by most of the fandom but is subtly controlled or guided through indirect channels. Some female Cosplayers, however, suggest a fear of the fandom changing due to more of a male presence and influence, as well as fear of harassment and assault. The latter, however, does not seem a concern to many because currently the harassment and assault is primarily coming from outside the Cosplay fandom.

In a fan subculture where female members set the standards, ideals, and values, the male voices are likely to be overwhelmed and even silenced. It can be argued that the women in the fandom guide its direction through peer discussions and sweeping public admonishments instead of specific confrontations. Still, with male membership on the rise, there is the threat that males may dominate the subculture, potentially impacting the social structure and presence of the fandom overall.

Hazing and gatekeepers

"Haters" and "trolls" are derogatory identifiers for persons who prey on members from any fandom, usually online, both internally and externally to the groups. They frequently consider themselves experts regarding specific genres, characters, and/or storylines, and offer their critiques that highlight their knowledge or opinions. Regarding the Cosplay fandom, haters and trolls also proclaim expertise costume design and construction skills.

In addition to critiquing Cosplayers for costumes and even performances, haters and trolls may also quiz Cosplayers about their knowledge of characters and storylines. In this way, haters and trolls establish their perceived authority and expertise within the fandom. Giving harsh critiques to younger or newer fans about knowledge of genre, character, and storyline functions as hazing and gatekeeping for the fandom. While some members of the fandom abide by the practice of hazing, many Cosplayers recognize that it has the potential to impact the fan subculture negatively. Novices might not return after being disillusioned by the gatekeepers' high expectations for thorough research, developed construction skill sets, accurate costumes, and creative performances, the standards usually set for veteran or professional Cosplayers.

Consequently, Cosplayers actively discourage bullying, hazing, and trolling. Instead, the Cosplay fandom promotes inclusivity and diversity while openly condemning negativity toward Cosplayers, even from outside the fandom. As the Cosplay fandom realizes its importance despite organizers not fully acknowledging the significance of Cosplayers at fan conventions, they solicit convention organizers to address the undesirable issues being experienced by the Cosplayers.

Cosplay fan inclusivity

Most fandoms experience a certain amount of inclusivity of diverse individuals, where the focus of the fandom is their commonality to build relationships while not being based solely on race, ethnicity, or nationality. Still, these groups are rather homogenous, frequently reflecting the specific demographics related to the fandom's focus. Further reinforcing the group's homogenous composition, members of fandoms, often inadvertently, cause those who differ to feel uncomfortable when trying to participate in the fandom.

On the contrary to examples of most fandoms, which are primarily male dominated, the Cosplay fandom attempts to be inclusive of differing races, ethnicities, ages, abilities, sexualities, and genders because this inclusivity mindset brings in a wider array of source characters. While these demographics and inclusivity are commonly not topics of discussion within the fandom, they are evident in their interactions, appearances, and behaviors. The fandom recognizes the negative impact of discriminations and is actively addressing better ways to practice fulsome inclusivity.

The Cosplay fandom's efforts regarding inclusivity and diversity are significant factors in the fandom's continued growth and composition. The fandom's welcoming social structure encourages explorations of self and character not commonly available in other settings. Moreover, the Cosplay fandom focuses on the character, not the individual beneath the costume. Cosplayers can escape the trappings of expected everyday identities, and, instead, are encouraged to focus on the character's persona appearance.

Cosplay is NOT consent

The Cosplay fandom is primarily comprised of females who actively negotiate the fan spaces, once dominated by males, without compromising their character's sexual identity and gender. At the same time, male convention attendees navigate their changing territory without the knowledge of its final topography. The changing fan landscape is challenging for all convention attendees and fandoms. Further complicating this situation for the Cosplayers is the intrusive "male gaze" (Mulvey 1975), which depicts women and the world from the perspective of the stereotypical male point of view and attitudes. Since so many fandoms are male dominated and conventions spaces are filled with boys and men, female fans often feel like prey at fan conventions. The ways the male gaze impacts Cosplay is problematic because it defines a female-dominant fan subculture within and confined to stereotypical male perceptions.

When the Cosplay fandom is exploited and fetishized, the fandom is fertile for sexual harassment and other abuses. Consequently, outsiders or spectators sexually harass female Cosplayers in costume; Cosplayers crossplaying female characters are also similarly hounded. Since crossplay characters are further eroticized as the exotic Other, this judgment presents additional situations of vulnerability for female Cosplayers. Some Cosplayers speculate that the harassment toward female Cosplayers happens because those outside the Cosplay subculture interpret costumes as implied consent. Subsequently, spectators and non-Cosplayers touch and grope costumed female Cosplayers with inappropriate and sometimes illegal behaviors. Most Cosplay groups and conventions have now instituted rules about limiting interactions with Cosplayers.

Cosplayers also began their own campaign—"Cosplay is NOT Consent"—to extend protection to female-representing Cosplayers by educating convention attendees. The campaign's objective is to inform convention attendees that Cosplayers are not objects and the costume is not an invitation to be objectified. In addition, the movement assists female-representing Cosplayers in occupying and (re)claiming their space within the convention environments safely.

The resulting graphics and signage that states "Cosplay is NOT Consent" is posted and carried on signs throughout conventions. These graphics and related actions place responsibility on the harassers but also assume dress is the influencing factor for the unwanted behaviors. Convention organizers take cues from the "Cosplay is NOT Consent" initiative, and assume Cosplayers recognize their costumes are the enticement for the harassment.

The "Cosplay is NOT Consent" campaign brought to light that many female fans attending conventions do not feel safe. As a result, "Geeks for CONsent" was formed and petitioned convention organizers "to formalize and publicize anti-harassment policies" (Eventbrite 2015b). Convention organizers are making strides to make fan events safer: Calgary Expo, for example, is being praised for how safe all fans feel while in attendance (Eventbrite 2015a).

Fetishized characters and costumes

While "fetish" is commonly associated with a sexual deviance or variance from expected human attraction and sexual interactions, "fetish" is better defined as a strong attraction or desire for something (physical or intangible), sometimes imbued with magickal powers. Furries, for example, are assumed to be Cosplayers who are commonly associated with sexual fetish. Furries dress as real or fantastic anthropomorphic animals, usually donning faux-fur costumes that completely obscure the human form/corporeal body. Alternately, some examples of Furries use authentic animal furs, but most costumes are faux-fur. More rare, however, are Furries who utilize the human form within their hybrid fantasy animal characters, such as minotaur and centaurs. The fetish aspects of Furries are the tactile sensations created when touching, stroking, sucking, or smelling the fur, whether that fur is faux or animal in origin. Many Furries unite at conventions and other social gatherings for similar reasons as Cosplayers — belonging, entertainment, and socializing.

Also noteworthy, many Cosplay characters wear or carry fetishes that function as protection, magickal items, or weapons. For example, the Power Sword from *He-Man and the Masters of the Universe*, an animated television series, transforms meek Prince Adam into heroic He-Man by uttering a key phrase, and the Green Lantern (from the same-named comic book series) transforms an average human into an exceptional being with supernatural powers via mental control over his magical green ring. Villains can also carry fetishes — Skeletor's primary weapon and fetish is the other half of He-Man's Power Sword. Magickal fetishes are significant for anime and manga characters, especially in the case of common tropes of magical girls who use them to transform or gain powers. How could a Cosplayer portray the heroine Sailor Moon without her Star Power Stick, or Cardcaptor's Sakura without her Sealing Wand? Fetishes such as these transform characters with ritualized performances into their magical girl forms with associated powers.

While there is little research that would provide an understanding as to why Cosplayers are being sexually fetishized as hypersexual beings, it is speculated at great lengths without substantive data. Some of the assumptions about the Cosplay fandom result from the limited female character choices for Cosplayers, and the ones available are frequently hypersexualized with their physical appearance and costume. Subsequently, Cosplayers who accurately portray characters, who were originally illustrated as hypersexualized beings, are then deemed hypersexualized similarly to their characters.

While some Cosplayers may choose to participate in sexual fetishes associated with their chosen characters and storylines, this does not appear to be a norm. Cosplay, however, is enticing fodder for pornography. Cosplay pornography features people dressed in Cosplay-style costumes, who engage in sexual scenarios frequently including scenes similar to fan convention spaces and activities or roleplay fan fiction. Most performers in Cosplay pornography are not Cosplayers; these are actors who are dressed in costumes and use Cosplay as themes for the videos or photographs. Some performers are Cosplayers. Pixel Vixens, for example, is an online erotica website created by Cosplayers, which features actual Cosplayers in costumes roleplaying erotic scenarios.

Still, Cosplayers' connections to fetishes (i.e., objects imbued with magick or spirit) are critical to understanding the fandom, and the understanding/interpretation of the fetish may impact the Cosplayer's choice of character and subsequent costume. The incorporation of a fetish into a costume, whether an item of protection/transformation or tactile material, contributes to the overall understanding for the Cosplay character. Cosplayers are often unaware of these fetishized items, but reveal their importance and power in discussions.

Safe sex

Sex within fandoms has not been researched and is even speculative among fans. Still, time spent at fan conventions in the evening hours or visiting online discussion boards reveals that sex (or the lack thereof) is a significant part of the fan's life. Fan sex, however, does not always occur in person; it may take shape as phone sex, online sex, or fan fiction.

Fanfic, being not limited by ratings, censors, or audiences, may include storylines that describe sex between characters. In recent years, fanfic has even incorporated safe sex, concern about sexually transmitted diseases, and birth control, which reflects the growing presence of women in the fandoms. In this fantasy space created by fanfic, fans are free to explore relationships and storylines where they themselves can feel intimately involved.

Some fans speculate that because conventions attract growing numbers of diverse individuals who are together in a common space for several days, intimate, romantic, or sexual exchanges are inevitable (Peacock 2012). These fan convention relationships are often thought of as similar to a "summer romance" that will end with the conclusion of the convention without consequences. The temporal nature of fan conventions offers tempting opportunities for intimate affairs between fans. Additionally, conventions offer fans who are searching for companionship a concentrated pool of like-minded people. Tapping into this unique situation, some conventions have hosted speed-dating events for fans; New York Comic-Con, starting in 2009, hosted speed-dating sessions for fans, which became highly attended and extremely successful (Peterson 2011). Some conventions have earned reputations for more sexual activity than others. Fans sometimes refer to Dragon Con as "HookupCon." There is lore that CONvergence has specific floors in the hotels it occupies for sex rooms, which fans interviewed suggested was possible but not necessary since "sex is happening in every room" (Winge 2007).

Fan party rooms, regardless of the theme, may have bowls full of condoms, dental dams, and lubes encouraging fans to "be safe" in their intimate interactions. After-hours parties at fan conventions are infamous, assisting in "hookups" or having consenting intimate physical relations between fans. Accordingly, some fan conventions publish and post information about what constitutes "consent" in order to assure a safe environment for attendees. Unfortunately, outsiders or nonfans learn about the fan convention reputations and "crash" (enter the premises without paying for attendance) to search for sex with nerd/geek girls or molest and harass attendees.

Cosplayers and fans may flirt with each other as part of the Cosplay performance or the fan convention atmosphere. Some characters' personas and storylines provide Cosplayers with opportunities to roleplay a flirtatious or promiscuous character. Additionally, the costume may be used as an excuse to encourage emboldened interactions between Cosplayers and/or audience members.

Unfortunately, any flirtatious and provocative behaviors during roleplaying combined with the costumes contribute to the assumptions about Cosplayers. Some fans (and spectators) consider having sex with a Cosplay girl as an exotic challenge. "I wanna hook up with a Cosplay girl!" said one Cosplayer. Fans post online discussions about how they "scored with a Cosplay girl" or "smashed with a Cosplayer" (Winge 2017).

While most of these intimate exchanges are consensual, not all sexual encounters between fans are healthy and respectful. Also, individuals gain access to the convention spaces without being part of a fandom for many reasons, but it is most problematic for Cosplayers when these outsiders intend to pursue intimate relations with persons in costumes because it is seen as exotic and erotic. Consequently, the value of the fan convention security and attendee badges is immeasurable in maintaining the safety and protection of Cosplayers and all convention attendees.

In addition, not all fans are interested in a solely sexual encounter and pursue an intimate and/or romantic relationship with another compatible fan. After the conclusion of a fan convention, it is not uncommon for attendees to stay in contact with new friends or amorous interests via the Internet. In some cases, these long-distance and online relationships result in romantic and sometimes long-term commitments.

Costumed bodies: Transformation, conflict, and occupation

Cosplay offers opportunities for the construction of gender, sexuality, and identity within the tropes of fantastic characters, creating ritualized transformational spaces ripe with potential for conflict and agency. The Cosplay fandom is frequently the locus for transformation, conflict, and occupation of space at fan conventions.

As previously discussed in Chapter 4, the Cosplayer's body is ritualized when dressing in costume: a body in a state of transformation from the moment she first prepares the body to wear the costume to the moment the character's dress is completely disrobed. When becoming the character—donning the costume and makeup—the Cosplayer exists in liminal spaces with ritualized and rehearsed ways of achieving the fantastic persona. This transformation benefits the Cosplayer and the fandom but may cause issues within the greater fan community and at fan conventions.

The Cosplayer's costumed body confronts expected norms, even within the greater fan community at a convention, and further confronts the viewer and demands reaction, which is not always positive. Aggressive reactions or exchanges are often surprising and disarming to the Cosplayers because they do not understand why everyone does not appreciate their characters and resulting costumes. While there are very few incidents of violence toward Cosplayers, there is the potential for these tensions and conflicts to escalate into bodily harm.

Some Cosplayers describe these physical harassers as exhibiting "fanboy rage" or "fangirl rage" in their cruel and aggressive comments made to Cosplayers whose character portrayals do not meet the expectations of the observers. Fans assume ownership over characters and storylines they admire and even love, which they strive to protect from misinterpretations and representations. Cosplayers are subject to these fans' severe judgments about their character portrayals both online and at fan conventions.

The Cosplayer occupies both corporeal and conceptual spaces within their costumes and performances. Many Cosplayers attempt to defy the confines of their own corporeal bodies in favor of the fantastic characters' bodies. Cosplayers' consumption of space at fan conventions is a controversial issue. While Cosplayers attract media attention for conventions and are financially profitable for organizers and vendors, Cosplayers are also blamed for limiting attendees for accessing artists and vendors or worse: distracting attendees from purchasing merchandise.

Gender and the corporeal body

Judith Butler states, "Gender is instituted through the stylization of the body and, hence, must be understood as the mundane way in which bodily gestures, movements, and enactments of various kinds constitute the illusion of an abiding gendered self" (1988: 519). Gender is a socially constructed concept, which is both denied and reinforced within the Cosplay fandom. The role of gender and the corporeal body is complicated and often ritualized, especially when compounded within the Cosplay fandom. Judith Butler argues that gender is not fixed or binary but instead is performed (1993), whose performance is highlighted and exploited within Cosplay. Accordingly, Cosplayers and spectators alike are fascinated with the portrayal of gender intertwined with fantastic characters in ways that gender defies and extend the corporeal body.

Cosplay is inherently gendered because its sources of inspiration are characters with hyper-gendered identities. In fact, Cosplayers perform gender within the portrayals and dress of their characters. Viewers have preconceived notions and expectations of gender. When the Cosplayer fulfills or defies those expectations, this fulfillment or exception creates resolution or tension respectively. Subsequently, Cosplayers have the ability to influence perceptions of gender for their characters (and, likely, by extension for themselves) based upon revealed visual clues of dress, mannerisms, and/or body parts.

Still, "the artificiality of these [Cosplay] bodies places them outside the expectations of biological construction" (Anderson 2014: 26). Consider the ways Superman's costume allows the Cosplayer to wear prosthetic muscles without revealing the Cosplayer's corporeal body. Cosplayers commented about their conflicting feelings about the perceived powerful body in the costume and their flawed corporeal body. And, by virtue of Wonder Woman's skin- and cleavage-revealing costume, however, the Cosplayer must rely on her natural physique or else sacrifice expected details of appearance. The Cosplayer's corporeal body presents challenges in maintaining a perceived gender or expected physiques within the hyper-gendered costumed body. Moreover, as Cosplayers achieve agency through roleplaying their chosen characters, designations such as gender are becoming more complicated in the ways it is revealed or denied on the corporeal body.

Sexuality and gender in costume

The intersections of sexuality and gender occur within the chosen creative constructions of costumed characters of Cosplayers, which may include hidden sexual and/or gendered identities. Cosplay offers unconventional gender construction and sexuality within understood popular culture tropes of fantastic characters, which creates ritualized transformational spaces ripe with agency and empowerment. Cosplayers incorporate fetish, gender, and the corporeal body, and crossplay into the fandom in dramatic ways.

Both Cosplayers and spectators are fascinated with the portrayal of gender intertwined with the fantasy of Cosplay characters. Cosplayers are drawn to characters for reasons beyond their sexual or gender identity but still they must contend with the manifestations of sex, sexuality, and gender in costumes and performances when at fan conventions. "The expressiveness of the individual appears to involve two radically different kinds of sign activity; those they 'give' [verbal] and those they 'give off' [non-verbal cues]" (Goffman 1959: 2). Accordingly, the nonverbal language of the costume provides visual cues, which frequently open spaces for dialogue between Cosplayers and fans.

Cosplay, because it defies and extends the corporeal body, offers an accommodating space and social circles for crossplay. Crossplay adds a distinct, enhanced dimension to Cosplay, a visible manifestation of the costumed agency, affording the Cosplayers an array of character and gender choices. With growing interest in Cosplay, fan conventions need to address the risk factors and issues of harassment and bullying around Cosplayers.

The Cosplay subculture is facing a crisis primarily originating from outside the subculture; that is, Cosplayers are being sexually harassed both at conventions and online in social media sites. At fan conventions, female Cosplayers and crossplayers are the primary targets for verbal and physical harassment, unwanted photography, and even sexual assault. Crossplay is commonplace and not necessarily exoticized and eroticized internal to the Cosplay fandom, however, externally it is Othered. Conventions create rules that are continually reconsidered and rewritten to address the changing concerns and needs of attendees, which often reflect misunderstandings and harassment stemming from the mistreatment of Cosplayers in costumes. When on social media, all Cosplayers face the possibility of contending with bullies and harassment.

Further problematizing the exotic reputation of the Cosplay fandom are external critiques that conflate and fetishize the fan subculture. Frenchy Lunning, a Japanese popular culture scholar, states "Cosplay is a *drag* performance" (2011: 77). Lunning continues to compare Cosplay to "drag" and "camp" as a means of explaining why Cosplayers portrayed characters differently from their origin media (2011: 82–83). The primary implication of Lunning's argument suggests that anyone in costume is performing drag. Lunning's assessment further implies there are notions of crossplay or gender play in all Cosplay activities, where none may exist. Perhaps, the most troubling aspect of Lunning's assertion is that Cosplay character portrayals are being equated with drag further exoticizes the already hypersexualized Cosplayer projecting her as the Other. Furthermore, Cosplayers and crossplayers take exception with the opinion that Cosplay is "drag"; instead, Cosplayers suggest that Cosplay is about "play," as well as parody and subversion of fantasy characters beyond their original media.

Cosplay environment

Constructing the Cosplay environment happens both organically and strategically, with specific but mostly unwritten expectations from the greater fan community and the Cosplay fandom. Fan conventions offer opportunities for Cosplayers to experience "carnivalesque" (Bakhtin 1968: 10) within the larger spectacle of the fan community. In the surroundings of the convention, time and space are shaped into the fantastic chaos and crowds, where attendees are distinguished into smaller groups only by their dress. Among the crowds, the Cosplayer feels as if she is enveloped into the greater collective and able to assume her character's persona and cease to be herself. All convention attendees were considered equal during carnival (Bakhtin 1968: 10); these groups resist being distinguished by socioeconomic and political organizations (Clark and Holquist 1986: 302).

In these carnivalesque scenes, the Cosplayer is hyper-aware of her body and the costume that consumes it. In this way, the body is experienced by heightened senses: the tactile textures of the fabric against the skin, scents of makeup and hair products, and weight of the costume and props. The costume offers the Cosplayer an opportunity to exchange her identity for another or meld with her selected character. Clark and Holquist argue that, in these moments, the body experiences death and renewal inside the carnivalesque environment (1986: 303).

External stimuli are continually impacting the Cosplay environment and Cosplayers with unknown outcomes for the fandom. Consider the role of designated performance spaces for Cosplayers and the creative ways the fandom is claiming their space and drawing attention to the performances at the same time. The Cosplay environment requires the Cosplayer's immersion into the character's persona, as well as audience members being immersed into the performance experience. In turn, the audience's immersion and reactions encourage the Cosplayer's performance. To this end, Cosplayers use amplified music projected over PA system (similar to Cosplay competitions) with backdrops to add to the designated Cosplay areas. Accordingly, the music cues direct social order similarly to the musical cues in theatrical performances.

Still, there will always be hallway performances that organically initiate from Cosplayers. In July 2017, at the Indiana Popular Culture Con in Indianapolis, Indiana, Lily Pichu played corresponding theme songs with her melodica (a piano-key style harmonica) for the Cosplayers she randomly encountered (Ratcliffe 2017). Perhaps, Pichu was "enchanting" and possibly nicely "trolling" Cosplayers at this convention (Ratcliffe 2017). Nevertheless, the noise levels at conventions already compete with Cosplayer's dialogue and interactions with audience members, thus adding music would create another layer to the cacophony of sounds.

The Cosplay environment is best understood as using Bakhtin's concept of "carnivalesque" (1968). Cosplayers are encouraged to interact and pose with convention attendees and fans, which creates settings ripe and expectant for eccentric behaviors and performances. Even designated Cosplay spaces offer a carnivalesque environment for Cosplayers to perform with theatrical irreverence and satire.

Girl power

Historically, very few females were present in fandoms, and were only seen at conventions because they were in relationships (e.g., sisters, wives, girlfriends) with male fans. Males were once the primary fan convention attendees because the fandoms that composed the greater fan community were male dominant. Over the last few decades, females made inroads into the fandoms, and eventually the number of women began to grow to nearly equal proportions for fan convention attendance (Eventbrite 2015a). As more females participate in fandoms formerly dominated by males, they must negotiate patriarchal constructs, discrimination, harassment, and marginalization.

In 2015, Cosplayers comprised more than 65 percent of the attendees of fan conventions (Eventbrite 2015a). My research confirms there is a significant female presence: of the ninety-eight participants, seventy-four were identified as female Cosplayers (Winge 2006a, 2007, 2017). While this shift in fan demographics should create a power shift, it has not happened to date. Despite more females attending conventions, many fandoms still promote and reward the established hegemonic structures. In fact, women are at a great disadvantage and even at risk in many fandom settings.

Subsequently, it is not surprising that the Cosplay fandom promotes and supports activities commonly deemed stereotypical female in Western society. In the fandom, Cosplayers are empowered and rewarded for skill sets (i.e., sewing, styling, etc.) commonly perceived negatively within mainstream society. The Cosplay fandom embodies communal knowledge and practice, which is empowering for Cosplayers and reinforces the value of designing, construction, sewing, and styling.

Despite the Cosplay fandom being a female-dominant subculture, it does not demonstrate specifically feminist movements or activism. The Cosplay fandom, however, may have its greatest strength in its female members. Cosplayers are responding creatively to the issues laid out in this chapter, which reflects the female-dominant subculture that sets the standards, values, and ideals by which the fandom functions, even if the fandom in not fully aware of it. If the demographics change significantly, these markers will change and have rippling impacts for the structure of the fandom overall.

Summary

The Cosplay fandom is faced with numerous challenges but is responding with creative and innovative solutions. Historically, the strong female presence in the Cosplay fandom has served it well. The female influence encourages disseminating tutorials and supporting positive Cosplay. They also embrace the inclusivity and resulting diversity among Cosplayers. The fandom may find its best solutions in the social structure and communal knowledge. Furthermore, these issues reinvent the Cosplay fandom and environment, which impacts the lived experience of the Cosplayer.

In Chapter 6, I discuss the possible futures of the Cosplay fandom and resulting impacts for Cosplayers. The mass and alternative media exposure and changing demographics are impacting the composition of the fandom, as well as the internal and external criticisms. The Cosplay fandom is growing into a diverse subculture that may fracture into factions or unify to embrace its differences.

6
WORLDS OF COSPLAY FUTURE

Cosplay is growing in popularity, which is traceable to the fandom's prominence in social media, continued media coverage, and numerical increase of Cosplayers at fan conventions. There are benefits and drawbacks to this increasing popularity. While Cosplayers have more access to fan conventions and merchandise, they also face exploitation without permissions, compensation, or consideration.

The Cosplay fandom extends beyond its expected, traditional subcultural spaces (i.e., fan conventions). It is positioned within the larger fandom communities/subcultures, as well as within the popular, Internet, and global culture. Subsequently, Cosplayers have far-reaching influences that are felt in mainstream and fan subcultural economies, popular culture, and fandom subcultures. At the same time, internal and external forces pull and push it into new and unexpected forms, cyclically impacting the Cosplay fandom. The support for the Cosplay fandom grows because of its captivating visual and continual presence on social media and mass media exposure with images of Cosplayers in costumes.

Furthermore, Japanese anime and manga continue to be significant stimuli for the Cosplay fandom. The anime/manga fandom offers opportunities and challenges for Cosplayers in its continued recursive and rebounding association with Japan, which contributes to assumptions about Japanese popular culture and the origins of the Cosplay subculture. I attempt to unpack the misunderstandings surrounding the connections to Japanese popular culture and anime and manga.

As contemporary innovations and creative technologies become more accessible, Cosplay costumes advance to new levels of achievement for desired fantastic bodies and performances. The Cosplay fandom is in the hands of the members who feel committed to the character costume and roleplaying. The supportive social environment of the fandom encourages its growth and inclusivity by promoting meritocracy.

The future of the Cosplay offers opportunities for the fandom to grow into a diverse and unified group, or splinter into factions along the fractures created from issues and disagreements. Mainstream acceptance, mass media exposure, and changing demographics will impact the composition of the fandom. In recent years, the fandom has come under internal criticism for no longer being about fun; instead, it focuses on perfection, which is perceived as encouraging harsh judgments and bullying.

Cosplay popularity and impacts

The increasing popularity of Cosplay is evident around the world. According to the International Costumers' Guild website, there were more than 900 conventions that feature Cosplay events and activities in 2016–17 (ICG 2017). There are continually new fan conventions and Cosplay competitions. Despite the Cosplay fandom's growing popularity, there are very few Cosplay-focused conventions (not counting Furry conventions, where not all Cosplayers feel comfortable or welcome). In recent years, more Cosplay-focused conventions emerged, with enthusiastic response from Cosplayers. Cosplay America, for example, takes place annually in October in North Carolina, United States, and began in 2013. This fan convention focuses on Cosplay activities, placing Cosplayers at the forefront of the convention instead of limiting them to performing in designated spaces and times.

Shuto Con is a fan convention primarily focusing on Cosplay, along with anime/manga and gaming, which was organized by Stefanie Shall and first held in spring 2011, in Lansing, Michigan. Shuto Con is also one of the first conventions that practices "interactive Cosplay," which encourages Cosplayers to not only dress and perform as their favorite characters but also actively interact as their characters with other attendees, whether in costume or not. Shuto Con also has secret Cosplay judges who circulate throughout the convention and interact with Cosplayers in order to select the best character representations to serve as Cosplay Queen and King each year, who are featured on the convention's website (see shutocon.com/intcosplay.html).

Fan conventions focusing on Cosplay or at least making it a primary concentration create space for the fandom in new and noteworthy ways. Frequently, these conventions are organized by Cosplayers for Cosplayers with panels, vendors, and attractions of particular interest to Cosplay, such as costume booths, performance spaces, and costume designers and performers as featured guests. Cosplay conventions, however, bring new pressures for attendance and expenditure necessary to make it profitable and repeatable. Despite the growing popularity of Cosplay and demand for Cosplay celebrities for sponsored events and fan conventions, there still are limited numbers of solely Cosplay-focused conventions.

Cosplayers enjoy interacting with other Cosplayers because the in-person exchanges and communications not only share communal information but also affirm social connections. Interactions between Cosplayers commonly result in positive escalating energy levels, manifesting as louder dialogues or increasingly flamboyant gestures. Moreover, Cosplayers' performance antics escalate as they vie against each other in order to secure the audience's attention. Within the Cosplay fandom, Cosplayers are both audience members and performers, sometimes at the same time, which influences and impacts the performances.

The appeal of fan conventions for Cosplayers is the intentional attentiveness and responsiveness to Cosplay activities and needs. An added benefit is how many more spaces can be secured for Cosplayers' performances and safety. Attendees at fan conventions acknowledge the importance of security personnel, controlled entrances and exits, and attendee badges, which assure fan activities, events, and competitions (Eventbrite 2015b). Furthermore, Cosplayers rely heavily on the convention organizers' security measures to keep them safe while in costumes and performing, especially when nonfans exoticize and eroticize members of the fandom as a focus for sexual harassment and abuses.

Making room for Cosplay

The Cosplay fandom's rapid growth and continuous external attention results in new pressures for Cosplayers, which is further complicated by fan conventions also growing in number of attendees and related sales (Salkowitz 2012). Convention organizers are challenged to find locations large enough to accommodate the growing numbers of fans and events. And, every year there are more fan conventions emerging to meet the demands of these growing fandoms. Consequently, all fandoms are experiencing an influx of attendees, which, combined with intense media attention brought by the Cosplay fandom, will impact the greater fandom community overall. The continued pressures on the members of these fandoms results in disputes and issues, especially regarding fans who consume space and interrupt the flow at conventions.

Superficially, Cosplayers may appear more extroverted than many other fandoms' members because of their public performances. Instead, many Cosplayers cope with performance anxiety, and still others are introverts who have difficulties even interacting within the fandom. In fact, the people who are typically drawn to fantasy characters with such deep devotion are often introverts who enjoy the escapism of a story over the fearfulness of real life. Furthermore, new, young, and more introverted Cosplayers struggle with the multiple demands and expectations from the fandom, fans, audiences, and other fandoms.

Fan conventions have become a safe space for like-minded individuals to enjoy sharing their love of genre, story, and/or characters with others. Attendees, recognizing the difficulties for introverts and socially awkward individuals, employ "geek lures," such as caffeinated drinks and sugary and salty foods, roleplaying games, comic books, and anime viewings, in the private rooms with plenty of signage to attract like-minded people. The result is floors and floors of "party rooms," each with its theme and unique lures catering to vast arrays of geek fetishes.

For Cosplayers, each party room becomes a performance space to practice their quick wit or rehearsed dialogue, and the hallways host photography opportunities as well as the occasional sword or lightsaber duel (with prop weapons). It is rare to find a Cosplayer hosting a party room, which more directly reflects their need for space to accommodate all of their costume elements and time to prepare and dress in their costume more than their desire to host. When Cosplayers host party rooms, however, the space becomes a competitive performance space with each new Cosplayer demanding her moment on the stage.

Cosplayers attract large crowds in the public spaces of the conventions, which cause serious congestion issues for movement, viewing, and shopping. Since many conventions are at maximum capacity for the venues, the additional congestion caused by Cosplayers posing for photos or performing in hallways and open spaces becomes points of contention. Moreover, when Cosplayers or their fans (and gawkers) block vendors', artists', and dealers' tables, there are more issues that require the attention of convention organizers.

Cosplay everyday

Many fans enjoy being Cosplayers to the degree that they desire to extend their Cosplay experiences beyond the fan convention or occasional party or event. The ways that Cosplay manifests in their everyday lifestyle reflects the individual's commitment, devotion, and possible obsession, such as social media posts updating friends and fans of their latest character selection, costume design, and construction progress.

The Cosplay lifestyle manifests beyond simply wearing costumes at fan conventions but usually includes the costume (or portions of it) to some degree. Cosplay activities outside of but relating directly to the fandom convention range from preparation for the next convention to socializing with other Cosplayers to supporting the fandom: Cosplayers participate in the lifestyle when learning skills for making costumes, producing tutorial videos, socializing with other Cosplayers, competing in competitions, posting images of Cosplayers in costume to social media sites, and similar online sites. Cosplay is a comprehensive lifestyle that has the potential to consume a significant amount of Cosplayers' time and money.

In addition, one of the more formal ways that Cosplayers extend the Cosplay experiences in everyday life is by practicing Disneybound, which is dressing similar to a Disney character without wearing a costume, that is, dressing in everyday fashions in color combinations and proportions similar to a specific Disney character, with an accessory that calls attention to special details. Disneybound Bambi is accomplished by wearing light brown clothing and a scarf with white dots, or Disneybound Mickey Mouse wears high-waist red shorts and black T-shirt with white socks and yellow tennis shoes.

In 2012, Leslie Kay created and popularized Disneybound, which encouraged Disney fans to abstractly dress as characters while at the theme parks (Disneybound 2012). Kay began Disneybound because Disneyland's dress code does not allow visitors over fourteen years old to wear costumes (Liddane 2015). Disneybound allows older fans to show their love for characters by strategically dressing in representative types of dress selected from current fashions that reflect the character they want to portray, which is wearing representative hues in similar proportions and locations on the body. A fan of Alice from *Alice in Wonderland*, for example, could wear a blue sweater over a white shirt, which shows the collar and cuffs, jeans, and a white hairband.

Kay created the Disneybound.com website, which suggests ensembles for Disney fans that mimic specific characters' dress. The Disneybound community labels images for social media dispersal of their Disneybound dress with hashtags such as #Disneybound or #DisneyboundChallenge posted on social media sites, such as Facebook, Twitter, Snapchat, Instagram, and Tumblr. In time, Disneybounders began wearing their costume-related dress to work and social occasions beyond the theme parks. This social media trend led to the addition of a Disneybound panel at 2017 San Diego Comic-Con.

In addition to the sartorial practice of Disneybound, there is Princessing and Princing, which range from dressing and performing as princesses and princess to wearing portions of costumes or clothes color blocked similar to a princess or prince character. "Princessing" is dressing and roleplaying a princess, usually a Disney princess, and "Princing" is where individuals dress as princes, again primarily Disney princes. Princing appears to be far less common than Princessing. Those who dress in costume may do it simply for purposes of entertainment rather than for charity and fund-raising.

Cosplayers participate in Disneybound and Princessing/Princing because it allows them to extend Cosplay into everyday life. These practices allow them to share their love of their favorite characters beyond the fandom too. A common trait among fandoms and often fan convention organizers is altruism. Subsequently, fan conventions and Cosplay groups commonly donate portions of the profits to charities and organize nonprofit groups who take part in charitable activities.

Second Life (SL) and virtual reality (VR) games offer innovative potential for the Cosplay fandom. Games such as SL and Sims extend Cosplay beyond the convention and into the digital and virtual realms. Cosplay is searchable on the SL Marketplace website, where digital costume designers post their Cosplay designs for sale, such as "M&I" Cosplay by Mustadio Gans and GateWay to Cosplay by Hathor Ronas. SL users, or residents, dress and style SL avatars as Cosplay characters and interact within the SL worlds. In addition, SL residents share images of their SL avatar dressed in Cosplay costumes on social media and personal blogs, such as Virtual Neko and Harmony Sandalphon.

Currently, VR requires equipment to fully experience the emersion of virtual worlds, but with Google Cardboard and a smart phone VR is more easily accessible. VR offers means for Cosplayers to interact with other Cosplayers in costumes without the need of a fan convention or even being in the same geographic location. It also makes it possible to design and wear elaborate costumes with details that are not achievable in the real world. VR enhances Cosplayers' performances with elaborate backgrounds, special effects, and extravagant costumes.

VR also poses problems for the Cosplay fandom as it creates limited-consequences spaces, where users may not be Cosplayers, or worse, and exploit the fandom. VRCosplay is a company that produces Cosplay pornography and virtual sexual activity, for example. This type of exploitation is not beneficial for the fandom, which is trying to humanize and protect the members of the subculture.

Successful Hollywood movies from the science-fiction and fantasy genres lead to the production and marketing of official merchandise and characters, which is consumed by fans and Cosplayers alike. Official merchandise, such as T-shirts, hats, and bags, is worn to demonstrate dedication and fan status to those who recognize the semiotics. As the apparel and accessories of fan merchandise become more costume-esque, Cosplayers will demonstrate character devotion within mainstream everyday dress.

Official fan merchandise that also functions as everyday dress serves a dual purpose for Cosplayers wishing to show the love of character and extend Cosplay into the real world. The Hogwarts collection adult clothing line from BlackMilk Clothing, for example, features shiny leggings and dresses in four colors and corresponding emblems for each house from Harry Potter: versions of Ron Weasley's sweaters with large "H" or "R" initials on the front; Hogwarts's emblem overall shorts lined with the four houses' colors; crop tops and skirts with graphics inspired by the *Harry Potter* books; and a draped top/dress that resembles Harry Potter's invisibility cloak. This costume-esque style of official merchandise is a response to the popularity of Cosplay and Cosplayers' demands in the market in addition to the success of fan movies, literature, and anime/manga.

The informal costuming practices that Cosplayers incorporate Cosplay into their everyday lives include dressing in official merchandise that resembles portions of the character's costume. In this way, fans from any fandom wearing official fan merchandise are not necessarily distinguishable from Cosplayers in everyday life; that is, Cosplayers are read as fans instead of the characters with whom they identify.

Cosplayers also bring costumes into the real world, which extends the fantasy of the characters and storylines. Some Cosplayers wear portions of their actual costumes or official merchandise in real life, such as Disney princess' tiaras, *My Little Pony* socks and hats with pastel rainbow color schemes, and *Harry Potter*'s Hogwarts school scarves in the houses' colors. This type of official fan merchandise is available through larger retailers and online.

There is a danger to the Cosplay fandom with this blurring of lines between the real world and fan activities and dress primarily reserved for conventions, competitions, and sanctioned activities. Despite the positive feelings associated with dressing as their beloved characters in everyday life, they risk being identified as a "Cosplayer" with the associated negative associations by the mainstream. The fandom also risks diluting the significance and meaning of the official gatherings and complete transformations into characters. The Cosplay fandom will need to redefine itself as it exists in the real world with these new expectations and limitations.

Buying and selling Cosplay

Cosplay is an expensive activity, and for the rare few Cosplayers there is money to be made. It is primarily outsiders, however, who are reaping most of the financial profit from the buying and selling of Cosplay. While the subculture is left to contend with negative byproducts (harassment, assault, etc.), those outside the subculture are financially profiting from the sensationalism of the fandom that attracts fans and spectators. The opportunities for internal profits are still relatively new for many Cosplayers, and exact figures have not been researched to date.

Cosplayers inadvertently promote companies that produce the films, literature, and animation disseminating their favorite characters. Cosplayers dressed as Wonder Woman celebrates their love of the character and storylines, but it also supports and promotes the media associated with the character, such as the 2017 film *Wonder Woman*. These character-driven promotions offer financial benefits to the corporations and fans, even if both Cosplayers and the corporations do not fully acknowledge the exchange.

An analysis of the fandom's character trends could offer corporations useful data for producing and marketing media reflecting fan trends. The

Cosplay fandom's demands on the market could lead to more character-driven productions and female leads. Closely related, the potential for financial profit derived from the sale of all types of goods and services associated with the Cosplay fandom drives the expanding availability and market of merchandise, stores, and services for Cosplayers and their fans. While fans in general are the overall market, Cosplayers are the primary target audience. To this end, in recent years, official merchandise includes more costume-esque dress items and accessories, which offers fans the "Cosplay experience."

Both online and brick-and-mortar stores, as well as convention vendors, provide products for Cosplayers to create their costumes, such as fabric, wigs, contact lenses, props, and makeup. In addition, Cosplay merchandise includes books, magazines, posters, and signed photographs as well as novelty items and action figures of celebrity Cosplayers. These stores may also sell costumes and related props that are suitable for mainstream Halloween costumes but would not be of the quality demanded by Cosplayers.

Fan conventions commonly have vendors' and/or dealers' rooms, which is usually a relatively large space that accommodates numerous vendors with an array of fan merchandise. Vendors and dealers cater to numerous types of fans with merchandise that ranges from handmade to digital to high-end production official merchandise. Vendor and/or dealer booths at conventions are all located in one space that is usually crowded with shopping fans. Very little of the merchandise would qualify as costume elements for Cosplayers, but this depends on the convention. At conventions heavily populated with Cosplayers, there tends to be more costume-related products and services available.

Services for Cosplayers are some of the least organized or marketed because the need is difficult to anticipate in any specificity or predictability. Those persons with marketable skills commonly advertise their services to their target market online. Subsequently, Cosplayers tend to find services, such as hirable craftpersons to make weapons or armor, by word of mouth at conventions or other social gatherings, as well as through social media. This is changing for fan entrepreneurs with e-commerce and social media business accounts. Etsy, for example, includes many vendors who offer Cosplay costumes, props, weapons, and other accessories or dress items.

Many Cosplay vendors are also Cosplayers, who intimately understand the market and its demands from internal fan experiences. These Cosplayer entrepreneurs propel the growing Cosplay economy, as well as market and sell products and services back to the fandom with expected details and quality. Furthermore, the availability and use of e-commerce provides the fandom with an inexpensive venue with low overhead and access to the Cosplay market from which to purchase and participate as entrepreneurs. Cosplay costume designers' services and goods are available at conventions and online.

The benefits of visiting a costume designer at a convention affords Cosplayers opportunities to select fabrics and secure proper measurements for custom costumes, in addition to trying on premade costumes in a dressing room/area and having the costume custom-fitted to the body. Some Cosplay costumers run a shop from their hotel rooms or booths in the vendor spaces during fan conventions, where they sell Cosplay costumes.

The Cosplay fandom is not self-sustaining now, nor has it ever been, as it relies on other fandoms for most of its conventions and genres for characters, as well as merchandise and even portions of costumes. Cosplay, however, is moving toward independence from other hosting fandoms even if they are not completely aware of this movement. Cosplayers are doing so by creating Cosplay-focused events, activities, and competitions, as well as conventions solely for the Cosplay fandom.

The buying and selling of Cosplay is most notable in the use of licensed and branded official merchandise. This type of merchandise allows fans to wear apparel and accessories bearing the signs and symbols that demonstrate their love of and loyalty to specific characters and storylines. In addition, official merchandise is also available as complete costumes for Halloween, which may be adapted and improved for more detailed character costumes for fan conventions.

Economic impacts

In *The Week*'s article "Why the Rise of Cosplay Is a Bad Sign for the U.S. Economy," James Pethokoukis predicts dire outcomes for the United States' economy if Cosplay continues to grow in popularity (Pethokoukis 2014). Pethokoukis reaches these conclusions by comparing the lifestyles of un/underemployed young adults in Japan to those in the United States. He further suggests that the cause-and-effect relationship between Japan's increasing interests in Cosplay is the result of young adults having excess time available for leisure activities, which contributes to their economic struggle. Offering a contrary point of view, Adam Ozimek's article in *Forbes* "No, The Rise in Cosplay Is Not a Bad Sign for the U.S. Economy" refutes Pethokoukis's claims noting the distinct differences between the economic structures of Japan and the United States before the popularity of Cosplay (Ozimek 2014). The latter article further notes the additional complexities impacting both economies. But, both two articles have sparked additional debates that continue to be discussed in regards to the popularity, consumption, and economic expectations related to Cosplay.

In 2014, Eventbrite sold US$1.5 billion in fan convention ticket sales for 180 countries (Eventbrite 2015a). US fan conventions earned US$600 million in gross ticket sales in 2013, with increases each subsequent year (Eventbrite 2015a).

In 1992, Gen Con broke records for attendance at any gaming fan convention with 18,000 attendees. I attended Gen Con that year in Milwaukee, Wisconsin, and in many subsequent years. In 2017, I attended Gen Con's fiftieth anniversary with more than 200,000 attendees in Indianapolis, Indiana. Emerald City Comic-Con in Seattle, Washington, for example, began with 2,500 attendees in 2003, and in 2015 there were 80,000 attendees, and in 2016 the convention sold out (Whitten 2015). Furthermore, the economic impacts for businesses within a few blocks of the convention site are likely to secure eight times the revenue of fan convention ticket sales, which were more than US$5 billion in 2014 (Whitten 2015). The challenge for fan convention organizers is to find spaces large enough for the growing numbers of fans who want to attend (and securing competent staff).

Also contributing to Cosplay's global economic impacts are costume and costume-related sales. In 2012, sales of Cosplay costumes (not including props or technology) collected US$11.7 billion in revenue on the global market, and CRI predicts that Cosplay costume sales will increase to US$23.6 billion by 2019 (CRI 2014). Japanese Cosplay costumes' annual sales total 40 billion yen ($500 million) in 2009 from the Yano Research Institute (A.K. and K.N.C. 2011). China Partytime, in China, the largest retailer for Cosplay wigs and costumes in 2014, had annual sales of US$179.8 million for wigs and US$181.1 million in Cosplay costumes in 2014 (Quamnet 2016).

Regardless of the specific outcomes from these debates, the discussions demonstrate that the growing popularity of Cosplay has the potential to influence economic realms that reach beyond the fandom. It further suggests Cosplay has the capacity for significant financial profit (even if not necessarily for the Cosplayers). Subsequently, it is difficult to dismiss Cosplay as a simple "hobby" when it is also considered a predictor for economic outcomes for entire countries.

Cosplay subcultural economy

Drawing on Pierre Bourdieu's culture capital theory about capital contributing to social status and life (1986), McCudden (2011) and Brownie and Graydon (2016) suggest that fandoms participate in a fan cultural economy with capital feeding the production and distribution channels, as well as the social structure. Fiske further extends Bourdieu's metaphor of culture as an economy by describing the fan cultural system as a "shadow cultural economy," where the use of the term "shadow" reflects how the fandom's cultural economy exists outside of but parallel to the mainstream cultural systems (1992: 30, 40). Fan cultural capital is not readily available to every fan equally, which creates a dynamic and competitive social system (Fiske 1992).

The cultural capital in the Cosplay fandom ranges from merchandise and costumes to images and social media posts to poses and performances. The Cosplay fandom demonstrates its shadow cultural economy with products and services offered and consumed by Cosplayers. The fandom's cultural capital and economy contribute to the subcultural social structure. Fiske suggests that access to the fandom and its social status is denied to those who exhibit accurate cultural capital (1992: 47–48). The Cosplay fandom, while not a strict gatekeeper, will evaluate peers harshly for inaccurate or poorly designed costumes. There is a social hierarchy, however, and outsiders may feel intimidated to participate in the fandom. The Cosplay fandom's social assets provide mobility within the fandom.

The Cosplay shadow cultural economy lurks in the recesses of the mainstream culture. The Cosplay cultural economy is highly dependent on other fandoms, such as anime/manga, science fiction, and Steampunk, for its success. Furthermore, Cosplayers impact other fandoms, especially those who nourish the Cosplay lifestyle. The anime/manga fandom provides Cosplayers with characters; in turn, Cosplayers' portrayals stimulate the interest in elements of Japanese popular culture.

In the shadows, the Cosplay fandom grows unfettered into unfamiliar spaces with a cultural economy that dwarfs other fandoms. The mainstream markets co-opt subcultural economies and capital for economic profit. Cosplay is also a financially profitable fandom, which has demonstrated significant growth potential for fan convention organizers and vendors.

Challenges to the Cosplay fandom

Cosplayers are at times subject to harassment and public scrutiny (Thomas 2014: 32). Female Cosplayers in costume have mentioned being harassed by outsiders or spectators, as have Cosplayers who crossplay as female characters. Some Cosplayers speculate the harassment toward female Cosplayers happens because those outside the Cosplay subculture interpret the subculture as exhibiting blatant sexual overtones and thus the costumes imply sexual consent. Subsequently, spectators and non-Cosplayers touch and grope female Cosplayers in costume with inappropriate and sometimes illegal mannerisms, even in public settings. In general, Cosplayers are growing concerned about the increasing harassment, not only from sexual assault but also from damage to their costumes. And, especially in the case of Furries, costumes are very expensive to create and to maintain; it is not acceptable to "pet" or stroke a Furry Cosplayer without prior permission so as to prevent soiling or mutilation of the fursuit.

In general, most Cosplayers I spoke with noted harassment, threats, and unwanted sexual advancements to them and friends at fan conventions, but primarily recounted examples of bullying happening on social media. These aggressions, however, are not confined to specific environments or focused on particular Cosplayers. Instead, bullying and harassment happen across the larger fandom community, and Cosplayers are convenient targets when dressed in costumes.

Fortunately, in-person violence toward crossplay Cosplayers is rare, but it does happen. In 2013, in Guangzhou, China, a man walking home from an anime event while costumed as a female character was attacked by six men, who verbally and physically assaulted the crossplay Cosplayer because they felt the male Cosplayer had fooled them into believing he was an attractive female (Tackett 2013). Once outside the fandom or convention spaces, Cosplayers are evaluated by mainstream values, which may expose them to discrimination and even violence.

Sexuality and gender contribute to the complexities of and dangers to the Cosplay fandom. The observed ritual and fluidity associated with gender, sexuality, and even the corporeal body is highlighted when Cosplayers crossplay characters. Cosplayers indicated that crossplay provides agency and additional attention from the spectators and the media. This attention from outsiders, however, sometimes turns aggressive, harassing, and exploitive.

Cosplayers experience financial challenges associated with attending conventions and participating in Cosplay activities in addition to those associated with constructing the costume. Attending a fan convention has expected expenses, including attendee badges (tickets), travel, parking, food, and hotel lodgings. Additionally, financial expenditures associated with costumes vary depending on the character and Cosplayers' resourcefulness, but even inexpensive costumes require time and financial commitment.

Cosplay rules

Fandom conventions are creating extensive rules for Cosplayers in attempt to manage the associated harassment and complaints. The general rules regarding interacting with convention attendees, especially Cosplayers, are increasing under the pretense of protecting Cosplayers and making conventions safer. Some fans from other fandoms blame Cosplayers for the difficulties at fan conventions and resulting restrictions imposed from the new rules. As a result, Cosplayers experience marginalization from other fandoms, and, in turn, some Cosplayers dismiss members of other fandoms. In fact, Cosplayers are unwelcome at some fan conventions, but the financial revenue, additional media attention, and interest from attendees associated with Cosplay necessitate rules instead of Cosplay prohibition.

The fan convention rules governing Cosplay have complicated attending conventions and are found to be oppressive by some Cosplayers and other attendees when the rules impact fandoms at large. Furthermore, conventions' rules intended to make the space safer and family friendly tend to specifically target female Cosplayers to modify their costumes and roleplaying behaviors. Subsequently, Cosplayers who roleplay female characters are concerned about how the rules will compromise the integrity of their character and costume.

Following the examples of Asian fan conventions, European and North American conventions began designating safe spaces for Cosplayers in which to pose and where photographing Cosplayers are freely permitted. While these spaces are typically demarked with only taped lines on the floor and a few small printed signs, convention attendees acknowledge the space designated for Cosplayers. Amateur and professional photographers gather when interesting Cosplayers enter the space and pose for pictures. Outside of designated spaces, persons wanting to photograph or video Cosplayers are expected to ask permission prior. Some fan convention organizers post these rules/guidelines, but most attendees are familiar with the unwritten rules for Cosplayers.

Cosplayers are accused of distracting convention attendees from vendor booths and, when fans gather, they contribute to congestion that obstructs vendors and artist tables. They are also blamed for the congestion in narrow walkways and hallways, which complicates Cosplayers' positions at fan conventions. Addressing criticisms, convention organizers attempt to find creative solutions. In 2017, Gen Con held a costume parade at specific times on each of the three days of the convention along a predetermined path, and the participating Cosplayers were expected to walk quickly and not pause to pose or perform. Despite this parade being a way for everyone to view the Cosplayers and keep them from clogging the walkways, spectators complained about their inability to clearly view or photograph the walking Cosplayers, how rapidly the Cosplayers were forced to keep moving, and the lack of information about the actual path of the parade.

While fan conventions early on adopted weapon restrictions, rules related to Cosplay costumes are more recent incarnations of dress codes. Weapon rules focus on safety restrictions that protect everyone attending the convention, while costume rules restrict Cosplayers' dress in hopes to dissuade molesters and harassers. Regardless of the initial reasoning, Cosplayers are the focus of many fan convention rules, which places responsibility on the victims and situates dress at the epicenter of these continuing discussions and issues.

Pellet and BB guns and other types of projectile guns are forbidden at most fan conventions, and related weapon rules are becoming more strictly enforced. When Cosplayers are forced to surrender their prop weapons, specifically guns, they resort to holding signs that state "pew pew" or carrying pictures of the guns that should accompany their character costumes. In fact, the creative ways

Cosplayers in which adapt to the rules suggests as a fandom it will thrive as a dynamic system.

Some conventions have chosen to prohibit all prop and replica guns due to safety concerns, especially after an incident at the Phoenix Comic-Con in May 2017 (Burton 2017). While Cosplayers nearly universally comply with these requests/rules/guidelines (even if not posted prior to their arrival at the convention), they may express their resentments primarily through social media posts and social circles at conventions. Some Cosplayers, however, are upset about the bans on weapons because it disrupts the accuracy of the character's appearance (Burton 2017). The Cosplay fandom responds with clever ways to Cosplay characters and storylines without their weapons including holding signs poking fun at the weapon prop bans, such as "BANG" and "missing weapon due to prop weapons ban" are scrawled on cardboard with a marker, or pictures are taken before and after their convention attendance. The fandom's humor contributes to their resiliency to these external complications.

Unlike convention organizers, who have official channels to promote rules and guidelines, Cosplayers have some difficulties setting rules and limitations on access to the fandom from outsiders. In addition to harassment and bullying, Cosplayers are experiencing unique issues because as more families attend conventions, there are more opportunities for parents to leave their children to watch Cosplayers perform. While most Cosplayers are happy to interact with children, they are not caregivers and do not want the added responsibilities of minors. In recent years, Cosplayers are warning families not to leave children unaccompanied: "Cosplayers are not babysitters!"

Within the Cosplay fandom, there are unwritten rules or guidelines for Cosplayers. "Have fun, don't be a dick" is a common motto among Cosplayers, and is put into writing at some convention Cosplay events, on T-shirts, and bumper stickers. This motto is a reminder how the activity of Cosplay is an escape from everyday life into fantasy; Cosplay is not meant to cause drama and conflicts. The fandom encourages supportive and compassionate relationships among Cosplayers. Thus, Cosplayers causing drama are gently reminded that Cosplay is meant to be fun by someone saying, "Have fun, don't be a dick."

Of course, there are issues at fan conventions and within the Cosplay fandom that are not addressed by the rules. Cosplayers refer to many of these types of incidents as "drama." The Cosplay fandom's complex social system utilizes gossip as a valid means of communication. The role of gossip within the fandom and convention cannot be understated; gossip is essentially the primary way new information is disseminated. Unfortunately, this type of communication is not reliable and may lead to misunderstandings and disputes. Sometimes the drama and conflicts from interactions with other fandoms at conventions continue past the weekend and spills over to social media, which then publicly air disagreements and misunderstandings.

Consequently, all these factors are impacting and changing the Cosplay fandom in predictable and unexpected ways. Spaces designated for Cosplay posing, performing, and photography are necessities at fan conventions, for example, while it is unknown how these protected areas impact foot traffic and pathway congestion. Overall, Cosplayers serve as both attractions and detriments for fan conventions, which requires responsive rules that facilitate the needs of both the fandom and the convention.

Weights and measures of Cosplayers

While Cosplayers freely offer their costumed selves, characters, and performances for judgment in competitions and for feedback from fans and friends online, they are also the targets for criticism from many other directions. Attendees at fan conventions are annoyed with the inconvenience and "gawker" congestion created around Cosplayers posing for pictures and performing for an audience. In addition, the media criticize Cosplayers because of hypersexualized costumes and bodies, as well as provocative behaviors or performances.

There is a movement from various fandoms to criticize Cosplayers for a variety of concerns ranging from blocking vendors' or artists' tables to causing congestion in the hallways to wearing revealing costumes that are inappropriate for families and children. While these are all valid concerns, Cosplayers argue that the fandom is beneficial to convention vendors because they spend significant amounts of money on costumes and props, fan merchandise, and concessions. In addition, Cosplayers attract media attention for fan conventions, entertain convention attendees, and stimulate dialog about characters, genres, and storylines.

In addition, the Cosplay fandom has internal struggles as members are under attack from other Cosplayers. Some Cosplayers suggest their harshest criticisms are from inside the fandom, from their peer Cosplayers. While it is not commonplace, Cosplayers sometimes attack one another with online "flames" or harsh critiques about costumes and performances. Also, the Internet creates a (virtual) space fertile for additional external boldness and even malice toward Cosplayers for the mere participation in the fandom. Cosplayers who give punitive critiques argue they are attempts to protect the integrity of the character and the fandom. To this end, some Cosplayers use these types of critiques to improve their character costume and/or performances.

Cosplayers portraying female characters are the most prevalent focus of criticism (and harassment), which commonly concentrates on their revealing dress exposing their bodies. When many of the fantasy female characters in comic books, graphic novels, and movies are hypersexualized, emphasizing their bodies with minimal dress, it is not surprising that Cosplayers roleplaying female characters present similar bodies and dress. Some Cosplayers, however, interpret characters to be sexier with more revealing clothing than their original media. Consequently, Cosplayers who portray hypersexualized characters are susceptible.

Fans also critique Cosplayers, especially Cosplay celebrities and models. Their public identity/image makes them a convenient target. As previously mentioned, Yaya Han was heavily criticized for possibly having breast implants. Female Cosplayers, in particular, are under scrutiny for being women, for their character choices, or how they choose to visually represent a character.

The Cosplay fandom is highly responsive to external stimuli. Within days of the release of the movie *Wonder Woman* (2017), there were tutorial videos available online demonstrating how to create the specific armor and dress from Wonder Woman's two primary looks/styles in the movie. This type of nimble response is common in the Cosplay fandom, reflecting it is a living social system and culture. In a similar manner, they are responding to the criticisms of individual Cosplayers and the fandom overall with race-, sex-, and body-positive activisms and working with convention organizers to create safer Cosplay spaces.

Image-centric

As discussed previously, the Cosplay fandom is image-centric and this is unlikely to diminish in the future of the subculture. Instead, it is likely that new technologies and social media venues will increase the fandom's exposure to the public and continue to fuel the already image-centric behaviors. The importance of photographs to Cosplayers is unlikely to wane in the future, especially in the light of improving and new technologies and how they interface with social media platforms. As new social media platforms become more visual oriented, Cosplayers will quickly adopt and utilize these new platforms to share their Cosplay characters/personas.

The advances in smartphones and related applications provide even novices with high-resolution images and videos. The paths of dissemination for videos are similar to those of still images; however, currently there are fewer online platforms for videos than images. There are likely to be more video-friendly ways of sharing this format as the demand increases. Recent innovations offer the fandom still images imbued with movement that resemble the special effects used to create the moving photographs as seen in the *Harry Potter* movies. Similar to animated GIFs (graphic interchange format), the cinemagraph (video-photograph), Flixel (application), or Live Photos (an iPhone feature) allow static images to embed short videos. Live Photos, for example, captures a video vignette of a character's performance within a still image that is activated each time the image is digitally accessed.[1]

As the technology to make videos has become more accessible and user-friendly, Cosplayers utilize videos as tutorials for costume construction, makeup application, and performance choreography. Furthermore, the integration and use of videos into the fandom brings to life the characters with more consideration for the performances of Cosplay rather than just static images. Cosplayers are already accessing VR technologies in order to enhance and extend the Cosplay experience.

The Internet and fans

Cosplayers use the Internet as a virtual space to connect with their peers from the fandom, seek advice, create tutorials, and share characters. Social media sites provide ways to distribute Cosplay characters and costumes to a wide array of people. Forums offer opportunities to ask questions, seek support, and share accomplishments. Fan fiction and fan art sites allow Cosplayers to share their creative interpretations of characters and storylines. YouTube serves as a means to disseminate videos featuring costume construction tutorials, fan music and performance videos, and vloggers (video blog) videocasts.

Posting images and videos of their character costumes and performances make Cosplayers particularly susceptible to negative interactions online. While these online posts bring support and positive reviews, Cosplayers also risk bullying from outsiders as well as harsh critiques. Cosplayers who post images of themselves dressed as their chosen fictional characters online are vulnerable. Some sites monitor interactions and support reporting issues in order to protect online users and facilitate productive sharing of information and communications. Cosplayers are not alone in finding ways to cope with online issues; many fandoms complain about bullying and harassment on the Internet.

Mass media and social media

The mass media and social media function in juxtaposition to one another in the ways in which Cosplayers are exposed and revealed to the rest of the world. The mass media covers Cosplayers as the exoticized Other at fandom conventions with external interest. Social media provide an intimate view of the Cosplay fandom and individual Cosplayers revealing internal experiences. While Cosplayers take the coverage of the fandom in the mass media and social media for granted, they are essential for the continued growth and expansion of the fandom.

The future of Cosplay relies on maintaining this balance between internal and external impacts and outcomes. This balance assures continued interest for potential new Cosplayers and feeds the fandom's need for attention. The symbiotic relationship between the fandom and the media nourishes both with information and attention. Furthermore, the media has a dichotomous role in the Cosplay fandom. Both alternative and mass media operate in concert reporting on the Cosplay fandom. Media reports about the Cosplay fandom demystify portions of the fandom while further exoticizing it for mainstream consumption. These media stories encourage curious people to learn more about the fandom while at the same time expose the fandom's sensitive areas.

Regardless of external or internal mediated versions of Cosplayer and their characters, the fan identities exist in dichotomous paradigms. The character identity is constructed from personal love and appreciation of the character while its primarily exhibition and consumption is public. The ways Cosplayers' and their characters' identities are revealed in the media, and social media expose intimate details about the Cosplay fandom and its members.

Cosplay and Japan

Even among Cosplayers there are misunderstandings about Japan's role in the Cosplay fandom. Some Cosplayers even become angry when confronted with the knowledge that Cosplay did not originate in Japan or that it is not a popular activity among mainstream Japanese society. Still, Cosplay has undeniable and complex connections to Japan that defy straightforward explanations. Cosplayers demonstrate an increasing affection for anime and manga and associated Japanese culture. The increasing popularity of portraying anime and manga characters further seals the bonds between Cosplay and Japan.

In Tokyo, there are districts that cater to fandoms such as Cosplayers. Retailers and merchandisers support the Cosplay fan subculture by providing products that appeal to Cosplayers and their fans alike. There are even Cosplay cafés, where Cosplayers are welcome and the staff dress in character costumes. Despite recognizing the financial benefits from the Cosplay fandom, Japanese mainstream society continues to marginalize Cosplayers.

Japanese anime and manga continue to be driving forces behind the continued interest in the Cosplay fandom. The anime and manga genre(s) offer dynamic, three-dimensional characters with impressive costumes and styling that Cosplayers fall in love with and want to portray and perform. These storylines further offer opportunities to infuse creativity into Cosplay costumes, portrayals, and performances. Consequently, Japanese anime and manga is an enticing lure to many Cosplayers, ensuring a continued relationship between the genres and the fandom.

Cosplay costumes

Cosplay costumes are at the fundamental foundation of the fandom with the beloved characters and storylines serving as the foundations. Designing, constructing, styling, and wearing costumes define the Cosplayer, which in turn establishes and contributes to the subsequent interactions, poses, and performances. The costume further operates as a vehicle for the Cosplayer to engage fully with other Cosplayers, audience members, and other fandoms. Cosplayers rely on the nonverbal communication of the costume and overall appearance to attract an audience and visually establish the character with performances.

Cosplay costumes are constantly under evaluation from people both internal and external to the fandom. The criteria that determine a "good" or "bad" costume vary radically from insiders to outsiders. Effort and experience are rewarded within the fandom, whereas outsiders expect perfection and/or entertainment with the character's portrayals and performances. Members of the fandom, however, may evaluate experienced Cosplayers harshly for costumes lacking key elements or poor quality. In competitions, Cosplayers are often rewarded for costumes demonstrating lengthy construction processes and elaborate details.

The Cosplay fandom welcomes everyone or at least everyone who is willing to don portions of characters' costumes (posing and performances are optional but encouraged). Still, anyone wearing a costume is not necessarily a Cosplayer or wants to be identified as such. The various levels of Cosplay participation reflect the commitment of the Cosplayer to character immersion, which is usually evident in the level of detailed elements and costume design.

Costume technologies

Cosplayers have an intimate relationship with technologies that are often overlooked because it is disguised within the costume and performance. Inside the moving extensions of the human body, costumes frequently hide motorized armature as well as associated software that programs and controls the movements. Even the standard sewing machine represents a significant mode of technology used by most Cosplayers, which becomes easier to use with new iterations and computerization. The availability of specialized machines, such as embroidery and quilting machines, allows Cosplayers more direct control when designing and constructing their costumes.

Furthermore, close examination of the fandom's costume design and construction processes demonstrates their reliance on technologies and related innovations when they create complicated costumes, props, and weapons. Cosplayers and Cosplay costume designers are regularly accessing and adopting technologies spanning from sewing machines to Andio computers to 3D printers, as well as innovative materials, such as Worbla.

As technological advancements are made accessible to the general public, it also benefits the Cosplay fandom. Moreover, there is no gatekeeping for these technologies within the fandom. In fact, anyone interested in learning new skills and/or technologies will find open-source resources[2] and support from other Cosplayers. Furthermore, Cosplayers push technologies forward to meet their growing demands for intricate and complex costumes.

Cosplayer lived experience

Martin Heidegger (2010) suggests the experience of *being* for a person is understood in the individual's relationships to the constructed world, things, and others. There are three essential phases for the experience of *being*: (1) essential thinking of *being*; (2) dwelling in the vicinity of *being*; and (3) truth of *being* (George 2000: 153–86; see also Heidegger 2010). Furthermore, a person's thinking and belonging (togetherness) constitutes the identity of *being*, which can be understood within appropriation (Heidegger 2010: 36–42). Adding to Heidegger's understanding of *being* is Max van Manen's *lived experience*, which encourages research to understand the human experiences in the ways they are reflexively and socially constructed (1989: 35–39).

The lived experience of *being* a Cosplayer occupies a distinct space within larger fan communities. They experience *being* as part of the Cosplay fandom and any fandoms from which they select/create characters. Balancing their multifaceted positionality across so many fandoms is wrought with complications. Cosplayers, however, value their multiple fan identities because it provides access at fan conventions, insider fandom information, and a greater sense of belonging.

Being is about revealing and concealing identity within specific experience activities and "play" as the non-rehearsed performances in the fandom (see Heidegger 2010). Similarly, the identity of the Cosplayer is both revealed and concealed when wearing the character's costume. As the Cosplayer ritually reincarnates the self, she never truly returns to her original identity because the Cosplay experience forever changes her. The authentic essence *being* the Cosplayer is to experience the world through her beloved character. Accordingly, Cosplayers highly value character recognition from peers and audience members.

The Cosplayer's lived experience includes aspects of theatre. Cosplayers dress in costumes and perform for themselves as much as they do for others. Theatrical settings seem to spring forth when Cosplayers in costume begin to pose or perform. In these theatrical settings, the costume signals the gathering of audiences and pending performances. Fan audiences familiar with characters and storylines enjoy interacting with the Cosplayers during hallway and other performances.

The Cosplayer in costume and performing at the fan convention are only fractions of the lived experience. The experience of *being* a Cosplayer personalizes the complexities of the Cosplay social networks, economic structures, and fandom patterns, which often manifest with the character costume and performances. Within the Cosplay fandom, the Cosplayer is supported and challenged to bring fantastic characters to live, which stimulates and benefits the Cosplay subcultural social system.

Cosplayers demonstrate sentimental attachment to their character costumes, reflecting the significant time, energy, and financial commitments they invest. They demonstrate their creativity and innovation in their character costume designs and construction techniques, as well as with their performances. Cosplayers highly value character recognition, which relies heavily on the accuracy of the costume.

The Cosplay fandom's ability to acclimate to new demands and adapt to members' needs will be key to its survival and continuation as a living social system. Systems theory provides a way to understand the intricacies of the Cosplay fandom's social system. Individual parts impact the whole system and the sum of the parts does not equal the whole. Emerging from the examination of the social and cultural systems of the Cosplay fandom is the empowerment and agency gained from being a Cosplayer.

The future of Cosplay is female

This research study revealed that the Cosplay fandom's unique composition results in unique opportunities and challenges. The future of Cosplay has exciting possibilities if the subculture is able to address disconcerting issues and acknowledge itself as a global phenomenon instead of being tied to an individual country or genre. The immediate future of the Cosplay fandom is one that reflects its dominant female population but its demographics are rapidly changing.

Most notably, girls and women have influence in the Cosplay fandom, which manifests in various manners. It is present in the fandom's multigenerational composition, which could benefit the future of the fandom. Families raise children within the fandom with the hopes that many will continue to participate in Cosplay in the future. Their guidance is also evident in the inclusive and diverse composition of the fandom.

These girls' and women's impact on the fandom is present in the skills (such as sewing, embroidery, and knitting) valued by the fandom, despite their marginalization in mainstream Western society. In addition to skill sets often deemed domestic or "women's work," the fandom encourages and tutors

Cosplayers to learn to use tools and technologies that assist in the construction of their fictional character costumes. Subsequently, girls and women are empowered with new skills and experiences, which build self-confidence and agency.

Fandoms, in general, are experiencing an influx of girls and women. To this end, new fan conventions are being organized for girls and women. In 2011, the GeekGirlCon in Seattle, Washington, was launched to empower girls and women. The annual fan convention features panels about comics, game design, science fiction, STEAM, and technology, as well as spaces for Cosplay and Cosplay Repair Station, DIY Science Zone, exhibitors, gaming, and vendors. The GeekGirlCon also recognizes the paramount roles of women in arts, fandoms, leadership, sciences, and technologies that they describe as "woman-positive geekdom" (GeekGirlCon 2017).

In fandom and convention settings, girls and women are empowered to address any issues that arise. At GeekGirlCon, for example, the organizers have the strictest *code of conduct* regarding the interactions between fans at the convention, highlighting

- "No" means no.
- "Stop" means stop.
- "Go away" means go away.
- Attire is not consent. (GeekGirlCon 2017)

The entire GeekGirlCon Code of Conduct is very thorough and includes policies about harassment and reporting violations. These types of guidelines for convention attendees not only establish the rules that everyone should adhere to, but it also suggests that the organizers recognize issues specifically facing female fans.

See you at the next con

When the convention concludes, many Cosplayers express being "depressed" or "lost" until they begin work on planning their characters and costumes for the next fan convention or designing and constructing the next costume. Black Widow summarized her feelings at the conclusion of the convention (see Plate 6.1):

Everyone understands your love for these characters and stories, and shared your excitement, and you didn't have to feel judged by people who didn't get it. Coming home to real life was a big bummer.

At the same time, Cosplayers are euphoric about experiences at fan conventions and immediately begin discussing and planning which characters they will roleplay at the next convention.

The fan convention is positioned as a powerful nexus for creativity, socializing, and performance with significant implications for identity, reflection, and even mental health. Cosplayers have a symbiotic relationship with the fan convention. The Cosplay fandom is reliant on the convention to provide a relatively safe setting to express fan appreciation. At the same time, the Cosplay fandom serves the fan convention as entertainment and lively representations of characters and storylines that affect all observing attendees.

The positionality of Cosplayers is precarious to the larger fan community. This is visually evident at fan conventions, where Cosplayers stand distinct from other fans with their fantasy character costumes and performances. Their striking visual presence demands attention, which serves Cosplayer and observers as valuable escapes and connections to greater fan community via mutual character admiration.

Convention organizers recognize the attraction to Cosplayers and their performances, as well as the potential for financial profit in connection to the fandom. Subsequently, organizers increase events (masquerades, parades, etc.) and spaces (designated Cosplay areas) for Cosplayers at fan conventions. In addition, organizers, frequently Cosplayers, create new Cosplay fan conventions, where Cosplay activities dominate the schedules and Cosplayers are the main focus.

Online relationships beyond the fan conventions sustain Cosplayers and the fandom overall. Furthermore, the use of social media allows Cosplayers to extend their fan identity beyond the physical limitations of fan conventions. Cosplayers contend that the potential for positive interactions and recognition outweighs any negative outcomes encountered online.

With few limiting impediments and its exotic visual allure, Cosplay fandom grows unchecked in ways that most subcultures have not experienced. Cosplay is popular because of its members' celebration of beloved characters and stories, which they portray and roleplay for everyone to enjoy. The trajectory of the Cosplay fandom suggests the need for more Cosplayer-focused conventions in order to support the growing population and needs of the fandom.

Summary

When I was introduced to Cosplay, I was intrigued and drawn to the subculture because of the gorgeous costumes and creative portrayals of characters. As my research allowed me to uncover layer after layer of the Cosplay fandom, I discovered that the subculture is a dynamic system that offered fans ways to intimately connect with characters and storylines. My research with the Cosplay fan subculture revealed common themes highlighting the Cosplayers' experiences. I found Cosplayers to be open, creative, and humorous; they were always willing to share their fan lives with me. Their thoughtful reflections about the fandom and their fan identities revealed the Cosplay and Cosplayer experiences.

The future is promising for the Cosplay fandom with a growing, diverse population, if the fandom addresses Cosplayers' concerns about assaults, harassment, and bullying. The Cosplay fandom relies on members sharing information and being supportive of peers' merits. Accordingly, Cosplayers respond rapidly and creatively to new stimuli and issues. The fandom, as it continues to impact and be influenced by popular culture, is shaped in meaningful ways by its female Cosplayers.

The lived experience of *being* a Cosplayer is unique even among the greater fandom community. Cosplayers establish their fan identity by wearing a fictional character costume, which is commonly designed and constructed by the wearer. These vibrant costumes and energetic performances facilitate escapism for Cosplayers and observers alike. Cosplayers' experiences in the fandom, because of its meritocracy structure, lead to feelings of empowerment and agency.

Plate 1.3 The Cosplayer Phoenix portrays the protagonist character Taako from *The Adventure Zone* podcast, against the futuristic architecture of the Eli and Edythe Broad Museum. Photo: Therèsa M. Winge.

Plate 1.4 Cosplayers portray Superman and Batman at the 2013 Comic-Con in New York City. Photo: Neilson Barnard/Getty Images.

Plate 3.1 Even the meekest character, such as the adolescent and irrelevant Milk, from *Super Milk Chan*, offers the Cosplayer with a disguise from which she finds refuge from the realities of everyday life and the chaos of the fan convention. Photo: Therèsa M. Winge.

Plate 3.2 Cosplay characters' tattoos are applied with so much precision and detail that it is difficult to determine whether these body modifications are permanent or temporary. Photo: Timothy A. Clary/AFP/Getty Images.

Plate 3.7 These Cosplayers portray the same character—Cloud Strife from *Final Fantasy VII*—who wields the enormous Buster Sword made from a wooden dowel, foam slab, duct tape, and paint. The character in the lower image is crossplaying Cloud Strife, a female Cosplayer portraying a male videogame character. Photo: Therèsa M. Winge.

Plate 3.8 The Cosplayer portrays dark, cute Ashley from the *Warioware* series in the videogame series by Nintendo. Photo: Therèsa M. Winge.

Plate 3.9 As part of the charity challenge for GISHWHES, Jodie Gustafson cosplayed her version of a Donna Reed/June Cleaver character costume. Photo: J. Gustafson.

Plate 3.10 Vergil, from the *Devil May Cry 3* videogame, an avid Cosplayer, stated that he attends "five or six conventions a year." Photo: Therèsa M. Winge.

Plate 4.1 Cosplayer posing as the strong female heroine Storm from *X-Men* at 2013 Comic-Con in New York City. Photo: Laura Cavanaugh/Getty Images.

Plate 4.2 An older Cosplay couple portrays Wonder Woman and Batman at 2014 Comic-Con in New York. Photo: TIMOTHY A. CLARY/AFP/Getty Images.

Plate 4.5 A Cosplay couple portrays Steampunk versions of Bane and Catwoman from *Batman* at 2013 Comic-Con in New York City. Photo: Neilson Barnard/Getty Images.

Plate 4.6 Lady, also known as Mary, from the *Devil May Cry 3* videogame. Female Cosplayers gain agency through portraying powerful characters wielding props of oversized, formidable weapons. Photo: Therèsa M. Winge.

Plate 4.10 The Cosplay team known as Deep Dive portrays Asuna and Kirito (Alfheim Online versions) from *Sword Art Online* demonstrating choreographed swordplay. Photo: Erin and Justin Inveninato/PhotosNXS.

Plate 5.2 A family cosplaying together at 2013 Comic-Con in New York City. Photo: Laura Cavanaugh/Getty Images.

Plate 5.3 Wonder Wobear is a humorous Cosplay portrayal of Wonder Woman, at the New York 2013 Comic-Con. Photo: Laura Cavanaugh/Getty Images.

Plate 6.1 Erin Inveninato is a well-known Cosplayer and judge (with her husband Justin Inveninato) at Dragon Con. Here, she cosplays Black Widow from the Marvel *Avengers*. Photo: Erin and Justin Inveninato/PhotosNXS.

NOTES

Chapter 1

1 The Cosplayers' parade is comparable to the Mummers parade held annually in Philadelphia, where participants dress in costumes and perform humorous skits for viewers, begun in the mid-seventeenth century (Highsmith 2016). Different from Cosplayers, Mummers' dress fits into one of four primary categories/divisions: Comic, Fancy, Fancy Brigades, and String Band (Highsmith 2016). The Mummers parade, while similar to the costumed parade of Cosplayers, does not have the same purpose or comparable costumes.

2 A weeb or weeaboo (meaning "wapanese") is a person who is not but wishes she or he were a Japanese, and usually a fan of CGDCT (cute girls do cute things) style anime. An "otaku" is a person obsessed with something usually referring to anime or anime related. Both terms are deemed negative with ethnocentric/racist connotations.

3 In Japan, Tsutomu Miyazaki is known as the Otaku Murderer because he abducted and murdered four young girls; he was a cannibal, serial killer, and necrophile (Ryall 2008). His interest in violent anime earned him the moniker "Otaku Murderer." With additional murders committed by persons who also watched anime, the Japanese police deemed the murderers a cult despite not having all of a cult's common hallmarks.

4 Gen Con is an annual gaming convention, originally located in Lake Geneva, Wisconsin. The convention later moved to Milwaukee, Wisconsin, in 1985, and since 2003 has been held in Indianapolis, Indiana. The convention has grown to attract fans of science fiction and fantasy.

5 Marc Hairston is an academic and an anime scholar, as well as a frequent presenter for Schoolgirls and Mobile Suits. He was a Cosplay judge with me because of his extensive experiences with anime and manga.

6 I served as a Cosplay judge with other academic and celebrity presenters at the Schoolgirls and Mobilesuits: Culture and Creation in Manga and Anime (SGMS) academic conference in 2003, 2004, and again in 2007. The name of SGMS eventually changed to Mechademia: Conference on Asian Popular Culture to coincide with the title of the *Mechademia* journal published by the University of Minnesota.

7 Mary Cotter is a 103-year-old Wonder Woman, who volunteers at Montclair Senior Center in her costume (Thompson 2015).

8   Due to human subject research restrictions, I interviewed Cosplayers over the age of eighteen years. I did not request proof of age for privacy considerations, but I asked my participants if they were at least eighteen years old. Some Cosplayers I initially met were ultimately unable to participate in this study because they were minors.

Chapter 2

1   My research with subcultures indicates individuals frequently belong to several subcultural groups simultaneously and throughout their lifetime. The individuals interviewed in my subcultural research accepted the "subculture" term for their rejection of mainstream fashions, homogeny, ideologies, and lifestyles. Conversely they commonly refused to identify themselves as belonging to any specific subculture, because as postmodern individuals with disjointed existences they are resistant to being defined or labeled. Accordingly, my definition of "subculture" allows groupings of individuals with specific commonalities (i.e., dress, geography, language, technology, etc.) to be understood as subcultural groups, and accounts for individuals to freely move into and out of other groups, even existing simultaneously in different groups. This definition is particularly useful in subcultural dress research, where all aspects of appearance are indicators demonstrating adherence to more than one group (Winge 2012).

2   Fans write fanfic to expand the storyline or story-arc of the character beyond the source material. Fanfic also can continue and keep a story or characters alive after the conclusion of a series, film, or book. In addition, fanfic sometimes contains sexual and graphic content not found in the original source due to television censors prohibiting sexual conduct, editors trying to reach a broader market, violence implied in source material but not specified, etc. Furthermore, fanfic reaches a fan audience and can even provide the writer with fan fame and acclaim.

3   Some fans readily adopt the labels of "nerds" and "geeks," while others take great offense because of the negative connotations. Both labels have trended positively in the mainstream media since the 1980s, but both lose favor and receive negative feedback reflecting their positions within mainstream society (Westcott 2012).

4   A "fetish" is understood as the magickal quality assigned to material objects and is not necessarily sexualized. Cosplayer's costume, for example, is imbued with sentimental qualities for the wearer, which is fetishized by the creator and wearer accordingly. The costume's sexual qualities (if any exist) may not be reflected to the Cosplayer's feelings imbued into the costume.

Chapter 3

1   A visual kei band is a Japanese contemporary pop rock band that offers highly stylized presentations and performances.

2   There are many different photographers, videographers, and Cosplayers who organize large Cosplay gatherings at fan conventions for image documentation. Distractotron, Beat Down Boogie, and the Superhero Costuming Forum organize

photography and videography opportunities for Cosplayers at fan conventions. Videos of the gatherings can be found on YouTube.

3 Themed weddings, even those where the bride and groom are wearing character costumes, are not necessarily that of Cosplay (see also Winge and Eicher 2003). Still, some Cosplayers dress as their favorite characters and hold their weddings at fan conventions.

Chapter 4

1 Gijinka is a fan activity that extends beyond the Cosplay fandom or the fan convention.

2 Lamerich as a first-time Cosplayer agreed to roleplay a character that was decided by her friends (2014).

3 Worbla is the brand name for a type of nontoxic thermoplastic material that is moldable when heated, and is commonly used by Cosplayers to create armor, weapons, and ridged props. Typically, sheets of Worbla are available in white, brown, or black with thermal adhesive on one side. After the Worbla is shaped and cooled, it can be painted or covered in gems, resin, or objects.

4 Joanne B. Eicher's definition of "dress": A system of nonverbal communication that enhances human beings' interaction as they move in space and time. As a coded sensory system, dressing the body occurs when human beings modify their bodies visually or through other sensory measures by manipulating color, texture, scent, sounds, and taste or by supplementing their bodies with articles of clothing and accessories, and jewelry (2000: 422).

Chapter 5

1 Judith Roof's research suggests that women are inclined to share knowledge and information, contributing to communal intellect in order to "democratize it" for all (Roof 2012: 525).

Chapter 6

1 A friend shared with me a "still" photograph of her nine-year-old son cosplaying Sebastian Black Butler. By holding her finger on the image on her smart phone, the figures in the image began to move for several seconds as a video play loop.

2 Originally the term "open-source" was used to designate software that was created using accessible coding and may be altered and disseminated by anyone. More recently, "open-source" has also been used to refer to any technology that meets the above criteria.

BIBLIOGRAPHY

(2011), "Cosplay with Me," *The Economist*. August 10. Available online: https://www.economist.com/blogs/schumpeter/2011/08/japanese-pop-culture (accessed June 1, 2015).

Alien (1979), [film], US: Brandywine Productions.

Anderson, K. (2014), "Actualized Fantasy at Comic Con and the Confessions of a 'Sad Cosplayer,'" in B. Boiling and M. J. Smith (eds.), *It Happened at Comic-Con: Ethnographic Essays on a Popular Culture Phenomenon*, pp. 15–28, Jefferson, NC: McFarland.

Aoyama, T., and Cahill, J. (2003), *Cosplay Girls: Japan's Live Animation Heroines*, Tokyo: DH Publishing.

Ashcroft, B., and Plunkett, L. (2014), *Cosplay World*, New York: Prestel.

Avatar: The Last Airbender (2005–08), [TV animated series], US: Nickelodeon.

Bacon-Smith, C. (1992), *Enterprising Women: Television Fandom and the Creation of Popular Myth*, Philadelphia: University of Pennsylvania Press.

Bainbridge, J., and Norris, C. (2009), "Selling Otaku? Mapping the Relationship between Industry and Fandom in the Australian Cosplay Scene," *Intersections: Gender and Sexuality in Asia and the Pacific* (April, Issue 20): 1–15.

Bainbridge, J., and Norris, C. (2013), "Posthuman Drag: Understanding Cosplay as Social Networking and Material Culture," *Intersections: Gender and Sexuality in Asia and the Pacific* (July, Issue 32): 1–11.

Bakamann. (2010), "Cosplay Mania Celebrates 10 Years of Philippine Cosplay," *Zen Otaku Honbu*. October 4. Available online: http://zenhonbuph.net/2010/10/cosplay-mania-celebrates-10-years-of-philippine-cosplay/ (accessed July 2017).

Bakhtin, M., and Iswolsky, H. [trans.]. (1968), *Rabelais and His World*, Cambridge, MA: Massachusetts Institute of Technology.

Baudrillard, J. (1998), *The Consumer Society: Myths and Structures*, London: Sage.

Beautiful. (2005), [music video], Artist: Moby.

The Big Bang Theory. (2007–present), [TV series], US: CBS.

Birch, N. (2013), "Star Trek: The Next Generation Uniform's Were Smelly, Painful Nightmares," *UPROXX News*. December 11. Available online: http://uproxx.com/webculture/star-trek-next-generations-uniforms-smelly-painful-nightmares/ (accessed June 9, 2016).

Bob's Burgers. (2011–present), [TV animated series], 20th Century Fox Television.

Bolton, C., and Rauch, E. (2010), "A Cosplay Photography Sampler," *Mechademia 5: Fanthropologies*, 5(1): 176–90.

Bourdieu, P. (1986), "The Forms of Capital," in J. Richardson (ed.), *The Handbook of Theory of Research for the Sociology of Education*, pp. 241–58, New York: Greenwood.

Bourdieu, P. (2014), "The Habitus and the Space of Life-Styles," in J. J. Gieseking, W. Mangold, C. Katz, S. Low, and S. Seegert (eds.), *The People, Place, and Space Reader*, pp. 166–222, New York: Routledge.

Brake, M. (1985), *Comparative Youth Culture: The Sociology of Youth Cultures and Youth Subcultures in America, Britain, and Canada*, New York: Routledge.

Braun, V. (2006), "Using Thematic Analysis in Psychology," *Qualitative Research in Psychology*, 96: 77–101.

Branscombe, N. R., and Wann, D. L. (1994), "Collective Self-Esteem Consequences of Out-Group Derogation When a Valued Social Identity Is on Trial," *European Journal of Social Psychology*, 24(6, November/December): 641–57.

Brownie, B. (2015), "The Masculinization of Dressing-up," *Clothing Cultures*, 2: (2, April): 145–55.

Brownie, B., and Graydon, D. (2016), *The Superhero Costume: Identity and Disguise in Fact and Fiction*, New York: Bloomsbury.

Bruno, M. (2002a), "Cosplay: The Illegitimate Child of SF Masquerades," *Glitz and Glitter Newsletter*, Millennium Costume Guild. October. Available online: http://millenniumcg. tripod.com/glitzglitter/1002articles.html (accessed March 20, 2005).

Bruno, M. (2002b), "Costuming a World Apart: Cosplay in America and Japan," *Glitz and Glitter Newsletter*, Millennium Costume Guild. October 2002. http://millenniumcg. tripod.com/glitzglitter/1002articles.html (accessed March 20, 2005).

Burton, B. (2017), "Fake Cosplay Guns, Real Problems at Comic Cons," *C/Net*. October 6. Available online: https://www.cnet.com/news/comic-con-fake-guns-weapons-props/?ftag=CAD-03-10aaj8j (accessed July 20, 2017).

Butler, J. (1988), "Performative Acts and Gender Constitution: An Essay in Phenomenology and Feminist Theory," *Theatre Journal*, 40(4, December): 519–31.

Butler, J. (1993), *Bodies That Matter: On the Discursive Limits of "Sex,"* New York: Routledge.

Carroll, L. (1865), *Alice in Wonderland*, London: MacMillan Publishing Co.

Casey, D. (2010), *Identity Crisis: Cosplay as Cultural Hybridization*, Medford, MA: Tuft University.

Chabon, M. (2008), "Secret Skin: An Essay in Unitard Theory," in A. Bolton and M. Chabon (eds.), *Superheroes: Fashion and Fantasy*, pp. 12–23, New York: Metropolitan Museum of Art.

Cherry, B. (2016), *Cult Media, Fandom, and Textiles: Handicrafting as Fan Art*, Oxford: Bloomsbury Publishing.

Clark, K., and Holquist, M. (1986), *Mikhail Bakhtin*, Cambridge, MA: Harvard University Press.

Clement, J., and McCarthy, H. (2001), *The Anime Encyclopedia: A Guide to Japanese Animation Since 1917*, Berkeley, CA: Stone Bridge Press.

Coppa, F. (2006), "A Brief History of Media Fandom," in K. Hellekson and K. Busse (eds.), *Fan Fiction and Fan Communities in the Age of the Internet*, pp. 41–59, Jefferson, NC: McFarland.

Cosplay! Crafting a Secret Identity. (2013), [documentary], USA: American Public Television.

Cosplayers: The Movie. (2009), [film], USA: Martell Bros. Studios.

Cosplayers UK: The Movie. (2011), [film], UK: Ed Hartwell.

CRI [China Research and Intelligence]. (2014), "CRI Cosplay Sales Report," *China Research and Intelligence*. Available online: http://ipo.yuanzhezixun.com/2016/03/03/industry-overview-of-the-cosplay-costumes-and-cosplay-wigs-market/ (accessed January 17, 2016).

Crossland, S. (2015), *Steampunk & Cosplay Fashion Design & Illustration*, Lake Forest, CA: Walter Foster Publishing.

CSI: Crime Scene Investigation (2003), [TV series]*, "Fur and Loathing" episode.* Aired October 30. USA: CBS.

Cubbinson, L. (2012), "Russell T. Davies, 'Nine Hysterical Women,' and the Death of Ianto Jones," in B. T. Williams and A. A. Zenger (eds.), *New Media Literacies and Participatory Popular Culture Across Borders*, pp. 135–50, New York: Routledge.

The Dark Knight Rises. (2012), [film], USA*:* Warner Bros*.*

Disneybound. (2012), "About Leslie Kay," *Disneybound*. Available online: http://disneybound.co/LeslieKay (accessed March 10, 2017).

Dr. Who. (1963–present), [TV series], UK*:* BBC.

Drazen, P. (2002), *Anime Explosion! The What? Why? & Wow! of Japanese Animation*, Berkeley, CA: Stone Bridge Press.

Duchesne, S. (2005), "Little Reckonings in Great Rooms: The Performance of 'Cosplay,'" *Canadian Theatre Review*, 121: 17–26.

Eicher, J. B. (2000), "Dress," in C. Kramarae and D. Spender (eds.), *Routledge International Encyclopedia of Women: Global Women's Issues and Knowledge*, p. 422, London: Routledge.

Ellard, A. (2016), "Professional Cosplayer Enako Reveals Her Lucrative Income," *Anime New Network*. September 15. Available online: http://www.animenewsnetwork.com/interest/2016-09-15/professional-cosplayer-enako-reveals-her-lucrative-income/.106485 (accessed April 5, 2017).

Epoch Talent. (n.d.), "Variable Cosplay," *Epoch Talent*. Available online: http://www.variablecosplay.com/ (accessed May 14, 2017).

Eventbrite. (2015a), "Eventbrite Fandoms Study Reveals Insights Into Con Attendees' Spending and Cosplay," *Eventbrite*. June 29. Available online: https://www.eventbrite.com/pressreleases/eventbrite-fandoms-study-reveals-insights-into-con-attendees-spending-and-cosplay/ (accessed January 10, 2016).

Eventbrite. (2015b), "Cosplay Is Not Consent: How to Make Your Con or Expo Harassment-Free," Arts & Culture, *Eventbrite*. October 30. Available online: https://www.eventbrite.com/blog/cosplay-harrassment-free-con-ds00/ (accessed February 4, 2017).

Fanboys. (2009), [film], USA: Weinstein Company.

Farscape. (1999–2003), [TV series], USA: Jim Henson Productions*.*

Fiske, J. (1992), "The Cultural Economy of Fandom," in L. A. Lewis (ed.), *The Adoring Audience: Fan Culture and Popular Media*, pp. 30–49. London: Routledge.

Flemming, K. L. (2007), "Participatory Fandom in American Culture: A Qualitative Case Study of DragonCon Attendees," MA dissertation, University of South Florida.

French, J. R. P. (1953), "Experiments in Field Settings," in L. Festinger and D. Katz (eds.), *Research Methods in the Behavioral Sciences*, pp. 98–135. New York: Holt, Rinehart & Winston.

Fursonas. (2016), [film], USA*:* Animal*.*

Galaxy Quest. (1999), [film], USA*:* Dreamworks*.*

Gapps, S. (2009), "Mobile Monuments: A View of Historical Reenactment and Authenticity from Inside the Costume Cupboard of History," *Rethinking History*, 13(3): 395–409.

Gauntlett, D. (2011), *Making Is Connecting: The Social Meaning of Creativity, From DIY and Knitting to YouTube and Web 2.0.*, Cambridge, UK: Polity Press.

GeekGirlCon. (2017), "GeekGirlCon," *GeekGirlCon*. Available online: https://geekgirlcon.com/ (accessed January 4, 2017).

Geertz, C. (1973), *The Interpretation of Cultures: Selected Essays*, New York: Basic Books.

George, V. (2000), *The Experience of Being as Goal of Human Existence: The Heideggerian Approach*, Washington DC: Council for Research of Values and Philosophy.

Goffman, E. (1959), *The Presentation of Self In Everyday Life*, New York: Doubleday.

Gunnels, J. (2009), "'A Jedi Like My Father Before Me': Social Identity and the New York Comic Con," *Transformative Works and Culture* 3. Available online: http://journal.transformativeworks.org/index.php/twc/article/view/161/110 (accessed October 11, 2016).

Hale, M. (2014), "Cosplay: Intertextuality, Public Texts, and the Body Fantastic," *Western Folklore*, 73 (1): 5–37.

Hank, H. (2013), "Costumed Fans Put a Gender Spin on Classic Characters," *CNN*, September 3. Available online: http://www.cnn.com/2013/09/03/living/cosplay-crossplay-dragoncon-irpt/ (accessed April 4, 2015).

Hebdige, D. (1979), *Subculture: The Meaning of Style*, New York: Routledge.

Heidegger, M. (2010), *Being and Time*, translated by J. Stambaugh, revised by D. Schmidt, Albany, NY: SUNY Press.

He-Man and the Masters of the Universe. (1983–85), [TV animated series], USA: Filmation Associates.

Hellekson, K., and Busse, K., eds. (2006), *Fan Fiction and Fan Communities in the Age of the Internet*, Jefferson, NC: McFarland Press.

Hellekson, K., and Busse, K., eds. (2014), *The Fan Fiction Studies Reader,* Iowa City, IA: University of Iowa Press.

Heroes of Cosplay. (2013–14), [TV series], USA: Syfy.

Highsmith, S. M. (2016), *Philadelphia Mummers*, Charleston, SC: Arcadia Publishing.

Hills, M. (2002), *Fan Cultures*, New York: Routledge.

Hills, M. (2014), "From Dalek Half Balls to Daft Punk Helmets: Mimetic Fandom and the Crafting of Replicas," in B. Rehak (ed.), "*Material Fan Culture*," special issue, *Transformative Works and Cultures*, no. 16.

Hlozek, R. (2004), Cosplay: The New Main Attraction, *Jivemagazine*. May. Available online: http://www.jivemagazine.com/article.php?pid=1953 (accessed March 20, 2005).

Hogg, M. (2001), "A Social Identity Theory of Leadership," *Personality and Social Psychology Review*, 5 (3): 184–200.

Hogg, M., Terry, D., and White, K. (1995), "A Tale of Two Theories: A Critical Comparison of Identity Theory with Social Identity Theory," *Social Psychology Quarterly*, 58: 255–69.

The Incredibles. (2004), [animated film], USA: Pixar Animation Studios.

ICG [International Costume Guild]. (2017), "Costume Conventions." *ICG*. Available online: http://www.costume.org/conventions.html (accessed May 26, 2017).

International Cosplay Day, (2012–present), *Facebook*. Available online: www.facebook.com/IntCosDay/ (accessed January 4, 2017).

Jenkins, H. (1992), *Textual Poachers: Television Fans and Participatory Culture*, London: Routledge.

Jenkins, H. (2006), *Fans, Bloggers, and Gamers: Exploring Participatory Culture*, New York: New York University Press.

Jeter, K. W. (1987), "Letter to the Editor," *Locus: The Newspaper of the Science Fiction World*, 20(4, April): 57.

Jung, C. G. (1972), *Psychology and Alchemy: Collected Works of C. G. Jung*, Vol. 12, 2nd ed., Princeton, NJ: Princeton University Press.

Jung, C. G. (1977), *Mysterium Coniunctionis: Collected Works of C. G. Jung*, 2nd ed., Princeton, NJ: Princeton University Press.

Jung, C. G. (1992), *Four Archetypes: Mother/Rebirth/Spirit/Trickster*, translated by R. F. C. Hull, Princeton, NJ: Princeton University Press.

Kelts, R. (2006), *Japanamerica: How Japanese Pop Culture Has Invaded the US*, New York: Palgrave Macmillan.

*Kick-Ass. (*2010*)*, [film], USA: Lionsgate.

Kotani, M., and LaMarre, T. (2007), "Doll Beauties and Cosplay," translated by T. LaMarre, *Mechademia 2: Networks of Desire*, 2(1), 49–62.

Lamerichs, N. (2011), "Stranger than Fiction: Fan Identity in Cosplay," *Transformative Works and Cultures* 7. Available online: http://journal.transformativeworks.org/index.php/twc/article/view/246/230 (accessed December 20, 2015).

Lamerichs, N. (2014), "Costuming as Subculture: The Multiple Bodies in Cosplay," *Scene*, 2 (1): 113–25.

LeBlanc, L. (1999), *Pretty in Punk: Girl's Gender Resistance in a Boy's Subculture*, New Brunswick, NJ: Rutgers University Press.

Ledoux, T., and Ranney, D. (1997), *The Complete Anime Guide, Second Edition*, Issaquah, WA: Tiger Mountain Press.

Lennon, S. J., Zheng, Z., and Fatnassi, A. (2016), "Women's Revealing Halloween Costumes: Other-objectification and Sexualization," *Fashion and Textiles*, (3, December): 21.

Lennon, T. L., Lennon, S. J., and Johnson, K. K. P. (1995), "Is Clothing Probative of Attitude or Intent? Implications for Rape and Sexual Harassment Cases," in M. E. Roach-Higgins, J. B. Eicher, and K. K. P. Johnson (eds.), *Dress and Identity*, pp. 209–17, New York: Fairchild Publications.

Liddane, L. (2015), "Can't Dress Up at Disneyland? Streetwear meets Disney in 'Disneybound' Style," *The Orange County Register*. November 8. Available online: http://www.ocregister.com/2015/11/18/cant-dress-up-at-disneyland-streetwear-meets-disney-in-disneybound-style/ (accessed March 2017).

Lunning, F. (2011), "Under the Ruffles: Shōjo and the Morphology of Power," *Mechademia 6: User Enhanced*, 6(1): 3–19.

Macias, P., and Machiyama, T. (2004), *Cruising the Anime City: An Otaku Guide to Neo Toykyo*, Berkeley, CA: Stone Bridge Press.

Marx, K. (2009), *Das Kapital: A Critique of Political Economy*, Washington, DC: Regnery Publishing.

McCarthy, H. (1993), *Anime!: A Beginner's Guide to Japanese Animation*, London, UK: Titan Books.

McCudden, M. (2011), "Degrees of Fandom: Authenticity and Hierarchy in the Age of Media Convergence," PhD thesis, University of Kansas.

Merton, R. K. (1968), *Social Theory and Social Structure*, New York: Free Press.

Miller, L. (2011), "Cute Masquerade and the Pimping of Japan," *International Journal of Japanese Sociology*, 20(1): 18–29.

Miller, F. G., and Rowold, K. L. (1979), "Halloween Masks and Deindividation," *Psychological Reports*, 44 (2): 422.

Miller, R. (2013), "Was Mr. Skygack the First Alien Character in Comics?" *io9*. September 19. Available online: https://io9.gizmodo.com/was-mr-skygack-the-first-alien-character-in-comics-453576089 (accessed June 11, 2015).

Misery. (1990), [film], USA: Castle Rock Entertainment.

Monty Python and the Holy Grail. (1975), [film], UK: Python (Monty) Pictures.

Muggleton, D. (2000), *Inside Subculture: The Postmodern Meaning of Style*, Oxford, UK: Berg.

Mullen, B., Migdal, M. J., and Rozell, D. (2003), "Self-Awareness, Deindividuation, and Social Identity: Unraveling Theoretical Paradoxes by Filling Empirical Lacunae," *Personal and Social Psychology Bulletin*, 29(2): 1071–81.

Mulvey, L. (1975), "Visual Pleasure and Narrative Cinema," *Screen*, Autumn 16 (3): 6–18.

My Little Pony: Friendship Is Magic. (2010–present), [TV animated series], USA: Hasbro Studios.

My Other Me: A Film about Cosplayers. (2013), [film], Canada: M.O.D. Entertainment.

Napier, S. (2000), *Anime from Akira to Princess Mononoke*, New York: Palgrave Macmillan.

Newtype USA. (2003), "What Happened to the Glasses!?" *Newtype USA*, August 2 (8).

O'Brien, C. M. (2012), *The Forrest J Ackerman Oeuvre: A Comprehensive Catalog of the Fiction, Nonfiction, Poetry, Screenplays, Film Appearances, Speeches and Other Works, with a Concise Biography*, Jefferson, NC: McFarland.

Okabe, D. (2012), "Cosplay, Learning, and Practice," in M. Ito, D. Okabe, and I. Tsuji (eds.), *Fandom Unbound: Otaku Culture in a Connected World*, pp. 225–48, New Haven, CT: Yale University Press.

Orisini, L. (2012), "Misa on Wheels Rolls Into Cosplay," *The Daily Dot*. February 8. Available online: https://www.dailydot.com/upstream/amanda-knightly-misa-on-wheels-cosplay/ (accessed December 16, 2016).

Orsini, L. (2015), *Cosplay: The Fantastic World of Role Play*, London: Carlton Books.

Ortiz, F. (1947), *Cuban Counterpoint: Tobacco and Sugar*, New York: A. A. Knopf.

Otaku Mode. (2016), "AnimeJapan 2017 Bigger Than Ever with Larger Main Area & 2 Business Area Days, Plus Family Anime Festa Gets Its Own Space!" *Tokyo Otaku Mode*. October 6. Available online: https://otakumode.com/news/57f46caaab6f6c2a7d103588/AnimeJapan-2017-Bigger-Than-Ever-with-Larger-Main-Area-2-Business-Area-Days-Plus-Family-Anime-Festa-Gets-Its-Own-Space! (accessed December 16, 2016).

Ozimek, A. (2014), "No, The Rise in Cosplay is Not a Bad Sign for the U.S. Economy," *Forbes*. October 14. Available online: https://www.forbes.com/sites/modeledbehavior/2014/10/14/no-the-rise-of-cosplay-is-not-a-bad-sign-for-the-u-s-economy/#b8bf1716f413 (accessed July 20, 2017).

Parrish, J. J. (2007), "Inventing a Universe: Reading and Writing Internet Fan Fiction," PhD thesis, University of Pittsburgh.

Patten, F. (2004), *Watching Anime, Reading Manga: 25 Years of Essays and Reviews*, Berkeley, CA: Stone Bridge Press.

Peacock, J. (2012), "Sex? At MY Comic Convention? It's More Likely Than You Think…," *Huffpost: The Blog*. September 5. Available online: https://www.huffingtonpost.com/joe-peacock/sex-at-my-dragoncon-its-m_b_1856216.html (accessed December 14, 2016).

Peterson, L. (2011), "The Joy of Dating at Comic Con," *Slate.com.* November 2. Available online: http://www.slate.com/articles/double_x/doublex/2011/11/speed_dating_at_comic_con_why_it_s_great_for_women.html (accessed January 27, 2018).

Pethokoukis, J. (2014), "Why the Rise of Cosplay is a Bad Sign for the U.S. Economy," *The Week*. October 9. Available online: http://theweek.com/articles/443181/why-rise-cosplay-bad-sign-economy (accessed July 20, 2017).

Plushies & Furries. (2001), [film], USA: Worlds of Wonder Productions.

Poitras, G. (1999), *Anime Companion: What's Japanese in Japanese Animation*, Berkeley, CA: Stone Bridge Press.

Poitras, G. (2001), *Anime Essentials: Everything a Fan Needs to Know*, Berkeley, CA: Stone Bridge Press.

Prideaux, E. (2001), "Japanese Trend Sees Teens Dress in Costume," *CNews*. Associated Press (Tokyo). February 7.

Quamnet. (2016), "China Partytime 1532," *Quamnet*. Available online: http://www.quamnet.com/marketipocontent.action?request_locale=en_US&cold=9143 (accessed July 20, 2017).

Queen of the Nerds. (2014), "The Top 4 'Professional Cosplayers' and Why They Annoy Actual Nerds," *Queen of the Nerds*. May 5. Available online: http://queenofthenerds.net/the-top-4-professional-cosplayers-and-why-they-annoy-actual-nerds/ (accessed August 13, 2015).

Rahman, O., Wing-Sun, L., and Cheung, B. H. (2012), "'Cosplay': Imaginative Self and Performing Identity," *Fashion Theory*, 16: 317–41.

Rastati, R. (2017), "Pro & Cons: The Rise of Hijab Cosplay in Indonesia," *Research Center for Society and Culture*. July 27. Available online http://pmb.lipi.go.id/pro-cons-the-rise-of-hijab-cosplay-in-indonesia/ (accessed October 4, 2017).

Ratcliffe, A. (2017), "Melodica Player Follows Random Cosplayers and Plays Their Characters' Themes," *Nerdist*. August 2. Available online: http://nerdist.com/melodica-player-follows-random-cosplayers-and-plays-their-characters-themes/ (accessed August 7, 2017).

Resnick, M. (2009), *...Always a Fan*, Rockville, MD: Wildside Press.

Reynolds, R. (1992), *Super Heroes: A Modern Mythology*, London: B. T. Batsford Ltd.

Reysen, S., and Branscombe, N. R. (2010), "Fanship and Fandom: Comparisons Between Sport and Non-sport Fans," *Journal of Sport Behavior*, 33(2): 176–93.

Richie, D. (2003), *Image Factory: Fads and Fashions in Japan*, London: Reaktion Books Limited.

Roach-Higgins, M. E., and Eicher, J. B. (1992), "Dress and Identity," *Clothing and Textiles Research Journal*, 10 (4): 1–8.

Roof, J. (2012), "Authority and Representation in Feminist Research," in S. N. Hesse-Biber (ed.) *Handbook of Feminist Research: Theory and Praxis*, pp. 520–43. Thousand Oaks, CA: Sage Publications.

Rosenberg, R. S., and Letamendi, A. (2013), "Expressions of Fandom: Findings from a Psychological Survey of Cosplay and Costume Wear," *Intensities: The Journal of Cult Media*, (Issue 5: Comic Book Intensities (Spring/Summer)): 9–18.

Ryall, J. (2008), "Nerd Cult Murderer Executed," *The Telegraph*. June 17. Available online: http://www.telegraph.co.uk/news/worldnews/asia/japan/2144503/Nerd-cult-murderer-executed.html (accessed March 12, 2017).

Sailor Moon. (1995–2000), [TV animated series], Japan: Cloverway International.

Salkowitz, R. (2012), *Comic Con and the Business of Pop Culture*, New York: McGraw Hill Education.

Schechner, R. (1988), *Performance Theory*, London: Routledge.

Schodt, F. L. (1996), *Dreamland Japan: Writings on Modern Manga*, Berkeley, CA: Stone Bridge Press.

Scott, S. (2015), "Cosplay Is Serious Business: Gendering Material Fan Labor on Heroes of Cosplay," *Cinema Journal*, 54(3): 146–54.

Shukla, P. (2015), *Costume: Performing Identities Through Dress*, Bloomington, IN: Indiana University Press.

Simmons, L. (2014), "Kirugumi, Dollers and How We See," [museum exhibit], Salon 94, Bowery, New York City: exhibited from March 7 to April 28.

Stalp, M. C. (2007), *Quilting: The Fabric of Everyday Life*, Oxford: Berg.

Stalp, M. C. (2015), "Girls Just Want to Have Fun (Too): Complicating the Study of Femininity and Women's Leisure," *Sociology Compass*, 9 (4): 261–71.

Stalp, M. C., and Winge, T. M. (2008), "My Collection is Bigger Than Yours: Tales from the Handcrafter's Stash," *Home Cultures: The Journal of Design, Architecture and Domestic Space*, 5 (2): 197–218.

Star Trek. (1966–69), [TV series], USA: CBS.

Star Trek: Deep Space Nine. (1993–99), [TV series], USA: Paramount Television.

Star Trek: The Next Generation. (1987–94), [TV series], USA: Paramount Televison.

Star Wars. (1977), [film], USA: Lucasfilm.

Stone, G. P. (1995), "Appearance and the Self," in M. E. Roach-Higgins, J. B. Eicher, and K. K. P. Johnson (eds.), *Dress and Identity*, pp. 19–39, New York: Fairchild Publications.

Strausbaugh, J. (2006), *Black Like You: Blackface, Whiteface, Insult & Imitation in American Popular Culture*, New York: Tarcher/Penguin.

Sullivan, J. L. (2013), *Media Audiences: Effects, Users, Institutions, and Power*, London, Sage.

Sweet, M. (2001), *Inventing the Victorians*, New York: St. Martin's Press.

Swimfan. (2002), [film], USA: Twentieth-Century Fox.

Tackett, R. (2013), "Man in China Beaten for His Incredibly Convincing Female Cosplay," July 7. Available online: http://en.rocketnews24.com/2013/07/04/man-in-china-beaten-for-his-convincing-female-cosplay/ (accessed April 22, 2015).

Tajfel, H. (1982), "Social Psychology of Intergroup Relations," *Annual Review of Psychology*, 33: 1–39.

Ted 2. (2015), [film], USA: Universal Pictures.

Thomas, C. (2014), "Love to Mess with the Mind: Engendering Crossplay," in B. Boiling and M. J. Smith (eds.), *It Happened at Comic-Con: Ethnographic Essays on a Popular Culture Phenomenon*, pp. 29–39, Jefferson, NC: McFarland.

Thompson, L. (2015), "The World's Oldest Cosplayer? 103 Year-Old Wonder Woman Can Still Go," *The Robot's Voice*. October 14. Available online: http://www.therobotsvoice.com/2015/10/worlds-oldest-cosplayer-103-year-old-wonder-woman-can-still-go.php (accessed January 12, 2016).

The Tick. (1994–96), [TV animated series], USA: 20th Century Fox Television.

The Tick. (2001–02), [TV live-action show], USA: Sony.

Todorov, T. (1973), *The Fantastic: A Structural Approach to Literary Genre*, translated by R. Howard, Ithaca, NY: Cornell University Press.

Toffler, A. (1980), *The Third Wave*, New York: Bantam Books.

Tomberry. (2014), "Sailor Bubba," *Know Your Meme*. October. Available online: http://knowyourmeme.com/memes/people/sailor-bubba (accessed July 13, 2015).

Turk, T. (2011), "Metalepsis in Fan Vids and Fan Fiction," in K. Kukkonen and S. Klimek (eds.), *Metalepsis in Popular Culture*, pp. 83–103. Berlin: Walter de Gruyter.

Turner, V. (1996), *The Ritual Process: Structure and Anti-Structure*, New York: Routledge.

United States Department of Justice. (2009), "American Disabilities Act," U.S. Department of Justice. July. Available online: https://www.ada.gov/cguide.htm (accessed May 2, 2017).

Unwin, T. A. (2005), *Jules Verne: Journeys in Writing*, Liverpool, UK: Liverpool University Press.

Usher, S. (ed.). (2011). "The Birth of Steampunk," *Letters of Note*. March 1. Available online: http://www.lettersofnote.com/2011/03/birth-of-steampunk.html (accessed June 11, 2017).

van Gennep, A. (1960), *The Rites of Passage*, London: Routledge.

van Manen, M. (1989), *Researching Lived Experience*, London, ON: Althouse Press.

Veach, M. (2010), "Mr. Skygack, From Mars," *Filson Historical Society Blog*. Available online: http://filsonhistorical.org/mr-skygak-from-mars/ (accessed December 19, 2014).

Veblen, T. (1899), *The Theory of the Leisure Class*, New York: Penguin.

Vogue. (2008), "Fashion Goes Pow!" *Vogue*. May, p. 62.

Weberstyle. (2016), "@Marvel Characters Inspire New Line of Suits. Weber Style Magazine," *Weberstyle*. September 6. Available online: https://webersterstyle. wordpress.com/2016/09/06/marvel-characters-inspire-new-line-of-suits/ (accessed December 16, 2016).

Westcott, K. (2012), "Are 'Geek' and 'Nerd' Now Positive Terms?" *BBC News Magazine*. November 16. Available online: http://www.bbc.com/news/magazine-20325517 (accessed April 4, 2017).

Whitten, S. (2015), "Comic Con Is Not Just About Cosplay: It's Big Biz," *CNBC*. October 14. Available online: https://www.cnbc.com/2015/10/14/comic-con-is-more-than-just-cosplay-its-big-biz.html (accessed July 20, 2017).

WikiMoon. (2014), "Sailor Bubba," *WikiMoon*. March 6. Available online: http://wikimoon. org/index.php?title=Sailor_Bubba (accessed July 13, 2015).

Williams, H. (2015), "The Photographer Who Allegedly Preyed on Cosplayers for Nudes," *Kotaku*. October 23. Available online: kotaku.com.au/2015/10/the-photographer-who-allegedly-preyed-on-cosplayers-for-nudes/ (accessed July 20, 2017).

Williams, J. P. (2011), *Subcultural Theory: Traditions and Concepts*. Cambridge, UK: Polity.

Willis, W. (1952), "The Immortal Teacup," *Science Fiction Digest*, (September): 3–5.

Wilson, E. (2008), "Stars and Superheroes at Museum Gala," *New York Times*, May 6. Available online: http://www.nytimes.com/2008/05/06/nyregion/06gala.html?_r=2& (accessed April 22, 2015).

Winge, T. M. (2006a), "Costuming the Imagination: Origins of Anime and Manga Cosplay," *Mechademia*, 1: 65–76.

Winge, T. M. (2006b), [unpublished research fieldnotes].

Winge, T. M. (2007), [unpublished research fieldnotes].

Winge, T. M. (2012), *Body Style*, Oxford: Bloomsbury Publishing.

Winge, T. M. (2016), [unpublished research fieldnotes].

Winge, T. M. (2017), [unpublished research fieldnotes].

Winge, T. M., and Eicher, J. (2003), "The American Groom Wore a Celtic Kilt: Theme Weddings as Canivalesque Events," in H. B. Foster and D. C. Johnson (eds.) *Wedding Dress Across Cultures*, pp. 207–18, Oxford: Berg.

Woerner, M. (2013), "The Company That Sold Controversial Cosplay Body Pillows Is Backing Down," *io9*. Available online: http://wwwio9.gizmodo.com/company-that-sold-controversial-cosplay-body-pillows-is-512453943 (accessed July 20, 2017).

Woo, B. (2012), "Alpha Nerds: Cultural Intermediaries in a Subcultural Scene," *European Journal of Cultural Studies*, 15 (5): 659–76.

Wonder Woman. (2017), [film], USA: Warner Brothers.

World Cosplay Summit. (2016), "Introduction of each team 2016," *World Cosplay Summit*. 2016. Available online: http://www.worldcosplaysummit.jp/en/2016/team/ (accessed October 3, 2017).

Xiaomi, T. (2006), "Cosplay: Bridging Reality and Fantasy," *Shenzhen Daily*, (June 22): 15. Available online: http://pdf.sznews.com/szdaily/pdf/200606/0622/s150622.pdf (accessed October 14, 2016).

INDEX